SOCIALISM,
ECONOMICS
AND
DEVELOPMENT

SOCIALISM, ECONOMICS AND DEVELOPMENT

ALEC NOVE

London
ALLEN & UNWIN
Boston   Sydney

Allen & Unwin (Publishers) Ltd,
40 Museum Street, London WC1A 1LU, UK

Allen & Unwin (Publishers) Ltd,
Park Lane, Hemel Hempstead, Herts HP2 4TE,UK

Allen & Unwin, Inc.,
8 Winchester Place, Winchester, Mass. 01890, USA

Allen & Unwin (Australia) Ltd,
8 Napier Street, North Sydney, NSW 2060, Australia

First published in 1986

British Library Cataloguing in Publication Data

Nove, Alec
    Socialism, economics and development.
1. Economic development – Social aspects
2. Economic development – Political aspects
I. Title
330.9   HD82
ISBN 0–04–335054–2
ISBN 0–04–335055–0 Pbk

Library of Congress Cataloging-in-Publications Data

Nove, Alec.
    Socialism, economics, and development.
Includes index.
1. Marxian economics. 2. Economic development.
3 Economics – Soviet Union. I. Title.
HB97.5.N599 1986   335.4   85–22819
ISBN 0–04–335054–2 (alk. paper)
ISBN 0–04–335055–0 (pbk. : alk. paper)

Set in 10 on 12pt Bembo by Phoenix Photosetting, Chatham
and printed in Great Britain by Anchor Brendon Ltd.,
Tiptree, Essex

Contents

Introduction

As the table of contents bears witness, this collection reflects a rather wide range of interests and experience, from the Chilean catastrophe to the Soviet social structure. Many of these papers appeared in somewhat inaccessible journals, symposia and festschrifts, and it is my hope that most readers will find something in these pages to interest them. I have made a very few cuts and even fewer updatings, usually of statistics. Where subsequent events have modified the picture to a significant extent, attention is drawn to this in an introductory note to the appropriate chapter.

Thanks are due to the various editors and publishers for permission to reprint, and to Catherine Hopkins for ingeniously putting together papers of varying age, size and degree of legibility. Remaining errors are all my own work.

ALEC NOVE

PART ONE

Development

1 The political economy of the Allende regime

This essay was originally published in P. O'Brien (ed.), *Allende's Chile* (New York: Praeger, 1976), pp. 51–78, and was written in the immediate aftermath of the military coup, that is, at the end of 1973.

I taught in the planning institute of the Universidad Catolica de Chile in September–November 1972, and revisited the country in March 1973. I tried to the best of my ability to understand what was happening, what the policy of the government was, and the causes of the economic troubles that were besetting it. What follows is an attempt to analyse the economic policies that, beyond doubt, contributed to the disaster that befell the Allende regime. It may be of interest to note that when I expressed many of the same ideas in Santiago in November 1972 I was criticized by most of those who heard me for a harsh and unsympathetic approach. I denied then, and I deny now, any harshness or lack of sympathy. The facts point to a lack of clarity and a great deal of contradiction and confusion, due partly to divided counsels, partly to political constraints and partly to a fundamental dichotomy in the economic-political strategy of the administration. Of course, defeat was due also to the actions of the government's enemies, but grave errors gave these enemies far too many opportunities to exploit. To pretend that the government merely fell victim to a conspiracy between the CIA and the extreme right is of no help to anyone, least of all the Chilean left – which is not to deny the obvious facts of conspiracy and sabotage. In any conflict in which one is defeated, it is self-evident that the enemy's actions made a major contribution to the outcome (and deserve more careful study than they will get in this essay). However, in any inquest on a lost battle attention is usually and rightly devoted to analysing one's own errors, and to discovering why one was not successful and the enemy was. The conspiracy-based explanation leads logically to far-reaching conclusions about the impossibility of a peaceful road to socialism. In one such version the onward march towards a just society was violently interrupted because it was in fact succeeding, whereas (in my view) by early 1973, indeed, by the second half of 1972, catastrophe faced the economy, with the gravest political consequences plainly discernible. It may indeed be true that there is no 'peaceful road' in Latin America (or Italy, or anywhere), but the case for this proposition should not rest on myths about Chile.

One first must take cognizance of the class structure of Chile. It is a country with a very large class of small shopkeepers, owners of workshops, artisans, owner-drivers of trucks, small peasantry, and other members of what must be called the petty bourgeoisie. There was, of course, a group of big businessmen, many of them linked with foreign corporations, and an upper stratum of senior civil servants, officers and professional people; the officers were (by Latin American standards) rather poorly paid, but took great pride in their disciplined nationalism, as could be seen each Independence day in their spectacularly precise goose-stepping. The tactic appropriate to a left-wing president was, it seemed, to attract or at least neutralize the petty bourgeoisie, while gaining peasant support by pressing ahead with land reform, which had been begun slowly under the previous president, Eduardo Frei. Allende, understandably, sought to reassure the petty bourgeoisie and promised to take action only against the foreign corporations and the few Chilean big monopolists. It was surely essential for the security of the regime not to antagonize the 'small men'.

I appreciate that constraints and limitations are not unchangeable, and that observers can and do differ in interpreting the limits of the possible. But it is sufficient here to stress that economic policies were conceived and carried out within a social and political structure that set limits to what Allende and most of his colleagues considered it possible to do.

The economic legacy of the Frei administration

Chile, when I first visited it in 1965, was facing economic difficulties. First, there was the chronic inflation, which had gone on for many decades. The behaviour of the price index in the years of Frei's presidency is shown in Table 1.1. Food supplies were adequate only because of substantial imports, and this for a country that, a generation earlier, had been a significant exporter of grain and meat. Agriculture had for too long

Table 1.1   Price rises (per cent)

	Retail prices	Wholesale prices
1967	18.1	19.3
1968	26.6	30.5
1969	30.7	36.5
1970	32.5	36.1

Source: Antecedentes sobre el desarollo chileno (Santiago: ODEPLAN 1971).

been in the doldrums, and this was attributed by most Chilean economists at least in part to the inefficiency or inactivity of the landed proprietors, whose liking for horse-riding in ponchos – and holding land as a hedge against inflation – exceeded their interest in productive activity. Frei's Christian Democrat administration did indeed adopt land reform laws, and we shall see that Allende's speeded-up land reforms were based on these very same laws.

Industrial output rose only slowly, or stagnated. Chile is not a populous country, and the industries that operated under cover of a high tariff wall were unable to benefit from economies of scale. A foolish policy of indiscriminate encouragement to foreign capital led to setting up more than twenty small car assembly plants, all far below optimum size. Unemployment grew, and there was much under-utilization of industrial capacity. The 1971 ODEPLAN figures (Table 1.2) give one some idea of the trend. Thus in the last three Frei years inflation rates rose, industrial output showed little upward trend and unemployment increased.

Table 1.2 Industrial output and unemployment, 1967–70

	1967	1968	1969	1970
Industrial output (per cent increase)	2.8	2.4	3.7	0.8
Unemployment (per cent, incomplete figures)	4.7	4.9	5.0	6.0

Source: Antecedentes, op. cit.

The balance of payments was a constant source of concern. With nitrates no longer significant, and an increasing food import bill to meet, Chile's exports consisted largely of copper, which accounted for around 80 per cent of the total. The country was thus very vulnerable to price changes of this one commodity. 'Import-saving' industrialization led to increasing imports of machinery and components, and the bulk of Chile's oil also had to be imported. In addition, Chile had to carry a large burden of debt, both governmental and commercial. Frei succeeded in coping with the balance of payments, building up reserves in the process (see Table 1.3). However, this increase in reserves was achieved by

Table 1.3 Balance of payments (US$)

	Net balance	Reserves
1967	−25.0	−91.5
1968	+127.0	37.7
1969	+222.8	220.0
1970	+108.2	343.2

Source: Antecedentes, op. cit., pp. 435–6.

damping down activity, and this contributed to unemployment of human and material resources.

The copper mines were, in the main, US-run, by the Anaconda and Kennecott companies. Frei decided to 'Chilanize' them, acquiring a 51 per cent controlling shareholding. However, the terms of the agreement proved highly favourable to the copper companies, who made and remitted unusually high profits in the years following 'Chileanization'.

Allende's economic programme

Allende's victory was unexpected, and there is some evidence that he was caught unprepared, with no defined plan of action. His programme promised to contain inflation, to redistribute income in favour of the poor, to carry out a rapid land reform, and to nationalize the copper companies, other foreign-owned corporations and big monopolies. Thereby it was hoped to weaken the economic-political basis of the right-wing parties, to strengthen the electoral popularity of the regime and to move onwards towards socialism. These onward moves were by no means clear. Nor were the ways in which the various elements of the immediate programme were to be carried out. There was, we may be sure, much improvisation.

Two factors must be stressed. The first was that the election of Allende touched off great expectations among the working-class supporters of Popular Unity (UP). Life would become better, wages would go up, they would soak the rich. The strength of these expectations, as well as the government's own commitment to income redistribution, made it politically essential to grant large wage increases, while simultaneously combating inflation. The other factor was disunity, or rather divisions, on the left. The trade unions were united under CUT (Confederacion Unica de Trabajadores), but within them the parties competed, with the Christian Democrats vying with the Communists, who controlled CUT, in promising or demanding immediate benefits. Politically, too, there were those who urged massive concessions to the workers, to win their enthusiastic support as a first and essential step towards mobilizing them for the march towards socialism. Some of Allende's supporters thought of the possibility of a plebiscite to amend the Constitution to give the government greater powers, and large benefits for the masses could mean votes. Some of the parties in the UP coalition, especially the socialists under their secretary Altamirano and two of the smaller parties (MAPU and the Left-Christians), were for a vigorous socialist offensive and for extensive redistributive measures in favour of the poor. Allende himself seems to have been nearer the Communists in urging caution. It was, above all, the Communists who sought to reassure the middle classes, insisting that legality should be respected and attention paid to economic possibilities. They were outflanked from the left not only by the MIRistas, who were urging seizures of property and challenging the very concept of legality, but by the other members of the coalition. (I recall the mocking tones of Chilean postgraduates whom I met at an international seminar in the summer of 1971; the Communists were a bourgeois party, they insisted.)

The government knew that it could nationalize copper with the over-whelming support of the people and of Congress. It promptly did so, virtually denying compensation by claiming that excess profits and unpaid taxes in the past should be deducted from the compensation entitlements of Kennecott and Anaconda. Whether it was wise to do this is a matter of opinion, for the government risked more trouble with the United States as well as with the firms in question; the latter were important as suppliers of equipment to the mines, the former could (and did) take steps to cut Chile off from credits which, possibly, might have helped to mitigate the balance-of-payments problem. It is worth inquiring whether the failure to compensate caused, on balance, more loss than gain. Chilean delegates could have dragged out compensation negotiations for years, while accepting the principle, thus weakening the argument of the government's enemies, who (as the ITT files show) were hard at work persuading American official agencies to take hostile action. (It is, of course, also arguable that the United States would in any case have done its worst, whatever the compensation paid for copper.) Could it be that the fine 'declaratory' value of the no-compensation principle was a luxury that Chile could not afford? Whether one accepts this view or not, there is no doubt at all that the action was popular. Even the right-wing deputies in Congress voted for it.

The nationalization of other enterprises was more difficult. A list of ninety firms was drawn up and submitted to Congress, which turned it down. There was thus no direct legal road, and so the government was forced to resort to a number of expedients. These included participation on a 51 per cent basis in the case of foreign-owned enterprises, a procedure that covered, among other things, some enterprises owned by ITT (such as the Sheraton hotel). Participation could be achieved by direct negotia-tion with the enterprises concerned, in the knowledge that their foreign ownership would give the government political strength in dealing with them. If the enterprises refused – as I was told Philips refused – they were sometimes allowed to carry on, because of the loss that would follow from their withdrawal. Chilean-owned big firms would be, and were, tackled on the basis of existing legislation or by indirect forms of executive ingenuity, as follows.

(1) The government acquired control by purchasing controlling shares. For example, this was how banks were acquired, and some industrial

firms also. The process was in some cases facilitated by related actions; demands for large wage increases, price control and denial of import licences could, separately or in combination, cause sufficient losses to 'persuade' the directors to sell.

(2) Use was made of legislation adopted in 1932 under the short-lived rule of a left-wing president, Davila, and never repealed. This provided for control over (not nationalization of) enterprises that were not being operated in a vaguely defined public interest. The government put in an *interventor*, who replaced the board of directors. By this means, state control was much expanded. Again, the incomes of owners could be reduced by a combination of price control and wage increases.

(3) Finally there was action from below, often encouraged by one or more of the UP parties but sometimes spontaneous (or MIR-inspired), in which workers occupied factories and/or demanded that the government take over control from the owners.

By these and similar means the so-called *area social* (Social Property Area), that is, the state-controlled sector, was substantially expanded by stages. But these methods caused not only bitterness but also confusion and uncertainty – bitterness because they were seen as a way of evading legislative opposition to nationalization, confusion because there was uncertainty about who might be nationalized or 'intervened' next. It would have been better and clearer if Congress had passed the law nationalizing the ninety named enterprises and the government had combined this with a clear guarantee that other firms were free of the danger of takeover. Of course, it was not Allende's fault that Congress refused to pass the law. But the fact remains that, as things were, business nervousness increased, paralysing private investment and causing many conflicts with particular firms, who used the press and the commercial radio to lambast the real or alleged efforts of the government to nationalize them. I recall the daily 'commercials' on behalf of the large Chilean-owned paper company, Papeles y Cartones, whose losses, due to price control, were suspected of being a deliberate prelude to a state takeover; the commercial ended with the words, shouted in chorus: 'La Papelera: NO!' At the other end of the scale, the nervousness of owner-drivers about alleged plans to nationalize road transport contributed to the mobilization of these key petty bourgeois against the government in 1972, with deplorable results. Of course these fears were played upon by right-wing elements.

The government did make friendly declarations towards small business, and the banks that it controlled were generous with credit. Allende announced: 'Although monopolies will be abolished, because that is in the greater interests of the country, for this same reason we guarantee that middle- and small-scale businesses may rely on the close collaboration of the state to ensure the sound development of their activities.'[1] Maximum interest rates were reduced from 44 per cent to 31 per cent.[2] But one factor – probably not the most important – in alienating the medium- and small-scale business community was the method by which state control was expanded.

It is noteworthy that, of the ninety enterprises originally scheduled for nationalization (or for mixed state-private ownership), twenty were foreign-controlled, that is, over 50 per cent of their capital was held by foreign companies. Of these, only six were to be nationalized outright; the others would be mixed, that is, Chilean state organs would operate them in joint ownership with the foreign interests. Progress was in fact not very rapid, as the situation in December 1972 shows (see Table 1.4).

Table 1.4 Nationalization of Industrial Enterprises (December 1972)

	Number of enterprises	Percentage	Percentage share of production
Social and mixed area	103	12.7	13.4
Requisitioned and 'intervened' enterprises	99	6.9	8.5
Total	202	19.6	21.9

Source: Facultad de Economia Politica, *La economia chilena en 1972* (Santiago: Universidad de Chile, 1973), pp. 134–5; with acknowledgement to Cristobal Kay for help in finding these and some other statistics.

Although it was intended to expand the Social Property Area in 1973, the large majority of industrial production (around 70 per cent) would still have remained in the private sector even if Allende had survived to the end of that year and carried out his programme. This underlines the vital importance to the health of the economy of enabling private industry to function effectively.

Land reform proceeded rapidly but, while the government could take credit for carrying out its promises, once again there were unfortunate consequences, attributable partly to the actions of the ultra-left, and partly (perhaps mainly) to the legal provisions upon which the reform process was based. There was also a persistent dispute among the government's supporters concerning the maximum size of holding that was to be exempted from redistribution. The reform proceeded on the basis of 80 hectares (much more than this when the land was of inferior quality), but many left-wing critics demanded limits of 40 hectares or even less.

There were two disruptive features of the reform as it was carried out (and in my view the second of them was the most serious). First, the owners were, under the Frei land reform law, allowed to remove their assets, and this meant loss of equipment and, in some cases, also of livestock. Second, the fate of the redistributed land was uncertain. The peasants did not, as a rule, acquire it as personal property; it was run on a semi-co-operative basis under the name of *asentamiento*. This was an ill-defined and provisional arrangement, pending a final settlement that could be either private ownership or collective or co-operative farming. There were differences of opinion about what was to be done and what the peasants wanted, and great unclarity over how the *asentamientos* were to be run, how the peasants were to work within them, and how the produce was to be disposed of and the resultant income distributed. Since many peasants also had private holdings, all this greatly confused the system of incentives; how much co-operative work should the peasants undertake, and what remuneration should they receive? Since a black market soon grew up, these issues became linked with the problem of selling through legal channels at legal prices.

The government set up institutions for land reform, but these never had clearly defined powers or an agreed strategy. Credits were lavished upon agriculture, but these were seldom repaid. In these circumstances, it is hardly surprising that output and marketing did not come up to expectation.[3]

One example of lack of control of the reform process was the speed-up of migration from rural to urban areas. According to statements made to me in Santiago, this was because many landless labourers casually employed on estates were denied any land, as the estates' land was divided among existing regular labourers (or rather, that one had to be such to be a member of the *asentamiento*. These labourers often also cultivated small landholdings of their own.) This was a consequence of local influence on the process of reform. Since smallholders could not afford to employ labourers, many casual labourers on the old estates had no alternative but to join the slum dwellers whose shacks disfigured the outskirts of Santiago and Valparaiso.

Finally, the MIR encouraged illegal land seizure, presenting the government with a dilemma. To use force against the peasants would be to outrage much of the left. Not to use force would greatly upset the constitutionalists among the military (upon whom, in the last resort, the government had to rely) and also contradict the government's claim to keep within legal norms, a claim that it relied upon to secure acceptance of its measures by its more moderate opponents. Obviously, the intransigents would be against all its actions, but the moderate centre of public opinion was not to be too greatly antagonized, and certainly not on an issue – land reform – on which the government could legitimately claim that it was carrying out Christian Democrat policy based upon Frei's own legislation, which Frei himself had not speedily enforced. In the event, the government compromised, offending both the extreme left and the centre by repressing some illegal seizures and tolerating others. Allende's speech on the subject made on 21 December 1970 in Santiago is an example of the discomfort of the authorities faced with this problem.[4]

The unsound policies of 1971

Large increases in wages followed the election of Allende. In a country with a long tradition of inflation, regular wage rises were a feature of life. Allende's first year was not out of the ordinary. The exact extent of the rise in money and real wages depends considerably on the months chosen for the comparison, hence the evidence of a number of different estimates. The figures in Tables 1.5 and 1.6 seem reasonably reliable.

It seems clear that, in the first year, money wages did not rise faster than in the last year of Frei's presidency. The difference, as can be seen, was entirely due to the behaviour of the price index and this, in turn, was due to tighter price control. Probably in holding down prices the government hoped that money wages would not rise so fast. If so, its hopes were disappointed. It should be added that the magnitude of the increase was due in part to autonomous trade union actions, and to the willingness of many employers to concede large claims to 'buy off' possible demands for

Table 1.5 Percentage increases in real wages, 1970–1

	Wages and salaries	Retail prices	Real wages[a]
January–January	43.2	28.1	11.8
April–April	53.0	20.2	27.0
July–July	54.9	19.1	30.1
October–October	51.9	16.5	34.1

[a] Derived from first two columns.
Source: La economia chilena en 1982, op. cit., p. 265.

Table 1.6 Percentage increases in real wages, 1968–71

	Wages and salaries (index, unknown base)	Percentage increase over previous figure	Price increase	Real wages percentage increase
October 1968	1,187.0	—	—	—
October 1969	1,605.4	35.2	27.2	6.2
October 1970	2,450.7	52.7	35.6	12.6
July 1971	3,529.3	44.0	12.2	28.3

Source: Informe annual, 1971 (Santiago: ODEPLAN, 1972), pp. 27–8 (calculated from figures there given).

nationalization or 'intervention.' So the rises were not solely the consequence of deliberate government policy. However, the large increase was
a fact.

Powers to control prices had existed long before Allende, but his
government sought to exercise them with greater toughness to prevent
the money wage rise from evaporating through inflation. The effect was
remarkable; in the period from October 1970 to October 1971, inflation
was brought down to a mere 16.5 per cent, as measured by the retail price
index against an average of 29 per cent in Frei's last three years. This meant
a rise in 'real wages' of 34 per cent. It seems to me that in this single figure
one sees most clearly expressed the basic unsoundness of the government's
political-economic strategy. It was a fatal and large step on the road to
disaster.

It did not look that way at first. The large increases in purchasing
power, under conditions of under-employment of human and material
resources, had favourable effects on industrial production, which rose by
12 per cent in 1971. But common economic sense showed that this was
unrepeatable; once the slack was taken up, there could be no more increase
without investments, and investments (as we shall see) were reduced, not
only in the private but also in the nationalized productive sector (housing
construction and public works did increase).

In any case, part of the inflated demand of 1971 was met out of higher
domestic industrial production. But the bulk of the extra demand was for
food, and agricultural output was quite insufficient to meet it. So, at the
controlled prices, food had to be imported in ever-growing quantities, as
Table 1.7 demonstrates.

Table 1.7 Balance of Payments, 1970–2 (US$, millions)

	1970	1971	1972
Exports	1,129	1,076	853
Imports	1,020	1,123	1,287
Balance of services	−39	−45	−10
Net commercial balance	+71	−122	−444
Net foreign remittances	−129	−90	−120
Net current account	−57	−212	−564
Capital movements	+149	−100	−17
Net balance of payments	+91	−311	−581
Renegotiation of external debt	—	—	200
Imports of foodstuffs	178.2[a]	314.2[a]	444[b]
Imports of machinery	—	178[a]	137[b]

[a] From pp. 47, 145.
[b] Estimate
Source: *Comentarios sobre la situacion economica* (Santiago: Universidad de Chile, 2nd semester 1972/3), p. 138.

The table is quite clear; imports of food rose very steeply, imports of capital goods fell (reflecting falling investments), total imports rose, and capital movements made matters worse. Reserves fell precipitately, indeed virtually disappeared by the end of the year, as we shall see.

An important factor was an unfortunate and unpredictable fall in copper prices from their 1969 peak of $66 per ton to only $48–9 in 1971 and 1972. This found reflection in the fall in export revenues shown in Table 1.7. Exports of other items also fell. There is absolutely no evidence that the fall in prices was planned by anyone, any more than was the sharp rise that occurred during 1973. It could not have come at a worse time from Allende's point of view. It made a bad situation worse, though it would have been bad even if copper had remained at $66.

The same requires to be said of the reduction of credits and aid. The United States did not help, it hindered (except, significantly, that military aid continued). Needless to say, if Allende had had aid from the United States on the scale of, say, US subsidies to Taiwan or South Vietnam, he might well have been able to ride out the balance-of-payments consequences of his policy. But one can hardly envisage a road to socialism, including confiscation of US assets, based on US aid. It has also been argued that, while new lines of credit were indeed fewer, renegotiation of past debts and drawings on credits previously negotiated continued to help the Chilean balance of payments.[5]

Why have I used the word 'disaster' about the policy of 1971? Because of the exhaustion of currency reserves – which fell from $377.6 million in September 1970 to $32.3 million in December 1971[6] – the impossible increase in 'real wages', the price controls, the inevitable material shortages, the exaggerated expectations of the workers and the fall in investments made a major crisis quite inevitable in 1972. When I argued this on an earlier occasion, a Chilean responded indignantly: 'We were not concerned with economic efficiency, we were concerned with power.' This meant that the aim of policy as he saw it was primarily of a short-term political nature; to secure a jumping-off ground to get mass support, either to amend the Constitution or to achieve 'workers' power' by mobilizing and 'ideologizing' the masses. It is pointed out that in the municipal elections of April 1971, when the costs of the policies were not yet apparent, the UP did win more votes, indeed very close to 50 per cent. Then, so the political argument ran, was the time to attack.

The chance, if it existed, was missed. But did it exist? Was such a strategy politically feasible? Much depends on the answer, but this basically economic survey is not the place to attempt to find it. We can agree, surely, that unless some drastic political change could have been engineered during 1971, it was likely that political disaster as well as economic chaos would ensue during 1972, and that economic inefficiency would threaten the hold on power. Even if a change in the power balance could have occurred, economic troubles would still have followed the utterly unsustainable and totally unsound increase in real wages. All that could be argued is that the government might have been in a stronger position to repress the resultant discontent.

The government chose not only to control prices but also to peg the official exchange rates. A growing gap developed between these and the black market rate, diverting transactions and currency away from official channels. (There were a number of rates, depending on the nature of the transaction.)

The statistics in Table 1.8 show Gross National Product (GNP) figures for 1970–2. The increase in industrial output in 1971 looked gratifying, but could not be maintained. The agricultural figure is likely to be inaccurate. The 1970 and 1971 figures are official (ODEPLAN); the 1972 estimates are those of the University of Chile's economic department.

GNP thus rose by 9.56 per cent in 1971, but only by 0.8 per cent in 1972.

Investments fell, according to the same sources, from 17.4 per cent of GNP in the decade 1960–70 to 13.3 per cent in 1971 and 12.4 per cent in 1972. They fell absolutely both in 1971 and 1972. Stocks of materials also declined.

Finally, the quantity of money in the possession of the private sector increased by 120 per cent in 1971, and by 140 per cent in 1972.[7]

The accelerating crisis of 1972

With no currency reserves to fall back on, the Allende administration found itself unable to meet demand at controlled prices. Wages continued to rise. Goods began to disappear. Black markets grew. As costs soared and output stopped rising owing to shortages of capacity, private business found itself in a squeeze. It was not inflation as such that was the sole cause

Table 1.8   Gross national product by sector   (millions of 1965 escudos)

	1970	1971	1972
Agriculture and fishing	2,015	2,130	2,032
Mining and quarries	2,259	2,324	2,240
Manufacturing	5,366	6,037	6,128
Construction	1,071	1,173	1,100
Public utilities	347	398	414
Transport and communication	996	1,049	1,065
Wholesale and retail trade	4,617	4,977	5,032
Other services	4,901	5,308	5,578
Total	21,357	23,396	23,590

Source: Comentarios, op. cit., p. 176.

of the trouble, at least until it accelerated in the second half of 1972. Latin American countries learned long ago to live with inflation. The trouble was the combination of cost inflation, price control and import restriction, plus unpredictability and uncertainty.

Since these circumstances greatly contributed to the alienation of the middle and petty bourgeoisie,it is necessary to dwell on them in a little more detail. To do so it is useful to imagine oneself to be a Chilean small businessman, say, a petty manufacturer, a shopkeeper, or an owner of two or three trucks, and to consider his difficulties and his frustrations. If he required spare parts, materials, or commodities from abroad, these would be subject to strict import licensing, because of the desperate shortage of foreign exchange. A licence might be unavailable. Or it might be available at one of a large number of widely varying exchange rates, according to the category of essentiality judged by the Central Bank to apply to the proposed transaction. By 1972 the would-be importer might or might not be called upon to make a deposit in escudos worth 10,000 per cent of the value of the imports for three months. (Provision for a 10,000 per cent deposit existed also under Frei, but applied to only a few goods. It was extended.) In so far as imports were involved, therefore, a high degree of uncertainty and frustration prevailed, as regards both the cost and the availability of the necessary permit.

Wages and material costs were subject to steep and sudden change. When, during 1972, the government began to allow large price rises, these were conceded reluctantly and after a long delay. Some foodstuffs, manufactures, or services might be held at 10 escudos for six months, so that production began to be carried on at a loss, and then suddenly the price was raised to 26 escudos, resulting in a profit for a few months until costs once again surpassed the authorized selling price. Wages were readjusted to keep pace with the rising prices, and price rises and wages increases speeded up and reinforced each other, as futile attempts were made to hold on to the excessive gains allowed in 1971. (The government was, of course, aware that these gains were in fact unsustainable and, as we shall see, tried to make a downward correction in the real wage level during the second half of 1972.) As price control was inevitably highly complex, and adjustments tended to be resisted until pressures built up, anomalies were extremely common. In September 1972 most bus rides in Santiago were 1.50 escudos, a daily newspaper was 4 escudos, the maximum price for cinema seats was 10 escudos, the toll for the Valparaiso road was 12 escudos, excellent wine was 25 escudos a bottle (but one had to bring a bottle), a portion of pizza cost 60 escudos, a tin of Paraguayan corned beef cost 120 escudos, and imported consumer durables cost thousands, but petrol (almost all of it imported) was phenomenally cheap. There was neither rhyme, nor reason, nor predictability. While cheap necessities may have been a form of redistribution of income, cheap petrol benefited the middle classes. Failure to keep prices of public utilities and of other nationalized industries ahead of costs necessitated large subsidies, which led to further money creation and stimulated inflation.

Many items at fixed prices became unobtainable. Others which were not controlled were available at high prices, so that, for instance, one could get cream but not milk. By September 1972, despite the price rise in August (see below), meat was exceedingly scarce and it was almost impossible to find sugar, flour, butter, margarine, rice or potatoes (though these latter did appear in October). It soon became very difficult to buy detergents, cigarettes, razor blades, toilet paper and toothpaste.

The government increasingly sought to supply the working-class areas with goods at official prices, using organizations set up for the purpose, the JAP (Juntas de Abastacimiento Popular – Popular Supply Committees), but this caused friction with traders and led to accusations of political favouritism. Undoubtedly the UP supporters in the industrial 'bidonvilles' around Santiago did reasonably well. In middle-class areas protests mounted, with housewives banging saucepan-lids every evening.

So the petty bourgeoisie had a difficult time as consumers and suffered great frustration in their professional capacities. Consequently, their hostility to the government mounted. Was this inevitable, given the desire to move towards socialism? Some have argued so. Others did not and do not agree. In a paper circulated in the summer of 1972, Jose Vera wrote the following. After listing the critical problems of the period (balance-of-payments deficit, supply shortages, deficiencies in economic administration, inflationary pressures due in part to excessive wage demands, and insufficient investments), he went on:

> The above-mentioned difficulties are the logical result of the peculiar form of the advance to socialism chosen by the government. In principle, the costs such methods imply are justified by the aim being pursued: to establish a just and dynamic socialist society. But it is clear that if the government cannot find speedy effective solutions which will permit a continued advance towards socialism, the aim will not be accomplished and the cost will no longer be justified. Furthermore the government would then face a period of grave political difficulties.

The author then made some suggestions, some of them socially very progressive, calling for reinforced government controls over the economy, and also for 'the creation of real and stable incentives for the private sector, which today faces a situation of great uncertainty and despair'.[8]

It is, of course, clear that Allende had no wish to antagonize the small man. It happened because of the economic crisis of 1972. The question is only, how far did the policies adopted earlier lead to this crisis and so to these consequences?

How far were these consequences foreseen? To some extent they were, or so I was assured in interviews before and after the coup. The initial economic strategy of 1971 was undertaken on political assumptions that proved unreal or inconsistent with the political strategy actually followed by the Allende administration. One view expressed to me is that calling the policies followed a 'strategy' would be misleading. There was *ninguna politica coherente*, there were several inconsistent strategies, reflecting the splits within the UP and the fact that key ministries were controlled by different parties (and also splits within parties, especially the Socialists).

In this connection, it may be interesting to quote the pro-UP (Marxist) publication of the Facultad de Economia Politica of the Universidad de Chile, *La economia chilena en 1972*. Noting the huge increase in real wages of 1971, the authors commented as follows: 'This line of economic policy aimed at demonstrating clearly the class nature of the revolutionary forces which controlled the executive power, with the ultimate objective of uniting with revolutionary forces sectors alien to them'[9] (that is, non-revolutionary and non-proletarian elements). After deploring the insufficiency of the organizational measures of mass activity, the authors noted that

> To isolate the 'powerful enemy', i.e. the big bourgeoisie and the imperialist interests, requires the support or at least neutralization of elements of vacillating classes . . . i.e. the petty bourgeoisie and also the middle bourgeoisie. But in an economy predominantly dependent-capitalist, which is subject to the law of value, commodity producers (whether capitalist or not) must respond to prices, and derive their profit margins from the difference between prices and costs . . . Consequently a policy designed to win or neutralize these middle-class strata . . . must be accompanied by a price-level linked with a certain level of profits, particularly if there exist upward pressures in levels in workers' wages.[10]

This is described as a 'contradition within an alliance of classes'. We shall see that by the middle of 1972 this view affected price policy. However, the authors do not show awareness that by then the damage had been done, and that the earlier policy ran directly counter to their own class analysis. Perhaps the way out they envisaged was a very large increase in the Social Property Area, which they imagined as withdrawn from the operation of the market and the 'law of value', plus a total change in the political balance, based upon mass activity. They do not make this clear.

It is also necessary to mention the government's policies in the fields of foreign exchange, industrial planning and agricultural procurements.

As inflation speeded up during 1972, the gap between the official and the black market exchange rates grew so wide that illegal transactions became normal. Thus in September 1972 the official 'tourist' rate of 45 escudos to the US dollar contrasted with a black market rate of over 300. When, in March, the official rate was belatedly moved to 90, the unofficial one approached 600. The few tourists were compelled to exchange a minimum at the official rate on arrival, but obviously the illegal market flourished. I was told by an American visitor how she went into a (nationalized) bank to change a traveller's cheque, and the bank clerk told her she was crazy to change it officially, offering to give her a much better rate if she would step outside.

As for planning, it was almost non-existent. The state sector's enterprises operated autonomously, and were as confused by the price pattern as was private enterprise. It had been understood that they were to make a profit. Indeed, one of the hopes placed upon nationalization had been that the state would be able to use industrial profits to finance its welfare and investment measures, independently of Congress's grip on the purse-strings. However, escalating wages and other costs, and price control, soon turned profits into losses in many cases. Far from contributing to the state budget, the nationalized sector became a charge on the budget. While market and price indicators lost their significance, the Allende administration was never able to make up its mind about what central planning powers there should be, or who should exercise them. Two 'competitors' emerged: CORFO, an industrial promotion organ originally set up in 1939, and ODEPLAN, the nearest equivalent to Gosplan. One reason for government indecisiveness was lack of clarity over the desirable degree of centralization. The parties were not of one mind on this. Allende himself spoke to workers and told them 'We are not your masters, you are your own masters.' Such sentiments would have accorded ill with the issuance of binding orders from Santiago. It would not be correct to assert that the government sought planning powers that were denied by Congress; the government probably did not know what powers it should seek. This would not have mattered too much if the state and private sectors had been effectively governed by the market, since this would have provided some sort of basis for operation. But the market was becoming hopelessly distorted.

Inflation speeded up for several mutually reinforcing reasons. Incomes had greatly increased in 1971, and continued to rise in 1972. Supplies could not be adequate at existing prices. So long as Pedro Vuskovic was responsible for economic policies, prices of necessities were kept low, despite the queues and empty shops. Then Vuskovic was replaced by Matus, who apparently decided that prices must rise to more realistic levels. The reasoning was that quoted on page 17 above, in the quotation from the Facultad de Economica Politica. The results are shown in Table 1.9.

Table 1.9   Rise in consumer prices, August 1972   (in escudos)

	31 July	31 August
Fillet steak	55.00	160.00
Stewing steak	29.00	70.00
Lamb chops	33.00	52.00
Chicken	18.50	33.00
Cooking oil	9.60	14.40
Tea	17.60	37.60
Coffee	17.50	31.70
Milk	1.70	3.50
Granulated sugar	6.00	12.00
Rice	2.90	7.10

Source: *El mercurio*, 23 September 1972.

This was to be part of an anti-inflationary strategy. Once set at more realistic levels, prices were to be frozen. However, this policy turn was half-hearted, doubtless because of its intense unpopularity, especially among UP supporters. Prices were still, as a rule, below the levels at which supplies balanced demand. Nor was it politically possible to reduce the level of real wages far from the unrealistic levels of 1971, especially as there was an election due in the following March.

Wages had to be raised to keep pace with rising prices. Thus in October 1972 the announced *reajuste* was 100 per cent, that is, a doubling of wages, and the consequences would naturally be a further major twist to the inflationary spiral. However, to the government's credit it did face the necessity of some decline in real wages, and this is reflected in the figures shown in Table 1.10.

Table 1.10   Percentage increases in real wages, 1971–2

	Wages and salaries	Prices	Real wages
January–January	52.5	24.8	+20.2
April–April	40.3	38.1	+1.6
July–July	44.9	45.9	−0.7
October–October	121.2	142.9	−15.0

Source: *La economia chilena en 1972*, op. cit., p. 265.

The 100 per cent increase was not to apply to everyone and it was calculated to incorporate increases already made during the year, except that the lowest paid were favourably treated. This policy caused irritation among the copper miners, who had been relatively well paid, and in 1973 this led to a damaging strike. Meanwhile, other forces were rapidly pushing up the supply of money. The nationalized industries required subsidies. The purchase of some private enterprises by the state was also financed by money creation. Indeed, the executive power to print money was a way round congressional financial control. Tax collection was not effective, and any new tough redistributive fiscal legislation would not pass Congress. Such desirable social measures as free milk for children, for instance, were in the last analysis paid for by the printing press.

Agricultural procurements suffered from the inflation and from the growing black market. Thus in late September 1972 the official price of potatoes was 4 escudos per kilo, the free or black price was 14 escudos. Peasants and middlemen naturally diverted potatoes (and many other products) to the black market. The one more or less sure source of supply under the government's control came from imports, and when they could be afforded. Agricultural production was also discouraged by uncertainty over the prices and availability of goods, which might obtain when the crop ripened. Because of the black market, and also the confusion between private and co-operative activities on the *asentamientos*, statistics of sowings and production became less and less reliable. Output was probably higher than was reported.

By September 1972 the situation was plainly deteriorating. The events of the following month would make a bad situation worse.

The general strike of bourgeoisie

The opposition parties were split over the tactic to adopt. Congressional elections in March 1973 would theoretically give them the opportunity to impeach Allende, provided they obtained more than a two-thirds majority. This seemed unlikely. The more extreme members of the right (Patria y Libertad, and much of the National party) seemed increasingly to have thought of persuading the military to intervene. But the military at this date were only likely to intervene to save the country either from a left-wing coup or from chaos. In the absence of a real danger of a left-wing coup, and given the grave economic situation that already existed, the best bet for the right seemed to be to worsen this situation by economic sabotage. This policy was facilitated by the bitter grievance felt by much of the petty as well as by the grande bourgeoisie. If the country could be made ungovernable, the army would have to step in. If chaos spread, then perhaps the disenchanted voters would abandon the UP by the time of the March elections.

The pretext chosen was a minor misunderstanding. In the distant southern province of Aisen, the provincial CORFO proposed a nationalized goods transport service, in an area poorly provided with transport. In intent it was certainly not more revolutionary than the activities of British Road Services in the Highlands of Scotland. However, the truck owners, mostly very small men, saw here the thin end of the wedge.

Nationalization, backed by the state's control over imports of trucks, buses and spare parts, was alleged to be threatening. Denials were of no avail. The truckers stopped work, in a country overwhelmingly dependent on road transport. Since so many of the truckers were owner-drivers, trade union action was no remedy. (A damaging strike by small truck owners in the United States in January–February 1974 reminds us that such troubles can also occur there.)

The government detained some of the ringleaders. This led to politically concerted action by other groups and associations (*gremios*). In mid-October, doctors, dentists, accountants, engineers, bank officials, pharmacists, shopkeepers, petty manufacturers and some university staffs stopped work. Allende declared a state of emergency (12 October) and tried a mixture of threats and negotiations, which ended in deadlock. The *gremios* presented joint demands, enshrined in a so-called 'Pliego de Chile', which included political conditions that amounted to surrender.

The CUT ordered its members to go on working. Volunteers loaded and unloaded railway wagons. Some trucks were requisitioned. The government improvised a distribution system for essential supplies, giving priority to working-class areas. However, disorganization of production was inevitable and considerable. Serious damage was being done, with the *gremios* repeating their determination to stay out, and Allende having no way of compelling them to return to normal activities within the bounds set by the constitution and legality.

Indeed, even within these bounds he was compelled to invoke the aid of the military. The state of emergency brought generals and admirals into the role of maintaining order. General Hector Bravo, for example, was appointed to command in Santiago and issued emergency regulations. Armed soldiers toured the streets and guarded the petrol stations, where long lines of motorists waited their turn. At this stage the military did their duty without fear or favour, but this did not include the use of violence against the strikers (as distinct from groups of demonstrators). Nor were they ordered to use such violence. The effect of their new role on the senior officers could have been significant for the future. A US correspondent in Santiago told me that as he was interviewing General Bravo, 'his phone was ringing, there was a line of petitioners outside his office. He was exercising power. And, you know, I thought he was beginning to enjoy it.'

A way out of the impasse was found, when the commanders of the army, navy and air force joined a reconstructed government. General Prats, commander in chief, became Minister of the Interior, which made him not only responsible for public order but also *ex officio* vice-president (this minister acts if the president is incapacitated, or abroad). Some of the less popular ministers were dropped at the same time. General Prats successfully negotiated an end to the general strike of the bourgeoisie in early November 1972. These events are not my primary concern in this essay. What matters in the present context are their economic consequences.

First, of course, industrial output diminished. The effect of this on inflation was muted at first by the strike of retail traders; the diminished output of consumer goods piled up in warehouses. Consequently, although a wage reajustment of 100 per cent occurred during this strike, the additional money chased more unsold goods in the short run. Second, while the crisis gave rise to some improvisations by the government in the field of planning, allocation and transportation, based in some degree on requisitioning, a precondition of the peace negotiated by Prats was a return to the status quo, that is, private capital assets had to be returned to their owners in so far as they had been acquired during the crisis. (The strikers had demanded more, including a reduction in the Social Property Area acquired or controlled in previous years.) A virtual guarantee had to be given that further nationalization would be halted. Third, this left the Allende administration with no further politico-economic perspective, except a vaguely defined consolidation of gains already made. Although Prats was a constitutionalist and acted at all times as a loyal servant of the president, in fact it was clear to all that the military members of the cabinet had a virtual right of veto; measures to which they took exception were unlikely to be adopted. There was little room for manoeuvre left.

The government was politically relieved, if economically further embarrassed, by the series of court actions by the Kennecott Copper Corporation, which sought to prevent payments being made by the purchasers of Chilean copper in Western Europe by claiming property rights to the (nationalized) mines. While these actions lasted payments were delayed, but the public in Chile supported Allende on this issue, and in fact even the right in Congress voted with the government over the Kennecott case.

The crisis showed a notable split in the Christian Democrat party, with contrasting speeches by the intransigent ex-president Frei and the more conciliatory and left-wing ex-candidate Tomic. Tomic clearly supported the compromise that left Allende in office with the military in the government (indeed, he told me so). It seemed at the time that Frei wished Allende's regime to fall, and it was therefore not surprising that in September 1973 Frei expressed support for the coup.

In November–December 1972 Allende visited New York and also Moscow. In Moscow he was given high honours. The Chilean Communist leader Corvalan was there too. No doubt they asked for immediate large-scale economic assistance. They got promises of delivery of Soviet equipment on credit, and some immediate help, but too little. 'We overestimated greatly the amount of aid we might get from socialist countries', said an official exiled after the coup. The USSR had its own balance-of-payments problem, and was pursuing détente with the United States.

The election and the deadlock

The civil-military government held on to power until the March elections, with inflation resumed at a rapid rate; there was a mixture, as before, of price controls, giving way at irregular intervals in the face of ever-rising costs; shortage of many foodstuffs and consumers' goods was a constant source of worry. January and February are summer holiday months, and everyone waited for March.

The elections were hailed by the left as a victory, because the UP vote was higher than at the presidential elections, and certainly higher than the left had anticipated – over 43 per cent of the total. Partly this must be explained by the fact that the Christian Democrats in March 1973 were aligned with the right, so that some left-wing supporters who had voted for Tomic in the presidential elections switched to the UP in the congressional elections. In fact, bearing in mind the economic chaos and social dangers of the situation, the result of the elections represented a fatal deadlock. The actual votes are shown in Table 1.11.

Table 1.11. Votes cast in the congressional elections, March 1973.

	(thousands)
Christian Democrats	1,005
National party	750
Socialists	700
Communists	570
Other UP (MAPU, IC, etc.)	330
Other right	220
Total UP	1,600
Total opposition	1,975

Allende had three more years to go. Could the country survive that long, with continuing deadlock between executive and legislature, and with economic disintegration threatening? The government could take no decisive action against the will of Congress and without the support of the military within its own ranks. At best it would hope to hold on to the social gains it had registered and survive until 1976. However, its chances were reduced when Prats and the other generals left the government after the elections. Their presence had been a source of irritation to the more left-wing members of the UP coalition; thus it was an open secret that the secretary of the Socialist party, Altamirano, opposed their participation. In retrospect, their resignation was a grave setback to the hopes of

Allende's survival. In fact it was the UP who wished them to resign, but the generals may well have been uneasy in a UP government, and under increasing pressure from their own fellow officers to withdraw, now that they had guaranteed the holding of free elections (they would in all probability have been free and honest anyhow, but the right had expressed deep suspicion on this point).

The accelerating inflation and growing sense of disintegration was faced in April to June 1973 by an all-civilian government, amid vigorous and often unscrupulous opposition from the right and from the majority of the Christian Democrats. The one external factor that turned favourable was an increase in the price of copper. But this proved to be too late to save the government, the more so because of the continuing high prices of items that needed to be imported, for instance, wheat. It might be argued that, without oppositionist sabotage, the government could have tightened economic controls and begun a programme of economic recovery. Allende did speak of the need for sacrifice and for increased productive investments. But the government's grip on power, the means available to enforce its decisions, had become dangerously weak.

What could Allende now do? He had not the power to impose any drastic economic policies; he faced a hostile Congress and a mainly hostile free press and radio; and the armed forces and carabineros, who had hitherto protected the Constitution, were watching from the sidelines, with increasing evidence of the emergence of a faction willing to consider the overthrow of the president. The ultra-left was calling for tough measures ('la mana dura', to quote a popular left-wing song of the period). Enforced how? There were militant (not military) working-class organizations, but to arm them would mean instantly provoking the military into decisive and overwhelming counteraction. The sad story of the last six months of Allende's rule was of a gradual slide into disaster, without any real means of averting it or of taking any new policy initiatives in the economic field. A precondition for action (other than a civil war that the army would win) was a coalition with the Christian Democrats, if a joint programme could be devised under some umbrella of a 'government of national salvation' with Allende still as president. Discussions along these lines were begun, very late because of opposition among many of the UP leaders. There was no time even to see whether something could have been achieved by this route, which was known to be favoured by the Communist party.

Two further setbacks weakened the government and disrupted the economy. One was the strike of many copper miners. This, the first major conflict with a group of workers, arose from their desire to maintain their position, won under the American companies, of being much better paid than other Chilean workers. The particular reason for their strike was that they demanded that the 100 per cent wage readjustment due in April 1973 should be added to a 40 per cent interim rise already granted them a few months earlier. The government refused, since other workers due a 100 per cent rise had not received this interim increase. A damaging loss of copper production and exports ensued in an obstinate dispute that lasted two months.

The second and ultimately fatal attack came once again from the *gremios*, again led by the road transport organization under the right-winger Leon Vilarin. Again paralysis threatened. Again the government mobilized its supporters and declared a state of emergency. Again it brought the military into the government. But history refused to repeat itself. The occasional acts of sabotage that had occurred in October 1972 became more frequent; electric pylons were blown up, one of Allende's own personal assistants was murdered. Inflation speeded up even further, to an annual rate of 400 per cent (the index for June 1973 was already 207 [January 1973=100]). Amid growing chaos, it became clear that, whatever the personal views of General Prats and a few other loyal senior officers, the bulk of the armed forces would not play any longer the role assigned to them. Allende must have pinned hopes upon a split in the military, who seemed more likely to split if he observed legality scrupulously. This was not altogether baseless. Prats went into exile, and some other senior and junior officers were dealt with severely by the conspirators after the coup. But in practice the conspiracy developed unhindered, while no steps were taken to organize 'unofficial' resistance for fear of upsetting the military. In fact, such feeble efforts as were made to form groups loyal to the UP, notably in the navy, were apparently undertaken by individuals without Allende's authorization (Altamirano was said to have played a leading part), and this helped the conspirators to present to vacillating officers a picture of a left-wing conspiracy to 'subvert' the navy. The last opportunity presented to the government was perhaps the premature rebellion of a tank regiment on 29 June (the Tancazo); this would have required drastic action, including mass dismissals of potentially disloyal officers. But the opportunity, if it existed, was not taken, and two months afterwards Prats was forced to resign by his fellow officers. Even in distant Glasgow I could see that this was the end. Meanwhile, with no means of enforcing any policy, the government could only watch the continuing collapse of the economy. Aware of the increasing likelihood of a coup, the striking bourgeoisie refused any compromise, did not negotiate, and waited for the political dividends that would flow from economic disasters. Allende had now neither policy nor power to impose a policy. He could only stagger on, improvising solutions to crises as they arose, until in the end the more ruthless elements in the armed forces destroyed him, the UP parties and the Constitution, on that tragic day of 11 September 1973.

The problem for the political economist is to draw any possible morals.

That errors were made is self-evident, but which of the errors were the fatal ones, which could have been avoided? Between the expectations and pressures of his own supporters and the objective difficulties, exacerbated by domestic opposition and foreign obstruction, how much room for manoeuvre was there for Allende? What could he do without a majority and without control over the legislature? Was there a more moderate policy that could have won the support of at least the left wing of the Christian Democrats in Congress? Or was such a policy, or a coalition that included Tomic, rendered impossible by the political attitudes of the UP supporters and of the leadership of most of its constituent parties? In any case, could it have been right so greatly to raise real wages and expectations, reduce investments and increase imports of food, and to use up all currency reserves and material stocks?

Among the errors that can be diagnosed was one that could be called economic naïveté, of a kind common in far left-wing circles in Britain and elsewhere. There is little realization that real incomes depend decisively on productivity. Wage restraint is equated with impermissible 'reformism' or with betraying the working class. By some UP leaders inflation was blamed airily on capitalism and curable by altering *los estructuras* (the structures), enlarging the Social Property Area, freeing Chile from subordination to foreign capital, and carrying out land reform. High output accompanied by price control would then halt inflation. (The above remarks on inflation are paraphrased from the *Programa basica del gobierno de la Unidad Popular*, cited from an editorial in *Panorama economico* devoted to *el desborde inflacionario*.)[11] A critic called this a *vision facilista*, and cited in illustration a speech by Millas made at the end of 1970, shortly after the Allende government took office:

> Until 3 November inflation galloped in Chile. From this day the problem begins to slow down. No more anti-patriotic devaluations of the escudo rate against the dollar! We will cancel various increases in price, for instance for electricity. Necessities will be subsidized. During the course of 1971 the new economic measures will take effect, with the result that rising prices will become a thing of the past, remembered as a burden carried in the days when governments served large-scale Capital.[12]

The fact that a large expansion of the money supply would stimulate a speed-up in inflation was either forgotten or regarded as unimportant. So was the pressure of rising wages upon costs. By contrast, there was a gross over-estimation of the anti-inflationary effects of price control, and an under-estimation of the effect of such control in stimulating imports. A large budget deficit financed by money creation, plus higher wages, plus strict price control, equals shortages and queues. This simple lesson may yet have to be learned in other countries. Falling profits, as costs rose, cut down the possibility of investing out of profits in the public and private sectors alike. The price adjustments that then had to be made in the middle of 1972 were so drastic that they caused the economy to stagger towards hyperinflation.

The editorial of *Panorama economico* makes a further important point: that while the organized working class did gain large increases in money wages, the price rises of 1972 hit a large and poor segment of the population that was deemed self-employed, or was in small workshops or petty services where no trade unions or wage regulations operated, or finally was poor peasants. 'The potential political consequences of this phenomenon are not difficult to imagine and could constitute another element of tension in the already acute process of political radicalization.'[13] How many of these, perhaps lumpenbourgeoisie as well as lumpenproletariat, turned to the radical right?

For an economist who writes and works in Great Britain, a further question poses itself. Certain errors not dissimilar to Allende's were committed under the Conservative government presided over by Edward Heath. Allende was a Marxist, Heath was a conservative. Britain too ran headlong into a crisis. Some of its elements had certain parallels with Chile. Heath reduced taxes for political reasons; Allende was unable to increase them for political reasons. But had a large and growing budget deficit, which contributed to inflation. Both faced a labour movement that demanded, and got, large wage increases. Both froze prices charged by nationalized industries, and had to subsidize their growing losses. A huge balance-of-payments deficit developed. This was made worse by a sharp worsening (in both countries) of the terms of trade. It was complicated, at a critical moment, by industrial action on the part of miners (copper and coal miners respectively). Given the balance-of-payments situation of 1973–5, suppose Britain had been faced with the prospect of paying its way without incurring further foreign indebtedness? Few would doubt that the resulting chaos would have had (perhaps still might have) profound effects on the British political system. It was only by vast borrowings that Heath, and after him Wilson, avoided disaster. Allende had no such choice; massive credits were denied him. (And where would Britain be today without oil revenues?)

These parallels serve as a useful reminder of the limitations of political power in a democracy. It is easy to say, why did Allende not impose a sound economic policy? A future historian might say the same thing about Heath or Wilson: why did they tolerate so high a rate of inflation (of course never as high as Chile's, but too high by European standards)?, why did they not balance the budget?, and so on. We who live in Britain know that, along with genuine errors of policy and judgement, Heath and Wilson were hemmed in by political and social constraints, by forces they could only partially control or could not control at all. To remember this is a first step towards understanding some of the causes of the economic failings of the Allende administration. They had the best intentions, they (or most of them) wished to conciliate the small businessmen, to reduce inflation, to redistribute income in favour of the very poor, and to nationalize key sectors in order to use their revenues for the public good. It is surely too simple, in the light of the evidence, to say that they were overthrown because of what they tried to do. Many of their policies led to results quite other than they had intended, and strengthened the hand of those who wished to eliminate the UP and all that it stood for. The present essay is written much more in sorrow than anger. It does not pretend to answer all the questions that it poses, directly or by implication. There is much more research to be done.

Meanwhile, we should (in my view) refrain from tempting generalizations about the inevitable failure of a parliamentary road, particularly if one bears in mind the fact of an anti-socialist parliamentary majority. One cannot legislate one's way towards socialism if the anti-socialists control the legislature.

Finally, a word on the junta's economic policies. Having eliminated political parties and suppressed trade unions, it made an attempt to raise prices to 'realistic' levels; they rose by 87.6 per cent in the single month of October 1973. This caused much hardship, as did the rise in unemployment that accompanied the attempts to impose deflation.

Perhaps the generals were hoping to follow the Brazilian model, where there has been an industrial boom based upon large-scale import of capital, a military regime, low wages and high profits. However, the Brazilian model may be quite inapplicable to Chile, with its much smaller population and relatively restricted internal market. The junta may well face political as well as economic crises, unless it receives aid from abroad. The outlook is still stormy.

Postscript (1983): A short-lived boom has been followed by a rash of bankruptcies, balance-of-payments crises and very high foreign debts. Strikes by copper miners and lorry owners recall similar events to Allende's last year. The outlook continues to be stormy.

Notes: Chapter 1

1 Speech of 5 November 1970 in Salvador Allende, *Chile's Road to Socialism* (Harmondsworth: Penguin, 1973), p. 65.
2 ibid., p. 84.
3 An excellent account of the whole problem was written by S. Barraclough and A. Affonso, 'Diagnóstico de la reformia agraria chilena', *Cuadernos de la realidad nacional* (Santiago: April 1973).

4 Allende, op. cit.
5 *Comentarios sobre la situacion economica* (Santiago: Universidad de Chile, 2nd semester 1972/3), p. 229.
6 ibid., p. 249.
7 ibid., p. 7.
8 *Documentos del consejo de rectores* (Santiago: Universidad de Chile, July–August 1972), pp. 43, 45.
9 Facultad de Economia Politica, *La economia chilena en 1972* (Santiago: Universidad de Chile, 1973), p. 40.
10 ibid., pp. 63–4.
11 *Panorama economico* (Santiago: October 1972).
12 *El siglo*, 13 December 1970, quoted in ibid.
13 ibid., p. 8.

2   *The explosive model*

This essay was originally published in the *Journal of Development Studies*, October 1966. Unemployment as a major social problem has become more acute since it was written. It remains of importance to note the achievement of more or less full employment in most communist-ruled countries, but there are exceptions; urban unemployment in China would multiply if migration from rural areas were permitted. Full employment has its costs, in economic inefficiency and weak labour discipline, but that is another story. So, after all, has large-scale unemployment.

This essay is intended to be a contribution to the debate concerning capital-intensive and labour-intensive investment. But at the same time its aim is to draw attention to what can become, perhaps is becoming, a major and dangerous contradiction between the supply of and demand for labour, which could well lead to social and political explosion. Finally I would like to look at the Soviet industrialization model, which does have some relevance to the points at issue.

Let me begin by describing a situation, elements of which can be found in a number of Latin American countries and probably elsewhere as well. If there is oversimplification and some cutting of analytical corners, the state of affairs described is closer to reality than most development models with which we are presented, especially by our more mathematically minded confrères.

The model contains the following three elements.

(1)   There is a landlord–dominated agriculture with little or no security of tenure for peasants, but with a government actually or potentially concerned with land reform. There is the possibility of legislation dealing with peasant rights to plots of land which they cultivate, or there exists, or is discussion of, minimum wage legislation for landless labourers. Under these conditions, prudent landlords try to reduce the number of peasants on their land. They make labour-saving investments, though of an extensive character which do not increase yields (for example, tractors not fertilizers). They show an understandable reluctance to allow peasants to establish any kind of squatters' rights which might conceivably be given legal force by a reforming government. As a result of all this, the normal drift of country dwellers to the bright lights of the city is swelled very considerably.

(2)   There is a rapid rate of population increase in both urban and rural areas.

(3)   Industrial investment in cities tends to be highly capital-intensive and employs relatively few of the additional labourers who come to seek employment. This is in fact the case in many countries at different stages of development. When I was in Latin America this fact was repeatedly stressed, while my colleague Emil Rado has kindly drawn my attention to his calculations which show that in a number of African countries there has been little or no upward trend in the numbers employed, as distinct from self-employed. Taking ten African countries, he has shown that the proportion of wage-earners in the total population fell in nine of them, in the ten years 1952–62. Even in absolute numbers there has been a fall, in a number of instances. In Latin America there is, as a rule, an increase, but it is far too slow to absorb the increase in the non-wage-earner force. In tropical Africa the phenomenon of landlordism is almost wholly absent, and so the first of the conditions of my 'explosive model' is absent too. It does operate, however, in many Latin American countries. This has the familiar effect of inflating the service sectors, greatly increasing the numbers of shoe-shine boys, and bringing about a potentially dangerous political atmosphere with a very large under-employed and discontented city mob.

This process creates a revolutionary situation and has evident political and social dangers. One can almost discern in the distance the American marines on the way to suppress the inevitable riots.

Why are capital-intensive investments made in such circumstances? Let us at once reject the tempting but incorrect notion that this is due primarily to the irrational predilection of underdeveloped governments for ultra-modern techniques, though it is true that some governments are attracted by grandiose projects. Private enterprise also chooses capital-intensive variants. It is a notable characteristic of industrial investments in these countries, whether these are made by domestic or by foreign capitalists, that they are labour-saving. Even a quite brief examination of actual investment projects can convince the analyst of this.

There are several reasons which help to explain this tendency, some of them of general application, some of them peculiar to certain countries.

Alexander Gerschenkron points out, by reference to the historical experience of developing European countries, that new industries tend to be modern and capital-intensive.[1] He shows that the beginning of wisdom in these matters is to cease to regard labour as a homogeneous and undifferentiated mass. While there may be surplus of totally unskilled peasants and ex-peasants, reliable factory labour is not abundant, and it often pays to save labour of types which is either scarce or inefficient. Gerschenkron also argues that the adoption of the most modern techniques borrowed from the most advanced countries is one of the few advantages of a late-comer, since long-established industrial countries inevitably have a much higher proportion of obsolete equipment. It could also be argued that a developing country is particularly short of men capable of designing equipment and initiating new productive processes; therefore, even granting that a different capital–labour ratio would be more apt to the circumstances of the case, there might well be no effective alternative to borrowing the techniques and methods which have been developed elsewhere. These points should be familiar to students of the subject, and it is not my intention to dwell on them, but only to add that these tendencies can be exacerbated by political measures which strengthen the endeavours of the entrepreneurs to save labour. These measures are common to a number of developing countries, particularly in Latin America. I refer to social legislation which greatly raises the costs of labour to the employer.

The classical case is that of Brazil. Very high social insurance contributions, very high severance pay and also job security all contribute to discourage the employment of more labour than is strictly necessary. In addition trade union restrictions keep open a wide gap between the incomes and living standards of the established working class on the one hand and of the new 'immigrants' (from rural areas) on the other. Institutional arrangements are such that it is not easy for labour or employers to cross this gap. This naturally encourages labour-saving investments.

However, it would be wrong to overstress the role of this factor taken by itself. Thus in the Russian Empire at the end of the last century the bulk of industrial investment was highly capital-intensive, even though there was no minimum wages legislation or social security contributions. So the tendency was there already, and populist pro-worker legislation only reinforced it.

In the model here described everyone is working in his own best interest. Landlords, investors and workers are all being rational according to their lights. It is logical for a landlord to get rid of sharecroppers who might invoke squatters' rights and so threaten his property and the value of his land. Capitalists also behave as economically rational men. Nor is it possible to blame workers for seeking higher wages and good sickness benefits. Yet the total effect is to create instability and perhaps precipitate a social and political explosion. This is a particularly vivid instance of the divergence of private and social interest. An explosion is not desired, but the behaviour pattern of various groups of individuals is such that they contribute greatly to its likelihood.

How, if at all, did Stalinist industralization avoid these difficulties?

Communist planners chose capital-intensive variants. They believed in introducing the most modern equipment and borrowed their techniques from the most advanced Western countries. In the 1930s whole plants were copied from Western models, with the United States and Germany particularly influential. Yet labour was pouring in from the villages. Of course in the USSR there were no landlords engaged in expelling sharecroppers and squatters. Instead there was collectivization, which in the years 1929–34 converted the peasant smallholder to a collective farmer, very much against his will in most cases. Migration to town was greatly speeded up in consequence. Needless to say, most of these migrants were totally unskilled, poor factory material, at least until after a prolonged period of training. But there was in fact no significant unemployment. Instead there was a shortage of labour in some sectors and areas.[2] Thus the explosive model did not apply to Stalin's Russia. We must now discover why not.

An interesting view has been expressed by David Granick.[3] He points out that the argument for capital-intensive investment choices, advanced by Galenson and Leibenstein, is irrelevant to the Soviet case, since their argument rests on the need to keep down the number of wage-earners in order to maintain a higher level of saving. In the USSR the level of savings/investments can be determined by the government. However, Granick cites the view (without clearly accepting or rejecting it) that there was 'unusual rationality' in the choice of production functions, and in capital-labour substitution, in the Soviet economy. This view would seem to rest on the fact that the scarcity of capital was recognized, that every effort was made to use capital assets intensively and that the abundant factor, labour, was applied, to the greatest possible extent, to maximize output.

In my view the facts were as he states them, but such conclusions may well be misleading. Equipment was indeed fully utilized. I recall one of my own early studies, in collaboration with Professor R. D. Laird, which analysed the use made of a threshing machine on a collective farm. It was worked by two shifts each of seventy peasants, and the man who invented such a remarkable way of using the equipment received a Stalin prize.[4] There were doubtless also many instances of the use of modern labour-saving machinery in factories, which were either themselves highly labour-intensive in the end, or were associated with unmechanized auxiliary processes which used a lot of labour. Furthermore whole sectors of industry were deliberately undercapitalized and under-equipped, for example, the clothing industry, since the capital that was available was allocated in accordance with state-determined priorities and not any measure of relative profitability. Therefore a very modern steel industry coexisted with old and worn-out equipment in less important sectors, or those judged to be less important.

Even in high-priority industries there remained some labour-intensive and high-cost plants, producing at a cost often several times higher than that of the modern plants in the same industry. This was due to a number of causes. One was a tendency to concentrate the bulk of new investments on new plants rather than modernization of old ones. Another was the impossibility of bankruptcy. The high-cost and inefficient plants were kept in production regardless of financial losses, since the overriding object was the maximization of total output. This produced some quite striking consequences in some industries. For example, in 1959 80 per cent of the electric power in the Soviet Union was generated in power stations employing only about 15 per cent of the total labour force engaged in the industry, while no less than 800,000 people were employed at 157,000 small and tiny generating plants which produced only a small proportion of the total electricity.[5] The same kind of picture emerges in analyses of Soviet production of tools, components, forgings and castings. In these instances the trouble arises mainly from the habit of many factories of producing those items for themselves by hand in small workshops, owing partly to the failure to provide for sufficient production in specialized plant and partly to uncertainties about supply. The common denominator in all this is an emphasis on production and a relative neglect of cost and profitability.

Was all this rational? Of course the Stalinist system did use its scarce capital very intensively. But it did so under conditions which, on any reasonable measure of efficiency, led to conspicuous waste of resources. The use of labour-saving machinery is justified economically by the labour it saves. If in the process of using it intensively a great deal of labour is employed, it would probably have been more profitable not to use the machine at all. I myself visited a Soviet farm on which a beet harvesting combine was followed on foot by four women who trimmed the tops of the beets by hand. They could have done almost all the work without any help whatever from the combine!

Over the economy as a whole it is quite probable that the cost of such lopsided mechanization helps to explain the contrast between the rapid growth of output and the very much more modest rise in living standards. This would certainly be the consequence one would expect from the inefficient use of resources. To put it in its simplest terms, the quantity of labour embodied in the equipment was often greater than the labour saved by its use. In the Stalin period it was impossible to calculate whether this was in fact so or not, since the price system was not adapted to such calculations. In any case this was the period in which the very concept of the rate of return on capital invested was regarded as un-Marxist and therefore sinful.

There is no evidence that the planners at this period consciously aimed at the result that was actually achieved. The labour force was persistently higher than had been planned or expected. For example the first five-year plan, when it was drafted in 1928, envisaged a total non-agricultural labour force of 12.9 million (maximum variant), an increase of about 3.7 million. The actual figure was 18.9 million, that is, the increase was 9.3

million.[6] In other words either the planners over-estimated the efficiency
of the labour force, or they were over-sanguine about the volume of
capital equipment which would be available, or both. They sought to
make good the deficiencies of their own plans by drawing in additional
labour, especially the surplus which still existed in agriculture. This was
not a deliberate and rational plan. They, so to speak, stumbled into it. The
aim was to go full-steam ahead while using the most capital-intensive and
the most modern technical variants in any industry judged to be of great
importance. But a decision to be capital-intensive does not, of course,
make capital as such any less scarce. Inevitably, therefore, the available
capital was exhausted on relatively few 'priority' projects or processes.
Having thus run out of capital, they continued to apply labour to the
greatest practicable extent. While real wages did fall in this period, it
would be wrong to regard the labour as being particularly cheap. Productivity was very low, and even at this time there were considerable social
security benefits, with contributions to the social security fund from the
various enterprises in proportion to the number of workers they
employed.

This entire policy would seem to have led to a very serious, perhaps
even appalling, misallocation of resources. Yet it did avoid the explosive
model. A Brazilian, Argentinian, or Indian private investor would not
invest in labour-saving and capital-intensive variants unless they really did
save labour. The Soviet investors – that is, the citizens in their capacity as
forced savers – could and did, while being totally unaware of it. The
planners too may have been unaware of it, and I have emphasized that in
their own published plans they envisaged much larger increases in labour
productivity, and therefore saving of labour, than actually occurred. It
would seem therefore that the avoidance of the explosive model was in
some sense conditional upon the irrationality of the Stalinist investment
policy. At least this thought is worth dwelling on.

Critical readers may well be feeling dissatisfied with the above argument. Why, they may well ask, was Stalin's investment policy irrational,
in the developmental sense of that ambiguous word? Is not imbalance a
necessary characteristic of development in a real-world situation? Given
that any large-scale project involves indivisibilities, part of the economy is
bound at some stage to be disproportionately and lopsidedly developed,
which may look irrational from the standpoint of static allocation criteria
but is none the less unavoidable and necessary. Nor is there anything
inherently irrational in mechanizing only part of the operation of a factory.
As Gerschenkron points out, it may well be that the main production line
is mechanized because, by saving the scarce kinds of labour, it affords the
greatest economy, while auxiliary tasks can be performed by unskilled
ex-peasants. All this is true, and it is indeed important not to jump to the
conclusion that Stalin could have chosen rationally if he had only been

converted to Western economic theory. In fact there were at this time no Western theories about investment criteria.[7] Even today few of us can be happy about the state of our ideas on investment choices in the context of rapid development.

Yet, after making all allowances for such counter-arguments, there is still an important sense in which the Stalin method wasted resources. It is literally true that, at any rate in the 1930s investment choices were made with little or no attempt to calculate either costs or rates of return. This refusal to calculate was justified by the assertion that choice was inherently a matter for politics, and this in turn was related to a purely qualitative assessment, expressing the priorities of the regime. Stalin did refer on occasion to profitability on the scale of the national economy, which was always to take priority over considerations of the profitability of any particular project. Few development economists would fail to recognize the possibility of a conflict between the interests of the development programme and the financial interest of some enterprise taken in isolation. However, Stalin had no way of defining or measuring 'national-economic profitability'; this was just a phrase, with no more meaning than the equally question-begging 'social welfare function', which we ought to maximize if we knew what it was. All this left the field wide open to arbitrary decision. Of course, there were instances in which investment choices were genuinely and consciously made on the grounds of political preference. For example, it may have been decided to build an industrial complex in the east for strategic reasons. In this instance the choice actually made cannot be criticized by economists on purely economic grounds.

However, in the majority of instances the investment choices actually made were not in this sense the expression of planners' preferences, nor were they a conscious choice between alternative means to an agreed end. The planners were unable or unwilling to compare the costs of alternatives. In some cases the decisions were the consequences of competition for investment resources between different branches of the administration. It would have been a miraculous coincidence if the investment plans actually adopted represented a rational choice, on any definition of the word 'rational'. Errors also arose in the process of execution of plans. An East European economist, commenting on an earlier draft of this essay, said that in his country investment projects were often drafted in a form in which a great deal of labour would be saved by complex mechanization; but at a later stage the investment allocation was cut (i.e. 'they ran out of capital'), and this left the designers no alternative but to abandon mechanization of auxiliary processes. The result, naturally, was the employment of additional labour and the failure to fulfil the labour productivity plans, as well as a much lower rate of return on capital than had originally been expected. There is also considerable evidence that the same problem is worrying Soviet planners today. They do now seek to calculate the rate of return, but repeatedly find that they have envisaged a much larger saving of labour than has in fact been taking place. The fact that, until very recently, there was no charge for capital encouraged over-application from below for investment resources, and overcapitalization was not reflected in cost calculations, either at enterprise level or in planning offices.

Of course, there is a great deal more which could be said about this whole complex subject. But perhaps we can agree that there was a connection between the refusal to base investment decisions on profitability calculations and the avoidance of urban unemployment, and also that no group of private capitalists could possibly have acted in the Stalin manner.

The Stalin manner included the suppression of independent trade unions and, in the first stages of Soviet industralization, a drastic depression of living standards. This was combined with a high rate of accumulation, and terror. This combination of circumstances renders the applicability and desirability of the Soviet model very doubtful indeed. So one is left with the problem of what advice can be given to developing countries on the subject of how to avoid the pitfalls inherent in the explosive model.

A beginning is a recognition of the importance of the problem, and therefore of the need to provide labour-intensive forms of employment more useful than the cleaning of shoes. Public works, especially in rural areas, road building, the encouragement of labour-intensive forms of agriculture such as fruit and vegetable raising, fewer financial penalties for the employer who does choose labour-intensive methods, these are a few rather obvious suggestions. It is significant, too, that in several Latin American countries land reform is regarded as a means of retaining labour in agriculture, and thus avoiding excessively rapid migration to town.

Some economists have urged the desirability of designing simpler and more labour-intensive kinds of factories for developing countries, which would fit their factor endowment. In so far as the use of modern capital-intensive methods stems from the non-existence of alternatives, this may well help. But for reasons already analysed at length, this is only one cause among others, and the results may be disappointing. Of course, it is necessary to study the circumstances of each particular country. Nor should one overlook the experiences and difficulties of China in endeavouring to combine highly labour-intensive rural works and rural industrialization with the development of a modern industry. To repeat, the contrast of the modern and medieval within a developing economy is not of itself evidence of irrationality. It is to some degree inevitable. In some economies it is thought desirable to combine the encouragement of labour-intensive cottage-type industries for the domestic market with a modern low-cost mechanized industry oriented largely to export. It may be of interest to realize that this thought is not new, as the following quotation shows:

Machines . . . if they reduce the number of those working, are harmful in a state with a large population. However we must distinguish between things made for domestic use and those which are intended for export to foreign lands. One cannot have too much economy of labour in making goods for export, since the other nations that receive them could obtain similar goods from their neighbours or from others who are in the same situation as ourselves.

The author is the Empress Catherine of Russia, the date 1768. The Empress's advisers are believed to have included some Russian former students at the University of Glasgow, who had attended Adam Smith's lectures. The document from which the statement is quoted is the famous *Nakaz*, Catherine's instructions to her officials.

Finally, it is noteworthy that communist-ruled countries which endeavour to reorganize the planning system, in an effort to ensure greater rationality in investment choices, also run into a problem of unemployment, or of job replacement. One sees this most clearly in Yugoslavia and Czechoslovakia, and these questions have at last been publicly discussed in the Soviet Union also.

Notes: Chapter 2

1 A. Gerschenkron, *Economic Backwardness in Historical Perspective* (Cambridge, Mass.: Harvard University Press, 1962).
2 Forced labour and deportation contributed significantly to labour redeployment in the Stalin period. However, this does not bear directly on the present argument.
3 D. Granick, 'On patterns of technological choice in Soviet industry', *American Economic Review*, vol. 52, no. 2 (May 1962), pp. 149–57.
4 A. Nove and R. D. Laird, 'Note on labour utilization in the kolkhoz', *Soviet Studies*, vol. 4, no. 4 (April 1953), pp. 434–42.
5 *Voprosy economiki*, 1961, no. 5.
6 Even the seven-year plan (1959–65) followed a not dissimilar course, there being in 1965 about 6 million more persons employed outside agriculture than the plan had envisaged. Granick, op. cit., argues that Soviet investment in early years produced above all an industrial labour force, i.e. it made possible mass training of raw ex-peasants. This is certainly an acceptable interpretation of what actually occurred, but it was evidently unintentional, at least in scale.
7 On this see the excellent book by J.-M. Collette, *Politique des investissements et calcul économique: l'expérience soviétique* (Paris: Cujas, 1965).

3 The poverty of micro-economics: an essay on the relationship of theory and policy

This was my contribution to the festschrift for Dr Tedy Prager (in a special issue of *Wirtschaft und Gesellschaft*, Vienna, vol. 8, no. 2, 1982), who had been a fellow-student at LSE about fifty years ago. It expresses my continuing dismay over what could be called myopic marginalism, which appears to underlie the ideology of Mrs Thatcher's privatization-and-fragmentation advisers. By the time this book is published we may hear much more about the consequences of such myopia, for example, in connection with the government's Bus Bill and the profit-oriented operations of British Telecom.

In his memoirs Tedy Prager kindly remembered how, as a fellow-student, I expressed scepticism as to the evidence given at the Moscow trials of 1937. Our paths diverged widely, geographically and ideologically, but I think we both share a concern for economics of socialism, and therefore also an interest in public enterprise in its many forms. Of course, activities do not become socialist merely by being public. Was it not Engels who remarked that, were it so, the first socialist institution was the regimental tailor. Some socialists are apt to dismiss the experience of nationalized industries in capitalist countries as irrelevant. However, they are wrong on two counts. First, most of the problems encountered in administering and evaluating the performance of nationalized industries occur in countries calling themselves socialist. Second, inadequacies in the operations of nationalized industries can help to discredit the socialist idea among the victims of these inadequacies, that is, the general public.

It is my contention that Western 'mainstream' micro-economics has not been helpful, indeed has on occasion been positively misleading, in the search for operational criteria. Furthermore, the teaching of economics has become less relevant, in these (and perhaps in some other) respects since the days when Tedy and I were at the London School of Economics.

It so happened that I was out of academic life, first in the army and then in the civil service, for twenty years. When I returned, I soon became aware how far out of touch I was with modern economics. But equally there arose a strong impression that modern economics was far out of touch with reality, indeed further out of touch than had been the case in my student days. True, there had been an interest in growth, a word which never seemed to have been mentioned in courses I had attended at the LSE. True also that there had been an emphasis on equilibrium. But it seemed to me that it was a different kind of equilibrium. If not exactly dynamic, it was none the less seen as a process. The market place was the scene of struggle. Competition was a battle with winners and losers. Hayek and Mises were pro-market, not because of the assumptions of perfect competition and perfect knowledge, which would have been equally applicable to perfect planning, but precisely because the real world was full of uncertainty and risk. An entrepreneur, it seemed evident, had an entrepreneurial function, and so had the firm. 'Pareto' optimality would seem to be a concept inapplicable to a competitive market, because quite plainly the success of any competitor meant damage, loss, borne by the less successful. Can *anything* of significance be done without damaging *someone*'s interest?

Instead I found myself face-to-face with some strange-looking concepts. Perfect competition, it seemed clear, was not competition at all, since its assumptions were inconsistent with any *process*; no battle, winners, losers, more or less efficient firms. Profits in equilibrium tended to zero, because in fact, on the assumptions underlying what purported to be the 'theory of the firm', there was no reason why firms should exist at all, and no real function (or, logically enough, reward) for entrepreneurship. Comically enough, this dry-as-dust construction was described by some Marxists as 'apologetics for capitalism', although, apart from its inherent unreality, it proposed no real role for capitalists, and treated everyone, capitalists and workers alike, as automata reacting to stimuli under conditions unknown in any world yet encountered. One example of our teaching may be worth quoting. I once was visiting in Oxford and was asked to discuss a draft thesis with a mature graduate student who was working on Yugoslavia. He had argued that, under certain circumstances, a Yugoslav firm would act in such-and-such a way. I objected that it would not do so, because, if it did, its competitors would gain at its expense. The student replied, coldly, that under the assumption of perfect competition, the firm would be quite indifferent to the actions of its competitors! (So it would, so it would . . .)

Many a reader will be saying to him or herself by now: this is too much, everyone knows that these abstract theories are not directly applicable to the real world, and their authors know this too and frequently say so. Quite right. But I will try to show that, none the less, certain theoretical simplifications do in fact influence advice that is given in real-world situations, partly because the fashionable mathematical apparatus requires these simplifications, partly because the relaxation of certain convenient assumptions stands in the way of desired quantification. In many instances, the problem is not a denial that certain real-world situations and complications exist, but rather an under-emphasis, or no mention at all, of matters of evident importance which would disturb the elegance or rigour of formal models.

Much of this essay will relate to advice given about the running of nationalized industries. I shall try to demonstrate that conventional micro-economics provided misleading guidelines to those charged with advising on economically rational behaviour by state enterprises. One reason among several is that they failed to use an adequate definition of commercial behaviour in real-world markets by real-world firms. Another is that they fell into the yawning gap between micro- and macro-economics. Still another is an unimaginatively narrow view of monopoly theory. Finally, there is the tendency to misuse marginal analysis, in situations in which externalities, indivisibilities, complementarities, *systemic* factors, are important, as they often are. Business studies are not guilty, or not so guilty, of the oversimplifications and omissions of which I speak. But economic theory has had regrettably little connection with business studies, despite Marshall's phrase about 'the ordinary business of life'.

There are certain concepts, certain words, of quite evident importance in 'real' micro-economics, which are not to be found at all in most textbooks. Let us look at a few of these, and consider the reasons and the consequences.

Let us begin with *quality*. A check on the index to a dozen textbooks showed either no entry at all under this head, or one related to product differentiation: that one way in which firms can behave under imperfect competition is to supply the product in different qualities, and at different prices (for instance, cars). This does at least suggest to the student that quality can vary, while in most books the word 'product' is silently assumed to be homogeneous, clear and unambiguous, and any variation (for reasons of 'product differentiation' or any other) then becomes simply a different product.

Kevin Lancaster wrote, and rightly, that any good or service possesses 'a bundle of characteristics'. Indeed it is so, and one must express astonishment that this needed saying at all. It may be simpler to confine the analysis to quantity and price, but there are other dimensions too: durability, packaging, punctuality, after-sales service, taste (whether relating to a dress or a restaurant meal), sharpness (of a knife or a razor-blade), and so on and so forth. Under competitive conditions there will be pressure to take these matters into account. But to do so involves trouble and expense. Quality of a given good or service can deteriorate, indeed is very likely to deteriorate, if competitive pressure is weak or absent. This seems to be

overlooked when economists advocate commercial behaviour by nationalized quasi-monopolies, with consequences which I shall discuss.

Oddly, there is very little discussion of either the quality or motivation
of labour and management. If not seen as homogeneous, labour is
differentiated by specialization: even the most blinkered micro-economist
would agree that there are differences between, say, miners, accountants
and pilots. But persons of the same speciality can work well or less well,
behaviour of management and labour can be affected by the indicators by
which their performance is judged, morale and attitudes affect outcome.
Obvious? Yes, but how often referred to in books on micro-economics?

To continue my list, let me take *goodwill*. Usually this is not mentioned
at all. It is to be found in Samuelson, but only in the form of a note to the
effect that it is a saleable asset. But this leaves out of account the underlying
economic meaning of goodwill as an asset: reputation for performance.
Conversely, there is badwill. If a firm provides a defective good, fails to
deliver in time, cannot supply spare parts, then its reputation suffers and so
does its business – if the customer can go elsewhere. There are two
consequences. One is that one cannot ignore the sum total of a firm's
activities; one transaction affects, for good or ill, other transactions. This
explains why theorists avoid the issue; it makes marginal analysis untidy,
since rigour and elegance require isolation of transactions from each other
(their link is with the market). Such selling slogans as 'Open always', 'We
will take you anywhere', 'You *will* be seated', 'We are never knowingly
undersold', are goodwill-creating means of pleasing the prospective customer. They do *not* necessarily imply that each transaction will yield the
required rate of profit; indeed it is quite likely that it will not. The chosen
strategy is expected to be profitable. A second consequence is that, if a
monopoly situation exists, there is no 'commercial' reason to acquire, no
commercial penalty for losing, goodwill. If the customer *cannot* go elsewhere, what does goodwill matter, in terms of the profit-and-loss account?

Let us pass on to *purpose, aim, role* of the enterprise. In a competitive
market, this is simple: to make a profit. The firm chooses its role in
relation to market opportunity. It can and does modify this role, selecting
the *strategy* which best suits its situation. Other firms in the same line of
business may select a different role. Let us take garages. Some may be open
on Sundays and/or all night, others not. Some shops open late on some
evenings, others do not. Once again, it does not follow that each of these
activities is at all times profitable if separately costed. Thus an all-night
garage probably does not make a profit between 3 and 5 a.m., but might
benefit from the fact that its customers know that it is always open. All this
assumes a competitive market. If, however, market forces are weak, or
there is a monopoly, then none of this would happen automatically. Why
should *any* garage be open at night, unless it is considered to be someone's
duty to ensure that some all-night facilities be provided? Or imagine a state

monopoly of retail trade. Apart from the question of convenience of opening hours, and the range of stocks carried, there is the not unimportant question of the saving of customers' time. Consider a monopolist retailer who is instructed to behave 'commercially', that is, to pay attention to profit, productivity per shop-worker, turnover per shop. These indicators would all look 'better' if the customers stood in line all day. So would the 'efficiency' of a bus service if all buses were full, with people standing on each other's toes. One really must introduce the question of 'efficiency for what', the *purpose* of the exercise.

Yet the late Denys Munby, an Oxford economist, who was then advising those in charge of (nationalized) transport undertakings, told the Select Committee on Nationalized Industries that, so long as the head of London Transport held the (to Munby) odd notion that he had a species of 'social contract' with Londoners, the efficient running of the business would be impossible![1] Surely, the exact opposite is true; unless those who are charged with providing public transport for London consider it their duty to provide the best possible service, subject of course to consideration of cost and finance, there can be no efficiency! This is so also for another reason, connected with the point made earlier about labour motivation. At lower managerial and operational levels, the staff are not and *can*not be aware of the effect of their actions or inactions upon the profit-and-loss account. They *can*, however, take pride in doing a good job, in pleasing the customers, in running trains or buses punctually, in not having people wait for twenty minutes in the rain. Even in a competitive situation, sensible firms urge their employees to provide good service. Of course, Denys Munby did not advocate bad service! But he seemed to have a concept of commercial calculation which excluded the idea of duty and purpose ('social contract') related to user needs. He and those who think like him tend to fragment, to disassemble a system, to concentrate on its parts, to advocate marginal cost pricing, for instance. Of the inherent ambiguity of 'margins' I shall say more in a moment. Now I would like to stress the doubtful conclusions which follow from such an approach, using public transport as my example. The first is the complexity of the fares structure. In most of the world, simplicity (and so cheapness in issuing and checking) is seen as desirable, hence flat fares regardless of distance in urban areas. These, of course, neglect marginal cost, perhaps because to take it into account is itself costly. No other management in the world would disassemble the transport system, or fail to consider its primary task, that of expeditiously moving people! In most countries there is some standard charge by distance for long-distance rail transport. In Britain our economists advise discriminatory charges ('what the market can bear'), in other words to exploit monopoly power if and when it exists. Yet such practices were curtailed when the railways were in private ownership.

This brings me to my last major point, the use and abuse of marginal analysis. Let me make it quite clear that I am not attacking marginalism as such, but what Paul Streeten once called 'misplaced marginalism'. One point has been made already: if a firm undertakes a bundle of activities which react upon one another, decisions cannot be taken in isolation, without considering the interconnections. It is similarly evident that complementarities and indivisibilities exist, and that one must take them into account if they are significant. No one, of course, would deny this. No one, for instance, is unaware that an electricity grid is an interrelated system, that one must consider the systemic effects of incremental decisions. But this tends to be treated as an exception to the general rule. But is this so? Is not a transport network also a network, a system?

This is relevant to the much-misunderstood issue of cross-subsidization, which many consider to be uneconomic. It is surely essential to distinguish two situations. In one, a *separate* loss-making activity (factory, mine, service) is subsidized by another one which is profitable. It is a reasonable supposition that this is economically irrational, unless strong arguments to the contrary exist. However, where there is indivisibility, complementarity, system, the situation is much more complex. In my earlier work I have cited the following illustrative instance. Suppose an airline benefits from a feeder service (a bus link to town, or an air link to another airport), and would suffer loss if it were withdrawn. It would pay the airline to subsidize the company which provided the feeder service, so long as the subsidy was less than the loss that would be suffered if the service were withdrawn. This is a simple instance of the marketing of externalities. However, suppose that the link is owned and operated by the airline. What was an externality now becomes an internality, and the purist will qualify it as 'cross-subsidization', and so as irrational!

A different example is as follows. Imagine a suburban railway line, which originates at the central station A. There are then stops at B, C, D, E, F and G. Most passengers get on at A. By the time the train reaches F three-quarters have alighted. Clearly the cost per passenger-mile is now much higher. Should one, in the interests of economic rationality and marginal cost pricing, charge a higher fare per mile between F and G, or close that section of the line? It is such considerations as these which have led almost every country in the world to charge a flat rate (or a standard fare by distance) – every country, that is, except Britain, where the prejudice against subsidization has also led to a situation in which public transport fares are by far the highest in the world.

What *is* a margin? Some textbooks do mention that the concept is unclear and ambiguous, but is this sufficiently stressed? Thus if one advocates marginal cost pricing in public transport, say, in London, is one speaking of:

The No. 13 bus which leaves at 11.05 p.m. on a Sunday?
The No. 13 bus between Swiss Cottage and Golders Green?
The No. 13 bus?
Buses (all routes) which leave after 11 p.m.?
Buses at weekends?
And so on.

What, in this context, is the distinction between short-term and long-term? What of the 'external' (internal?) effects on other public transport in London? Is it sufficiently appreciated by our students that most margins are actually averages of sub-margins? Is it adequately appreciated that *margins are not, as a rule, one-dimensional?*

This last point brings together many of the arguments already advanced, about bundles, purpose, strategy, goodwill, system and complementarity, and is a criticism of *myopic* marginalism which, I submit, our textbooks unintentionally encourage, with unfortunate effects on the advice given to government departments.

Let me illustrate the principle of multi-level margins with an example that will serve also as the basis of a critique of conventional investment criteria. Suppose we have any large economic operation, say, the Alaskan oilfield exploitation. This requires an initial decision that Alaskan oil is worth exploiting. Once this decision has been taken, a mass of consequential choices and decisions of an incremental or marginal character follow, relating to drilling equipment, means of transportation, housing, pipe, pumps, supply of food and of building materials, and so on. Each of these, in turn, can be subdivided into its component parts. This represents a *hierarchy*, conceptually and administratively. Our textbooks generally imply that a marginal decision *within* this multi-level hierarchy of margins is taken by reference to the market. We sometimes remember the work of Coase and of Williamson, we are aware that *within* the firm activities are administered. What is seldom adequately stressed is that a wide variety of marginal decisions, whether on allocation of resources or on investment, are taken within contexts, that they only make sense within a network or pattern of other decisions. *Given* that Alaskan oil is being developed, there *must* be a pipeline (or tankers) to move the oil, housing *must* be built, pumps must be installed, and so on. The question is not *whether* but *what*, or *how*. The 'marginal cost' of not providing an essential part of a complex is the loss of the whole output of the project, just as a prolonged strike of twenty men at a car component plant could cause the loss of millions of pounds. (What, then, is their marginal productivity?)

Then do we distinguish sufficiently clearly between the authentically 'micro' decision (for instance, whether a producer in a competitive environment should increase the output of a given product) and the rather different situation relating, say, to energy policy, or the future of the steel industry? These matters are neither macro nor micro. Yet major decisions by nationalized industries, in Britain especially, fall into their intermediate category (mezzo-economics?).

It is clear from a study of Soviet experience that these problems do not disappear if the entire economy is placed under a central planning authority. In the place of market or commercial criteria, enterprises are guided by obligatory plan targets. In theory these targets embody the needs of society, and the means to meet output targets are administratively allocated. In practice central instructions are inevitably aggregated, and, because they issue from different government offices, are inevitably inconsistent and contradictory. A large book can easily be filled with quotations from the works of Soviet economists which show how hard it is to devise efficiency criteria, and how the plan targets give rise to undesired and frequently perverse results. Thus a plan target expressed in tons penalizes economy of metal; construction enterprises fulfil plans in terms of roubles of expenditure, and thus prefer expensive inputs; retail trade achieves higher 'productivity' by having customers stand in line, and avoiding handling perishable goods. Under conditions of monopoly *and* a seller's market, and with cost-based prices which reflect neither use-value nor demand, cautious attempts to give greater emphasis to profitability are ineffective, and not surprisingly so. At the same time some 'eastern' reformers with an excessive faith in the market tend to neglect externalities and adopt the attitude described above as one-dimensional marginalism. While I am firmly of the opinion that the market mechanism and supply-and-demand balancing prices are urgently needed if Soviet micro-economics is to function with tolerable efficiency, it must be recognized that in some sectors (such as electricity, public transport) and in some types of decisions (especially those with important economic and social external effects) there will remain an important role for government (and planners) as custodians of the wider public interest. It is therefore not a coincidence that a paper of mine on this theme was reprinted in a Hungarian periodical.[2] There is much here that is open to debate, in East and West alike.

If Western micro-economics is unhelpful, Marxist economics is almost wholly irrelevant. While one might not agree with Wiles's view that micro-economics is *non*-Marxist, it must be admitted that Marx had nothing useful to say on the subject, and that he tended to the view that socialist planning would be simple, that when production is for use and not for profit all will be 'clear and transparent'. The meaning and function of economic laws and commercial calculation under socialism remains a subject of doubt and controversy. There is much still to do for those who are working on economics of socialism, not least in the field of operational criteria for socialized enterprises.

Notes: Chapter 3

1 *First Report of the Select Committee on Nationalized Industries* (London: HMSO, 1953).
2 *Acta Oeconomica*, vol. 20, nos 1–2 (1978).

PART TWO

Problems of Marxist and Soviet economics

4 Marx, the market and 'feasible socialism'

This essay was originally published in Ulrich Gartner and Jiri Kosta (eds), *Wirtschaft und Gesellschaft: Kritik und Alternativen* (Berlin: Duncker & Humblot, 1979), pp. 351–62. This was a festschrift for Ota Šik, the Czech *émigré* economist, who would have played a major role in reforming the Czech economy in 1968 had not outside forces intervened. It had struck me how many of the objections to the fundamentalist-Marxist vision of a functioning socialist economy had been anticipated in Russia in the 1920s, and this was the principle theme of my contribution. For a longer and more systematic discussion of the whole topic, see my *The Economics of Feasible Socialism* (London: Allen & Unwin, 1983).

I recall first meeting Ota Šik in Bursa, Turkey, over twenty years ago. We swam in a circular swimming-pool watered by hot natural springs, and argued about socialist economics. Much water, hot and otherwise, has flowed since then, and we have all learnt much from experience, some of it tragic experience. It has set many of us, who view capitalism critically and pessimistically, towards a search for new ways, a 'third way', neither Moscow nor Chicago. *Laissez-faire* is neither practicable nor effective in an age of giant corporations and increasing instability. Inflation, unemployment, the breakdown of social consensus, indefensible extremes in the distribution of wealth within and between countries, promise trouble ahead. At the same time the economic consequences of central planning are well known, its political-social implications are deplorable, and anyone with any interest in socialism must seek alternatives.

In this task he or she is impeded by certain aspects of the Marxian tradition. Neither Marx nor Engels nor Lenin seemed to have the remotest conception of the complexities of the functioning of a modern industrial economy. They discouraged, and did not themselves undertake, discussion of blueprints of a socialist or communist economy. They did, however, believe that problems would not be serious. One must agree with Aron Katsenellenboigen that 'Marx failed to examine the mechanism' of the functioning of the future society because he believed that 'the planned, purposeful development of communist society would make everything clear and understandable, in contrast with the spontaneously developing market mechanism of a capitalist society', so 'it was senseless to waste effort on examining the details of the society of the future'.[1] Did not Marx compare the 'mystification', the 'commodity fetishism', which exists under capitalism with the clarity of perception of economic reality under socialism? Engels in a famous passage remarked that 'everything would be done simply without the so-called value', and that 'the seizure of the means of production by society puts an end to commodity production'. Bettelheim was correct in ascribing to Marx the view that 'in a socialist society even at the beginning, there would be neither commodities, nor value, nor money, nor, consequently, prices and wages'.[2] Katsenellenboigen was right: 'Since future society, in the opinion of Marx and Engels, would be based on the planning principle, the need for spontaneous market exchange would be obviated . . . [They] conceived of future society as a system in which everything would be obvious. People's goals would be obvious [and unanimous, A.N.], as would the available resources and methods of transforming them into products needed by the population.'[3] Lenin knew his classical texts and took the same view. In a well-known passage in *State and Revolution*, he wrote: 'The function of control and accountancy, becoming ever more simple, will be performed by each in turn.'[4] (And he was not even talking about the next century.)

Of course these are part and parcel of the utopian elements of Marx's thought, along with the transcending of the division of labour, the withering away of the state, the elimination of alienation, the self-fulfilment of each in unity with all mankind under conditions of abundance, in other words, heaven on earth. I do not know what to make of this aspect of Marxism; of what conceivable significance, other than of a religious kind, is a definition of socialism in which, *as part of the definition*, every known political, economic and social problem is assumed not to exist? In the present essay attention will be focused solely on problems connected with planning and organization of production and distribution. However, Marxist concepts on these matters are linked with these 'utopian' aspects; thus the overcoming of scarcity and alienation is apparently to be associated with a new Man and Woman, who will need no incentives and who will do the right thing for the benefit of all, it being also assumed that 'the right thing' is clearly and unambiguously visible. Evidently under such conditions much of the discussion that follows would seem irrelevant, and no doubt this is why 'millenarian-fundamentalists' of the New Left are satisfied with evading the problems of the present day or any likely future. This guarantees them a role in eternal righteous opposition to any conceivable regime calling itself socialist, since 'anything that exists is guilty of compromising with reality', in the (satirical) words of Regis Debray.

It may seem paradoxical, but the most likely opportunity for Marx-inspired socialist planning will come under conditions not of abundance but of its opposite, a degree of scarcity with which market-type institutions and liberal political philosophy will be unable to cope. And not just in developing countries. The present tendency for excessive sectional demands, generating inflation, and also unemployment, plus the objective difficulty of even maintaining existing Western living standards, and of obtaining supplies of raw materials and fuel from the increasingly recalcitrant Third World, spell trouble to come. Exhaustion of natural resources or their effective control by producers (such as OPEC) would then compel strict economy and conservation measures, the very opposite of Marxian 'abundance', but calling for imposed social discipline and planning, for society's survival, with real sharing of sacrifice. There is a case for rethinking one's model of a socialism with such considerations in mind, and this has important implications; thus the existence of scarcity makes it plainly impossible to envisage the end of selfish acquisitiveness, and so this would have to be harnessed in the form of incentives. Consideration of economic use of resources, of efficiency, would be of vital importance. However, even on more optimistic assumptions the need for efficiency remains, since without it there is and can be no approach to abundance.

Given the traditionally negative view of market relations in Marxism, what sort of basis was envisaged by Marxist thinkers for economic calculations under socialism? There was a limited literature on the subject before 1917. Apart from Barone's seminal article,[5] there were some thoughts by Kautsky and the lesser-known Otto Neurath (*Vollsozialisierung*, 1910), but it remains true that until the Bolshevik revolution this was a very underdeveloped sector of socialist thought. Then came war-communism, with its 'illusions' about imminent communism, and the precipitous devaluation of the rouble under conditions of civil war and chaos. There was set up in 1920 a seminar on 'problems of a moneyless economy', under the chairmanship of the eminent agricultural economist A. A. Chayanov. Chayanov was not a communist, but some of the seminar participants were. They examined various models which were devised in 1919–20. A report and commentary may be found in the book written later by another of the participants in the seminar, L. Yurovsky.[6] Since the models and the discussions bear directly on contemporary controversies on the same subject, this is by no means of only historical interest. The book as a whole and this chapter in particular stamp L. Yurovsky as an economist of exceptional quality. Two years after its publication he was arrested on absurd charges and was never seen again.

Yurovsky began his exposition by analysing the functions of the commodity-money mechanism and of price. He showed himself well aware of their imperfections; he mentioned externalities, public goods, and inexactitude of amortization, the instability of the monetary unit (even under normal conditions). Yes, he admitted, there were instances when the welfare of society and the profit of a segment of the economy conflicted. There was no perfect solution known. He put the question thus: 'Can one envisage the existence of an economy, covering a wide area, with a large population and transport network, containing major factories and industrial establishments, which copes with production, distribution and consumption without the use of value-monetary calcula-tion?'[7] In this light he examined various models for a socialist economy.

The first models examined were those of M. Smit and S. Klepikov (Smit, a woman, died only a year ago). These sought a *technical* basis for calculation. Their efforts were first drafts only, according to the authors. Costs were classified under five heads: (1) human effort, (2) mechanical energy, (3) heat, (4) raw materials, etc., (5) machines and tools. The authors assumed that these five could be combined into two: man-hours and energy units. Subsequently it would all be expressed in standard man-hours, the content of this 'standard' being altered with changing techniques.

> Only in the distant future could we envisage so standardized a technique and so even a distribution of means of production among workers of all countries that the relationship between labour-effort and (mechanical) energy could be taken as a constant magnitude. For this, however, one must have two revolutionary storms, in tech-nique and in accountancy. Only when one has a World Economic Council (*Mirsovnarkhoz*), when the whole world will be the subject of economic and technical calculation, can one conceive of a constant relationship between human labour and the machine?[8]

Klepikov's variant envisaged 'combined human-and-machine energy units', and Yurovsky ironically commented that he (unlike Smit) did not consider it necessary to wait for a *mirsovnarkhoz*!

Yurovsky attacked this mercilessly as a nonsense. There is in the model *no* link between expenditure of energy and the end-result, no link with satisfaction of demand or need for any product, no realization that the same expenditure of energy can product a wide variety of highly unequal economic effects. Some kinds of energy (e. g. wind) are free, others are much more costly. The conversion of human labour into mechanical units would produce nonsensical results. 'To give these conceptions any economic sense would require more than the two revolutionary storms envisaged by Smit. One would also need a storm such as would change the character of organic and inorganic nature.'[9]

He then turned with much greater respect to the model devised by Chayanov, noting its similarity to that of Otto Neurath, though appar-ently Chayanov had no knowledge of Neurath's ideas. His model is as follows. The government determines on the basis of past experience how much of each product will be needed for the people. It seeks to determine

how best to produce this quantity and assortment. It then seeks to maximize the output per unit of labour and of available means of production.
There is no means of comparing cost and output, in the sense of determining net product or value-added, since costs and output are counted in
different units: 'Labour should be applied to obtain additional output up to
the point at which the burden of additional labour of society is equal to the
satisfaction of wants at the margin.' Yurovsky comments that no way of
calculating this is indicated. Costs should be minimized. 'Costs' are
divided into physical units of labour, materials, machinery, and so on.
These are to be weighted by coefficients, and the resultant combined costs
are then minimized by the government in choosing to produce the given
assortment where 'costs' in this sense are lowest. This is to be reinforced
by 'norms', set on the basis of past experience, of the quantities of inputs
(labour, fuel, materials, and so on) normally required to produce a given
item. Neither different categories of costs nor different products could be
measured in the same units.

Yurovsky commented that the (very intelligent) Chayanov worked out
correctly the logic of a moneyless economy with no common value-
denominator, in which, consequently, the government determined the
pattern of consumption and distributed products not in accordance with
consumer choice but according to its plan. It would also have to determine
the weights to be attached to the various elements of costs, and the inputs
too. (Chayanov in 1920 had theoretically established the necessity of
'material balances' or input–output norms.) It would be possible to operate
such a system, based on a set of relationships determined by the previously
existing market economy. There would, of course, be no means of telling
objectively whether the chosen pattern of production was better or worse
than another, and it would probably operate at a low level of efficiency and
consumption. It was not inherently nonsensical, as was the Smit model,
but in the opinion of Yurovsky it is still very implausible, for rather
evident reasons.

A further category of models, represented by Kreve, is based on the
adaptation of the labour theory of value. His unit of account is an hour of
socially necessary labour, or a man-hour utilized purposefully (tselesao-
brazno) for making a given product, with due allowance for the labour
content of the materials, machines, and so on, used. The basic unit of
labour-value (trudovaya tsennost) would be one hour of unskilled labour
fulfilling 100 per cent of his (her) work-norm. 'Conversion of skilled or
complex to unskilled labour would be a function of tariff wage-rates.
True, the tariff rates can be somewhat incorrect or unscientific, but that is a
question relating to wage-scales and not to labour values', wrote Kreve.
Existing stocks of goods would be valued at prewar prices divided by the
value of an hour of prewar labour, multiplied to bring them to the
production conditions existing in 1920. Kreve then proposed to add some

man-hour units to cover 'overheads', which include 'the maintenance of the local *sovnarkhoz*', the state's funds (including investment funds) and distribution costs. The worker would receive units specifying the number of man-hours worked, and would draw from the 'distributive organs' various products up to this labour-value. The enterprise would receive from the *sovnarkhoz* the materials corresponding (proportionate) to the value of its output measured in man-hours. The author proposed the creation of a Commissariat of Distribution and Supply, to carry out his scheme, 'and thereby drive the last stake into the putrifying corpse of the capitalist economy of Russia' (Kreve's words again).

Yurovsky commented that apart from such problems as how to calculate the additional labour-hours to be assigned to cover state expenditure and investment, there is a more fundamental objection, which is still relevant today. He stressed the importance in Kreve's model of the words *socially necessary* labour *purposefully* utilized. 'In a commodity-money economy the determination of what is purposeful and socially necessary is determined *in the market*.'[10] The Kreve model lacked any means of determining either social necessity or purposefulness. Yet such means must be provided. Yurovsky went on to question the desirability of assessing costs on the basis of labour-cost-plus, that is, on the basis of Volume I of *Capital*; this would make goods produced by industries with a high organic composition of capital 'cheaper' (again foreshadowing discussions which took place long after Stalin had him killed).

The next model to be considered was partly the product of K. Shmelev, and partly of Strumilin;[11] since the latter devised another and more complex model, I shall call this one Strumilin I. They prepared the draft of a decree 'on the labour unit of account'. This would bear the name *tred*, based on the Russian words *trudovaya edinitsa*. The Council of Labour and Defence was to determine how skilled labour was to be converted to standard *tred* units. All goods and service were to be denominated in *tred* units, revised at intervals. There was nothing said about how the social necessity of the labour expended would be determined, or how investment resources were to be obtained, and in this respect the model is inferior to Kreve's.

More subtle and ambitious was the model I shall call Strumilin II. He quoted Marx to the effect that the labour-time to be spent on production would, under socialism, be determined by the social utility of different products. It was a mathematical problem as to how to maximize satisfaction of need at minimum cost. Strumilin wrote that, though we cannot measure individual utility, *social* utility can be determined, measured and compared. He then assumed that 'as a first approximation, if volume of output (of any good) rises in a geometric progression, satisfaction rises in arithmetic progression'. Thus every additional unit of labour used in production gives diminishing marginal social utility. At some point the labour effort will produce insufficient social utility to be worth making, and this would represent the limit of production at the given level of productive forces.

The well-read Yurovsky could not forebear to point out that this sounds very much like Jevons, Menger, Walras, and so on, and he reinforced this with a quotation from Jevons in English: 'labour will be carried on until the increment of utility from any of the employment just balances the increment of pain'. Yurovsky commented:

> True, Jevons had in mind individual and Strumilin social utility. But the latter can scarcely be made up of anything other than individual utilities, and the saturation of social need as a result of increasing the volume of consumption can only take the form of the saturation of individual requirements. Old ideas of the so-called marginal utility school, in its more naive psychological variant, are fully expressed in the above-cited arguments. [12]

Strumilin's model of distribution was as follows. Each worker would have a work book in which was entered a sum of labour-values corresponding to his work, and this could be spent as the worker chose, Strumilin insisting that ration-cards were the consequence of 'war and beggary' and should give way to free choice. Of course, he also insisted, in socialist society there would be no money. Goods in the stores would bear 'price'-tags corresponding to their labour content, *tred* units. Strumilin's model was supposed to ensure that the marginal application of human effort in all spheres should produce an equal amount of utility or satisfaction. But how to achieve this, in the absence of a market? Strumilin would rely on expenditure budgets and research into how utility is affected by increased availability of specific products. Yurovsky commented that demand schedules could possibly be constructed by such methods in a highly egalitarian society. The government would have to observe stocks and increase or decrease production, in the light of the behaviour of consumers. It should also be possible to adjust supply to demand by altering *tred* valuations, but (Yurovsky commented ironically) adjustment of *labour*-values to changes in supply-and-demand relationships would conflict with doctrine, which relates these values solely to conditions of production. He warned that, if demand could not be met by increasing supply, there would cease to be freedom of consumer choice and the logic of rationing would take over. But certainly this model did stress that the task of production is to adjust to demand, even though the mechanics of doing so is problematical. Unless, that is, the adjusted and flexible *tred* units turned out to be money in a new guise, with the state stores acting as a retail *market*. He further noted that various productive enterprises would also demand goods (fuel, cloth, thread, and so on) and these would require to be measured, so as to be able to make essential efficiency calculations. It looked as if Strumilin was rediscovering money by a roundabout route.

Yurovsky then returned to an analysis of the measurement of cost in this model. Here again the 'organic composition of capital' is ignored, since there is no capital charge. The surrogate 'prices' would be proportionate to labour-costs alone. This would logically lead, in the course of the effort to adjust production to demand, to a redistribution of capital investments in the direction of capital-intensive industries, whose 'prices' would be (relatively) reduced, compared with a model in which valuations are based on an equal return to capital. But was this desirable? Why, he asked, should it follow from the fact that profit under capitalism was pocketed by the capitalist and that the revolution had eliminated the capitalist? Strumilin's reply was: 'Man is interested in economizing only his labour. Material and energy in nature are inexhaustible. Only to the extent that labour is expended on them should they be valued as costs.' Yurovsky strongly disagreed. First, they are not inexhaustible. Second, they are often scarce (land in city centres, oil-bearing land, and so on), and then they have to be 'valued' in order to be economically utilized. They could perhaps be valued in terms of the labour saved by their existence, but they cannot just be regarded as free. Then, third, how are investments to be distributed between different branches, on the basis of what calculations? How can the relative scarcity of machines and other means of production be brought into the calculations? How can the planning organs devise a criterion for allocating resources? Assets should be used to maximum effect, and this should be measured in the form of a yield on investments made. 'Only the memory of the fact that interest on capital formed a class income under capitalism can explain the psychological reluctance to use such calculations.'[13]

Yurovsky went on to classify these various models under two sets of two heads: those which envisage a single unit of valuation (for consumption and for production costs) and those which do not; and those which envisage consumer choice and those based on a ration or issue of consumers' goods. In the absence of any common valuation unit, there is no means of comparing costs with results, or different elements of costs and different products with one another, and this could only operate if the consumer is issued with a ration. Such a model could theoretically ensure balance between consumption and production, by strict regulation of both (the government distributes what is produced and is available), and then there is no need of money. But this kind of 'barracks socialism' is universally unpopular, and we have seen that even the communist Strumilin contemptuously rejected it. By contrast, consumer choice means issuing citizens with something very like money, and then expressing in these units the 'prices' of the products. The balance between supply and demand would then be achieved by altering price-tags and adjusting supply, as in a market economy. 'Prices' of this sort may also apply in transactions *between* state enterprises and organizations, though (and here again Yurovsky was far-sighted) much depends on the *degree of centralization.* 'The question of the limits of centralization should be decided by reference to the rationality of different organizational forms, and no one is able to anticipate what will be the rational degree of centralization at different stages of the development of a socialist economy.' But in any case it will be necessary to keep accounts of transactions in some standard, generally used unit. He then showed the superiority of a monetary unit over the *tred* and similar labour-value surrogates, as the latter fail to take into account 'the scarcity of means of production and the need so to utilize them as to maximize the satisfaction of the needs of society'.[14]

These quotations from Yurovsky appear to me to have considerable interest for the historian of economic (especially socialist) thought but, as already argued, they are still relevant today. Indeed, one has only to compare them with the thought-processes of modern Marxist 'fundamentalists' to realize that, far from there having been any progress, there has been regression. Take, for example, Charles Bettelheim's *Calcul économique et formes de propriété.*[15] With all of the USSR's experience from which to learn, he is still more or less where Smit and Kreve were in 1920. He attacks monetary calculation, advocating some sort of measurement of cost in hours (while appreciating the practical difficulty of calculating it). He denounces the use of a rate of return on capital, and declares that the criterion used by socialist planning should be 'socially useful effect', and this without suggesting how it should be determined or who should decide it. Nor is there a discussion of how to determine whether the hours of labour expended are socially more (or less) necessary. Bettelheim appreciates, correctly, the link between 'commodity production', that is, exchange relations and the monetary mechanism, and the autonomy of production units, but does not discuss what degree of autonomy the production units should have. Denouncing bureaucracy of the Soviet type, he and those who think like him attribute the distortions and inefficiencies not to the attempt to plan centrally, but to the existence of bureaucracy and privileged strata, the absence of democratic control by the 'associated producers'. It seems not to occur to him that the bureaucracy, as well as the micro-inefficiencies, are functional necessities, given the combination of centralization and the virtual elimination of price-and-market criteria. It is extraordinary how he and other 'new-leftists' have failed to think seriously about *how* the 'associated producers' (or the 'direct producers') *could* in fact control the vast complexities of a modern industrial economy with its millions of different products and multi-million interconnections and interdependencies.

Typical of Bettelheim's thought is his attack on the Yugoslav model for what surely are the wrong reasons: that the Yugoslav 'self-managed' enterprise is controlled not by its workers but by the market. But surely *any* group of producers should produce what the users of their goods and services require. To *that* extent it *must* be controlled by forces outside itself. In the Yugoslav model, the collective can study possibilities and choose between alternatives, within the limits set by the market, of course. The only known alternative is *orders* from above. If Bettelheim replies that his 'associated producers' are simultaneously producers *and* consumers, who can determine what is needed by comradely discussion, the rather obvious retort is that consumers are producers (and vice versa) *only* at the top of the hierarchical pyramid, at the level of the whole society, and that this is the logic of centralization, which has bureaucracy and alienation as practical consequences.

Lenin, after seizure of power, did learn that 'enterprises will be unable to function correctly if there is not a united will, connecting all the groups of toilers into a single economic organ, working with the precision of a clockwork mechanism'.[16] He also was appalled by the growth of bureaucracy. Did he have time, before his death, to connect the two? Trotsky, interestingly enough, did. 'In the course of the transitional epoch each enterprise . . . must, to a greater or lesser degree, orient itself independently in the market and test itself through the market . . . [and] be subject not only to control from the top, by state organs, but also from below, by the market.'[17] In the year 1936 he was attacking Stalinist planning for 'freeing itself from monetary (*tsennostnyi*) control, just as bureaucratic arbitrariness frees itself of political control'. He fully appreciated the logic and necessity of monetary-market relations and calculations for what he called 'the entire transitional epoch'.[18] True, Trotsky retained the vision of a full communism under conditions of universal abundance, but for the present (in this case the Russia of the 1930s) he actually advocated the *extension* of monetization, the use of 'economic monetary calculations developed under capitalism', of producers' self-interest, leading 'not to the reduction of commodity turnover but its expansion'.[19] This contrasts with the attacks of so-called Trotskyists today on the ideas of men like Ota Šik, or on the principles of the Hungarian reform model of 1968. Of course the market can cause serious social and economic distortions, requires to be limited, and must coexist with important centrally exercised state planning functions. Of course tensions can arise between local or sectoral and the general interest, between plan and market (as also *within* plan and market). But life without conflicts and tensions is not merely a utopian concept, it is also a very dull one. Equilibrium, as the admirable Hungarian economist Janos Kornai once reminded us, is not necessarily good; there is equilibrium between an impotent man and a frigid woman.

The search for a *dritte Weg* must continue. It is not an easy matter to find the right balance between centralization and decentralization, plan and market, freedom and discipline, short-term economic efficiency and other legitimate social objectives (such as greater equality, conservation of exhaustible resources, and so on). It is by no means impossible that a basic cause of our troubles is the logic of a modern industrial society and of repeated technological revolutions, which present insoluble social problems to us all. Given the population explosion in Asia, world poverty, limitation of natural resources, rising expectations, conflicts between groups, nations and classes, can any known system cope with the resultant problems? As was pointed out at the beginning, we are far indeed from Marx's 'abundance' and its implications. But the role and importance of planning is enhanced, both by the increase in the *scale* and complexity of production (the vast corporations of capitalist countries are internally *administered*) and by the unfortunate effects of uncontrolled stimulation of greed. We should indeed be aware of the *negative* aspects of a wholly market-oriented society, and of the strength of the case that can be made for planning and for social-political control democratically exercised, that is, for a species of socialism. However, hard and realistic thinking about *feasible* socialist economies requires, as a precondition, the open rejection of the utopian elements of Marx's thought. Neither he nor Lenin appreciated the inherent complexities of the problem, in its economic efficiency, social, or political dimensions. For them all would be 'simple'. We at least have no excuse for being unaware that it is all immensely complicated.

Notes: Chapter 4

1 A. Katsenellenboigen, *Studies in Soviet Economic Planning* (White Plains, NY: Sharpe, 1978), p. 29.
2 C. Bettelheim, *The Transition to a Socialist Society* (Hassocks: Harvester, 1975), p. 33.
3 Katsenellenboigen, op. cit.
4 V. I. Lenin, *Collected Works*, Vol. 25 (Moscow: Progress Publishers, and London, Lawrence & Wishart, 5th edn, 1964), pp. 426–7.
5 E. Barone's article 'The ministry of production in the collectivist state' is reprinted in A. Nove and D. M. Nuti (eds), *Socialist Economics: Selected Readings* (Harmondsworth: Penguin, 1972), pp. 52–74.
6 L. Yurovsky, *Denezhnaya politika sovetskoi vlasti* (Moscow: 1928).
7 ibid., p. 85.
8 ibid., p. 97, directly quoting M. Smit's article of 1921 about this model.
9 ibid., p. 99.
10 ibid., p. 105; original emphasis.
11 Strumilin died a natural death in 1973.
12 Yurovsky, op. cit., p. 109.
13 ibid., p. 118.
14 ibid., p. 125.
15 C. Bettelheim, *Calcul économique et formes de propriété* (Paris: Maspéro, 1970).

16   V. I. Lenin, *Sochineniya*, Vol. 36 (Moscow: 5th edn, 1962), p. 157.
17   Speech to 4th Congress of Comintern, 1922.
18   L. Trotsky, 'Chto takoye SSSR i kuda on idyot', mimeo., 1936, nos 58, 66, etc.
19   ibid.

5   The economy of the USSR and Marxism: What socialist model?

This appeared in Italian in *Storia del marxismo*, Vol. 3 (Turin: Einaudi, 1980), pp. 606–37, its object being to relate successive stages in Soviet economic structure and policies to the Marxist ideology which may (or may not) have inspired or justified them. Today also the debate about economic reform in the Soviet Union must take the legacy of Marxist-Leninist doctrine into account, reinterpreting or circumventing the labour theory of value and the role of 'commodity-money relations'.

'War-communism'

When power was seized by the Bolsheviks in November 1917, neither the Russian nor the West European Marxists had any clear notion of how a socialist economy might operate. Between the revolution and the establishment of the higher phase of communism there would be a transition period, coextensive with the 'dictatorship of the proletariat' prior to the withering away of the state, and Marx had indicated some initial steps which were to be taken in that period. However, neither the length of the transition nor the nature of the economic planning system which was to operate within it was defined. As is known, Marx and Engels were hostile to blueprints of a future society. However, they did indicate a number of features of communism as they conceived it: in a communist economy there would be no commodity production; society would plan its needs and take the necessary production decisions directly. It was thought by the founders of Marxism that this task would be simple, that the needs of society would be clearly seen, that men and women, their vision undistorted by class or sectional interest, would unanimously wish to do what needed to be done. The division of labour would be overcome or transcended. All would wish to give their work to society to the best of their ability, and take from the abundance of material goods in accordance with their needs. Resources were assumed, for all practical purposes, to be infinitely available, in a communist society which had overcome the contradiction between the forces of production and the relations of production. There would, of course, be no inequality, no money, no wages, no profits, no prices, no state and no law.

Of course, these 'utopian' aspects of Marx's thought could not apply to a transitional society, which would lack the levels of education, consciousness and productive capacity. However, Marx and Engels appeared to imply that the transition would not be a long one, and that steps in the direction of communism could be taken immediately. With the seizure of power, according to Engels, 'once society takes over the means of production, this will mean the end of commodity production, and with it the domination of the product over the producers'.[1] Money would speedily disappear, costs would be measured in labour-time. In the transition period rewards would be 'in accordance with work', not need, though it seems that Marx had in mind a quantity of work (i.e. hours), rather than envisaging unequal rewards for work of different skills. Even so, payments would be in paper certificates, which would not be money, as they would not circulate.

Lenin and his comrades had been brought up on such ideas as these. They had read hardly anything in Marxist literature about the problems of allocation, efficiency, or methods of planning. It is not unfair to say, with Katsenellenboigen, that 'the communists were romantics on this issue . . . The classical scholars of Marxism conceived of future society as a system in which everything would be obvious. People's goals would be obvious, as would the available resources for transforming them into products needed by the population.'[2]

Therefore, on the eve of the Bolshevik revolution, alongside such 'immediate' policy slogans as nationalizing the banks and distributing land to the peasants, Lenin put forward ideas which showed him to be unable to comprehend the *economic* problems of planning. One sees this in such well-known passages as: 'the function of control and accountancy, becoming ever more simple, will be performed by each in turn . . .'; 'A state bank, with branches in every rural district and factory, would constitute nine-tenths of the apparatus of socialism . . .'; 'Capitalism has so simplified the tasks of accountancy and control, reducing it to a relatively simple one of accountancy, that any literate person can do it'.[3]

There had been some discussion of the economics of a possible socialism before 1917. One can cite, for instance, Neurath[4] and of course Barone.[5] There was, however, no sign that these ideas had any influence on Russian socialists in any hue. Some of them, for instance, attended courses in economics (Bukharin had, in Vienna), but this produced only a more sophisticated denunciation of the bourgeois order. It would be wrong to criticize Marxism for not having devised blueprints or functioning models of socialist economies, for indeed experience would be a great and irreplaceable teacher. But it does seem appropriate to note that, within the

Marxist tradition, there was a powerful tendency to ignore practical economic problems which any socialist society would be bound to face, or to define socialism in such a way as to *assume* that these problems would be solved or transcended (*aufheben*).

Lenin and his comrades on the morrow of the revolution faced other problems too, notably that of survival in the face of powerful enemies, amid war, anarchy and economic and social collapse. It is still a matter of controversy among historians as to how far the system which came to be known as 'war-communism' was due to war or to communism, or explicable by ideological enthusiasm. To take two recent East European examples, Gimpelson tends to the first view,[6] Szamuely to the second,[7] though neither would deny that both factors played *some* role. War-communism was not imposed as part of a predetermined plan. Lenin could argue afterwards that early in 1918 he had considered a gradual path with, initially, a mixed economy, and he was already then in conflict with the fundamentalist 'left' of his party on such issues as workers' control and managerial prerogatives. Nationalization was sometimes insisted on by local comrades against the leaders' advice. Certain it is that no one intended the requisitioning by force of peasant food surpluses to be a normal way of relating to the peasantry.

Leaving this controversy to the historians, let us simply note that, by the end of 1919, in the midst of civil war, hunger and disease, there emerged both a system and an ideology. The words 'war-communism' were used to describe it after it had ended. Its essential features were: almost total nationalization, including the bulk of small-scale industry, a ban on private trade, extreme centralization of planning and control, partial demonetization (state enterprises supplying each other without payment, issuance of free rations to workers, later also the abolition of rent, tramway tickets, and so on). The peasants were left in possession of nominally nationalized land, but were under obligation to deliver all produce surplus to their family's basic requirements to the state, for which they were paid in fast-depreciating paper money with which they could not buy anything, as the few factories which still functioned produced primarily for the civil war fronts. In practice, there was a great deal of illegal or semi-legal trade, but those engaged in it were frequently arrested, their goods were confiscated, and they were liable to be shot as speculators.

These practices, in some part a response to dire necessity, had their counterpart in ideology. One can best see this in three sources. One was the first programme of the Russian Communist Party (1919). Another was the *ABC of Communism* by Bukharin and Preobrazhensky (1919). Finally there was Bukharin's *Economics of the Transition Period* (1920). It is often pointed out in Soviet sources that the last of these was criticized by Lenin (his marginal notes were published in 1929),[8] but at most key points relevant to our present theme Lenin expressed approval. In addition one can cite numerous other contemporary declarations to show that the large majority of the party's intellectuals thought that they were engaged in taking a short-cut to communism, that such phenomena as the ban on private trade and the elimination of money were part of the transition to the new society. Lenin, Trotsky and Bukharin all admitted that they had been affected in some degree by 'illusions', 'utopian hopes', though doubtless some had been more affected than others.

It is not part of my task to describe the dramatic course of events of those years, but rather to draw attention to issues of significance for the theory of Marxist socialism.

The first, surely, must be the basic Leninist belief in the seizure of power by a small party acting in the name of a numerically small proletariat in a backward, predominantly peasant country, in order later to create the preconditions for socialism (he hoped with the aid of the victorious proletariat of more advanced countries). On the implications of this view much has been written, and it need not be developed here, except perhaps to stress that this tension between Marxian socialist ideology and the reality of Russian backwardness underlay many of the theoretical and practical problems faced by Lenin and his successors.

Second, there was the issue of workers' control versus centralization and managerial authority. A portion of the intelligentsia-Bolsheviks and of working-class members was heavily influenced by syndicalist ideas, and envisaged management by workers' committees with no privileges, powers, or higher salaries for the managers, engineers, or other 'bourgeois specialists'. This led to a clash with Lenin as early as the spring of 1918, and a struggle with a 'left-communist' opposition which was to last until party factions were eliminated in 1921. Lenin had seen evident advantages in advocating workers' control when the object was disorganizing the efforts of the Provisional government. Similarly he was in favour of disrupting the army by subverting military discipline, urging control over officers by their men – as long as the army was in the service of the class enemy. But in both the military and in the industrial fields he strongly favoured discipline and subordination to authority as soon as he and his party *were* the authority. Earlier phrases about control by the armed workers came to mean control by the (centralized and disciplined) party acting on their behalf. While there was every practical reason for Lenin's attitude at the time, in the face of chaos and civil war dangers, some Marxists hold that Lenin's successful fight to snuff out workers' control at factory level had a highly negative influence on subsequent developments.

Third, there was a major (and somewhat confused) debate on the role of the trade unions, in production, in relation to the party and in relation also to their members. The claim that the trade unions should run industry, made by some of the 'lefts', was basically ill-conceived; if trade unions become the management, then in realistic terms they cease to be trade unions. Trade union *participation* at local level was a principle not in dispute, though, as indicated above, Lenin stressed the need for a clear line of responsibility and authority which enhanced managerial power. The dominance of the party in trade unions became a political question of practical importance, in a situation when acute hardships led to a resurgence of influence among workers of Mensheviks, anarchists and social revolutionaries, who still had limited legal rights until 1921, and indeed certain unions (railwaymen, printers, etc.) were in anti-Bolshevik hands and were 'captured' by police measures. Lenin was most conscious of the limits of his own party's grip on the workers. Thus he declared: 'The slogan "more faith in the forces of the working class" means *in reality* a strengthening of Menshevik and anarchist influences; Kronstadt has shown us this quite clearly in the spring of 1921.'[9] Lenin's idea of trade unions as a connecting-rod (*privodnyi remen'*) between party and masses implied the subordination of the unions to the party and its tasks. But he did not go as far as Trotsky who, in 1920, urged the *militarization* of trade unions, with labour organized in armies under quasi-military discipline.

Trotsky's position was not as different from Lenin's as might appear at first sight, and he was supported by Bukharin, who had attacked Lenin from a 'left' position in 1918. The situation at the end of the civil war was desperate, and labour mobilization for reconstruction was approved also by Lenin. But Trotsky and Bukharin went further; they constructed a theory of forced labour for the entire transition period. Bukharin specifically asserted that the general tasks of the proletariat, as seen by the party, required to be imposed on the proletariat itself. Trotsky argued that workers who did not go and work where ordered should be treated as military deserters.[10] The implications were clearly drawn; until such time as the working class achieved a high level of consciousness, did what had to be done willingly, they had to be coerced by the proletarian dictatorship. The Hungarian economic historian Szamuely linked this belief with the denial of the importance of material incentives; clearly, if men and women could not be induced to do what is necessary by either material or moral suasion, coercion was the only remaining alternative.

Of course the real situation of 1920–1 was one of hunger and want, and in retrospect we can say that Trotsky and Bukharin made a theoretical virtue of necessity. Their ideas would have made of the trade unions a part of the coercive apparatus, with union leaders acting, so to speak, as officers and sergeants of the labour army. (It is worth recalling that the notion of labour armies can be found in Marx's programmatic statements.)[11]

Lenin objected on principle. He was becoming increasingly alarmed at the bureaucratization and distortions which he saw around him. Workers needed to be protected from the consequences of these, and this was a vital task of trade unions. Unfortunately, this doubtless correct principle conflicted with that of party control over the independent manifestations of trade union power, under conditions of increasing bureaucratization of the party itself.

A fourth, and perhaps the most important, feature of the period related to the peasantry. The division of land among the peasants in 1917–18 had been elemental and uncontrolled, indeed uncontrollable. Lenin's willingness to accept the peasants' demands was a vital feature of the success of the Bolshevik revolution; the Provisional government procrastinated, claiming (understandably enough) that so complex a measure as land reform must await the Constituent Assembly. However, the elemental redivision of the land carried out by the peasantry caused major problems. Not only some efficient landlord estates but also many of the commercial peasant farms consolidated under the Stolypin reform were divided into strips under the medieval three-field system of cultivation, to the detriment both of productivity and of marketing. This was to create acute difficulties in food supply in the 1920s, and was an important long-term cause of the agricultural crisis at the end of that decade. The peasants in their capacity as petty-bourgeois element represented a potential danger to Soviet power; a country composed predominantly of smallholders, albeit on land nominally nationalized, meant that the party was a minority in what was repeatedly described in speeches of the time as a petty-bourgeois elemental swamp. This had very little indeed in common with the model implied by Marx's analysis either of socialism or of the transition period.

Some of the 'left' communists in Poland, Lithuania and Latvia, opposed the division of land among the peasants, and urged the setting up of collective and state farms. By such policies they alienated the peasantry and contributed to the victory of the counter-revolution. Indeed, Lenin himself was not wholly consistent on this issue. While on the one hand the very essence of Leninism was the utilization of peasant land hunger as a revolutionary force, he too saw the desirability of encouraging the setting up of state or collective farms, and his two-facedness on this issue was remarkably well understood by H. G. Wells, when he reported his talk with the man whom he called 'the dreamer in the Kremlin'. Quoting Lenin on plans to create large-scale state farms, overcoming the reluctance of 'selfish and illiterate' peasants, Wells remarked: 'At the mention of the peasants, Lenin's head came nearer to mine, his manner became confidential. As if, after all, the peasant *might* overhear.'[12] (Several Marxist writers, for instance, Bahro and Foster-Carter, have commented on the unfortunate consequences, in a predominantly peasant country, of regarding the peasantry as an object of social experiment, with its implications of revolution from *above*.)

Requisitioning during war-communism alienated the peasantry from the regime and discouraged production; it could only be a temporary, emergency measure. When he adopted the principles of NEP, Lenin derived from the bitter experiences of 1918–20 the need for gradualness. In one of his last works, 'On co-operation' (1923), he urged a cautious, step-by-step approach, with voluntary forms of co-operation weaning the peasants from their individualism. Stalin was later to claim that his collectivization drive was in line with Lenin's 'co-operative plan'. No one who reads Lenin's article can possibly doubt that Stalin's policy represented a total break with that indicated by Lenin's views as expressed in it.

The war-communism period produced a crop of highly original attempts to devise a model of a functioning socialist economy which could dispense with money and markets. A seminar was held in 1920 on 'problems of a moneyless economy', and various schemes were discussed (see pp. 53ff. above). But in view of present-day controversies among Marxists about 'market socialism' on the survival or elimination of commodity production, it seems important to note that the basic issues and possible models were discussed as early as 1920. It is now widely accepted among Marxists that money cannot be 'abolished' so long as the objective conditions for its existence are present. It has not existed for thousands of years without potent reasons! The market's functions, however imperfectly performed, cannot be easily replaced, and the effort to replace them by an all-embracing central plan, as we now know, leads to problems both of bureaucracy and of devising meaningful and workable economic criteria. The value of the discussions of 1920 is to show at how early a stage the basic issues were seen. As already suggested, it seems to be a valid criticism of the Marxian tradition that these issues were not perceived to be important *before* the revolution – just as contemporary critical Marxists such as Bahro and M. Vajda point out that Marx was wrong to refuse to take seriously Bakunin's prophetic warnings about a 'proletarian' dictatorship in which *former* workers became a new ruling stratum.

The abandonment of war-communism was rendered objectively necessary by the end of the civil war since the peasant majority could not accept the requisitioning and the ban on private trade, and once the danger of a White restoration faded rebellions did indeed break out, with the well-known Kronstadt revolt of the sailors as the last straw. On this interpretation, the Polish invasion (May 1920) and its aftermath postponed the introduction of NEP. However, some historians have another interpretation; when the Polish armies were compelled to retreat, Lenin saw the possibility of a link-up with a German revolution and, against Trotsky's warnings, caused the Red Army to advance to Warsaw. The defeat inflicted on the Reds by Pilsudski, and the evident refusal of the Polish workers and peasants to see the Bolsheviks as liberators, had far-reaching consequences. It may be argued[13] that this defeat led not only to NEP but also inexorably to 'socialism in one country', setting the seal on Soviet Russia's isolation.

Be this as it may, once peace was made with the Poles, and the last White army's Crimean stronghold was successfully assaulted, war-communism had to end. As Bukharin later remarked:

'The illusions of war–communism burst at the very hour when the proletarian army stormed the Perekop [the isthmus connecting the Crimea with the mainland].'[14]

NEP and the economics of a mixed economy

No more than 'war–communism' was NEP a consciously sought model. The decision of the Tenth Party Congress only envisaged the substitution of a tax in kind on the peasants for requisitioning. Relations with the peasants were to have been based on some ill–defined form of 'products-exchange' or barter (*produkto-obmen*). As Lenin explained, it proved impossible to hold this line, and private trade with small-scale private manufacturers and craftsmen was swiftly legalized. NEP, then, became a model of a mixed economy, with the state holding the 'commanding heights' (large-scale industry, most of wholesale trade, banks, foreign trade), but with the state sector itself operating in a market environment; management determined the product mix in negotiation with customers, costs had to be covered out of the proceeds of sales, the state plan was largely confined to investments. The peasants were left free to grow and sell what they pleased.

Was NEP a forced compromise, a bitter retreat? Or was it a return to the correct road, with war–communism seen as a sort of forced aberration? Lenin at various times expressed *both* views, and after his death the leadership split on this issue. Should NEP be persisted with 'seriously and for a long time' (Lenin's words), or should the offensive be resumed at the earliest possible date? And if resumed, what *sort* of offensive? Bukharin, in his moderate post-1921 posture, argued for economic competition; an efficient state production and distribution mechanism would drive the 'privateer'–NEPman out of business, and gradually the peasants too would see the advantages of co-operation and of collective production based on modern technique. Trotsky and Preobrazhensky, though opposed to Bukharin on the issues of investment policy and of the need to restrict the richer peasants (kulaks), did not explicitly advocate the use of coercion against the private sector. However, the party's war–communism traditions included precisely such coercion, and Stalin had widespread support, including part of the 'left' opposition, when, at the end of the decade, he led the campaign against private enterprise in town and country. There is here an important issue for Marxists. Marx himself never for a moment considered a situation in which petty-bourgeois production relations would manifest themselves spontaneously and police measures would be necessary to eliminate them. This is because he envisaged a transition to socialism in a highly developed capitalist economy, in which monopoly-capitalism had already destroyed the petty- and medium-bourgeoisie. But regimes owing allegiance to Marx have triumphed in underdeveloped countries. What, then, are they to do, in a situation in which the bulk of the people are not proletarian?

This dilemma has, of course, its political aspect. It is evidently no accident that 1921 saw both the introduction of NEP and the final elimination of all opposition parties, *and* also the ban on fractions within the Bolshevik party itself. The party became the instrument of long-term 'revolution from above'. This in turn was a consequence of backwardness, of 'unripeness' for socialism. The consequences of all this for the relationship of the party vanguard and its own rank-and-file members, and for democratic institutions in society as a whole, have been the subject of much comment by both Marxists and non-Marxists. Bahro's attempt to apply to the USSR Marx's 'Asian mode of production' and to combine it with the notion of an industrializing despotism, is among the most interesting. In his interpretation Lenin's entire strategy, as well as his elitist concept of the party and of its leadership, led towards Stalinism. In his view, the pathological excesses of Stalin's rule have tended to conceal the extent to which 'already *before* Stalin, in the first years after civil war, the basic features of the new social structure could be discerned in all essentials'.[15]

During this period there was a fascinating debate on economic laws under socialism, the best-known participants being Bukharin, Preobrazhensky and Skvortsov-Stepanov. The majority inclined to the view that the law of value survived only because of the existence of private enterprise and the lack of an all-embracing socialist plan. However, this left unsettled the question of what economic laws there would be once socialism was established. It will be recalled than when Bukharin, in his *Economics of the transition period*, asserted that political economy would not exist under socialism, Lenin in his marginal notes expressed disagreement. This whole issue was to be the subject of much subsequent controversy. (For a full and well-documented study of this question, see L. Baslé, 'L'élaboration de l'économie politique du socialisme', doctoral dissertation, Paris X-Nanterre, 1979.)

'Developmental socialism'

With NEP established and illusions of direct leaps into socialism shattered, what could Russian Marxists see as the next step in economic policy? In what ways could Marxist theory help them in their search for development strategies?

Evidently industrialization had to be resumed. It had been interrupted by war and revolution. Reconstruction was proceeding rapidly under NEP, but this could do no more than restore the previously existing structure. Major issues of political economy arose: how fast to go; what criteria should be used in making investment decisions; how far to rely on trade with capitalist countries; how to secure the necessary resources from the still-independent peasantry; what kind of plans to devise, and how to implement them; what role should be played by the private sector and by the market. A key political-economic issue was how to relate to the peasantry, which not only formed the large majority of the population, but whose marketed produce held the key to economic growth, being needed both to feed the cities and to secure essential foreign currency through export. I shall look in detail at the peasant problem in discussing the causes of collectivization, below. There were also differing interpretations of the stabilization of capitalism in the West, and of the role of foreign trade in Soviet development.[16]

The 'great debate' raised a variety of theoretical and political issues of high importance. Marxian thought had to be adapted to problems of underdevelopment and industrialization. Choice of economic strategy was deeply influenced by, and in its turn influenced, political strategy. The NEP compromise, based upon a *market* link with the peasantry, not only limited the possibilities of rapid capital accumulation, but also implied that priority should be given to investments with a short gestation period, directed towards satisfying the demand of the peasantry, thereby encouraging them to produce and sell more. Preobrazhensky and others on the 'left' argued that capital accumulation in the period 1923–5 was too small, that more should be extracted from the private sector (that is, the peasantry in the main), through an appropriate price policy. The theory known as 'primitive socialist accumulation' was, in its own terms, unexceptionable, and Bukharin's attacks on it as a theory smacked of political demagogy. But one must recall that at this period the weak and inefficient state industry was selling goods at high prices, that 1923 was the year of the so-called 'scissors crisis', which arose precisely because the terms of trade had turned too far against the peasant,[17] and that pressure was being exerted on state industry to reduce prices. No doubt all would be well if costs could be reduced even faster, but how could this be achieved? If Day is correct, Trotsky hoped to do so by importing Western equipment and know-how, but this would have required higher exports and therefore increased peasant marketings, unless large loans could be obtained, or concessions granted. In these circumstances, Bukharin and Stalin could counter-attack by pointing out that Preobrazhensky's policy would mean dangerously to rock the boat, that Trotsky's investment programme was unsound and adventurous, and that it was wrong in principle to speak of 'exploiting' the peasantry.

None the less, historians of Marxist thought will surely see profundity and originality in Preobrazhensky's analysis. The arguments set out in his 'New economics' were reinforced by a highly original adaptation of

Marx's model of expanded reproduction in the USSR, envisaging not only 'trade' between departments I and II but also between both and the petty-commodity (peasant and handicraft) sector. Preobrazhensky developed his model in an article in *Vestnik kommunisticheskoi akademii* (1927, no. 22),[18] which ended with the words: 'to be continued'. Alas, there was no second instalment. Preobrazhensky was silenced and, in due course, shot.

Of great importance, and wrongly neglected, were the professional economists and other specialists of the period. Mostly non-Bolshevik, but either within Marxism or very familiar with it, these men could be said to have been pioneers of modern development economics. For example, there was the very talented Bazarov, the already-mentioned Yurovsky, Maslov, Groman, Bernshtein-Kogan, Kondratiev, Fel'dman, Chayanov . . . Space forbids an adequate account of their thinking. They and other able and original theorists debated, at a high level of sophistication, such issues as: industrialization tempi, investment criteria in the context of abundant labour-supply, comparative costs and comparative advantage within a development strategy, agriculture versus industry, heavy industry versus light industry, the developmental capacities of peasant smallholders, the 'balance of the national economy' (the ancestor of input-output techniques), mathematical growth models, and all this when Western economists were totally uninterested in growth and development.[19] The argument between 'genetic' and 'teleological' planning is one which still rages in developing countries; what should be the role of existing patterns of demand and market forces, as against the objective of transforming existing structures? Bazarov, often thought to be the chief 'geneticist', in fact supported a wise compromise: change is indeed the objective, and certain key sectors had to be given priority and exempted from 'normal' rate-of-return criteria; however, plans which ignored the existing situation were unlikely to be sound or realizable. One is reminded of Bukharin's article, 'Notes of an economist' (*Pravda*, 30 September 1928), in which he warned against trying to build factories with bricks which were not there. Such sentiments were already being treated as evidence of right-wing deviation, later to be fatal to the accused. Perhaps because the professionals' arguments were similar to those of Bukharin, they were not only silenced but, with few exceptions, were imprisoned or shot. Other distinguished Marxist economists suffered a like fate; one has only to mention the highly talented I. I. Rubin, whose explorations of Marxian value theory are highly regarded today. The subsequent sterility of Soviet Marxism was a consequence of the destruction of many highly original minds, and the silencing of others.

The drafting of the first five-year plan (1927–8) took place at a time when the voices of moderation were being expelled at both the political and the technical-specialist level. This was the period summarized by the slogan 'there is no fortress the Bolsheviks cannot take'. It could be described as the psychology of the great leap forward. A great industry was required to be built in the shortest possible time, and military danger provided a strong argument for giving top priority to heavy industry and to achieving a greater degree to autarky. The priority of heavy industry, or more strictly of department I (making producers' goods) over department II (consumers' goods) has been widely regarded as a species of orthodox Marxism. While it is doubtless true that rapid growth does indeed require the more rapid expansion of department I, the great emphasis on this priority must be seen as a reflection of the policy decisions of Stalin and his leadership in the special situation of Russia of the time.

The actual five-year plan that was adopted, the higher of two variants, was itself swiftly superseded by ever more ambitious plans, creating acute imbalances and bottlenecks, which then became the subject of politically organized campaigns. The relative flexibility and market-orientation of NEP gave way gradually to a much more highly centralized structure, in which management was constrained to produce to order, for designated customers, obtaining its inputs from designated suppliers, all at prices fixed centrally. By 1931 credits could only be obtained from the State Bank (that is, enterprises were forbidden to lend to each other). Despite tight financial controls, the grossly excessive demand engendered by the grossly unrealistic plan targets, together with an increase in the labour force much greater than planned, led to strong inflationary pressures and to severe shortages. These included not only very serious lack of essential foodstuffs (many actually starved), but also shortage of industrial materials, fuel and transport facilities, and also of skilled labour. Endeavours to achieve the impossible led to overstrain and hardships, culminating in the extremely difficult year 1933, which also saw the worst consequences of collectivization (of which more in a moment).

Trotsky, in his exile, fulminated with reason against what he called 'prize-gallop industrialization', which he contrasted with his own earlier advocacy of rapid but balanced industrial growth (at a time when Stalin and Bukharin took a cautious line and accused Trotsky of adventurism).

It is difficult to relate the Stalin industrialization strategy to any theory, whether Marxist or not. Evidently its mainsprings could hardly be found along the line of Trotsky's analysis, with its stress on 'Thermidor' and bureaucracy. Stalin's cataclysmic 'revolution from above' was not a typical manifestation of bureaucracy! More fruitful is Bahro's approach: an 'industrializing despotism', perhaps reconcilable with Marx's vision of an Asian mode of production, but not, of course, with Marx's association of the Asian mode with traditionalist stagnation.

In the process of trying to transform the economy in record time, central control over resources was systematized into what might be called the command economy, or what Kosygin has more recently called 'directive planning'. Within this system managerial autonomy is in principle confined to finding the best way of obeying the orders received from above, and trade union activities are directed towards mobilizing the workers to fulfil the plan-orders. The 'Stalinist' industrial model is one in which workers' participation is minimal, in which the party-state hierarchy passes down commands, with obedience to these commands as the basic success criterion. Such has been the impact of Soviet experience, that many intelligent people supposed that such a way of organizing economic life is the translation into reality of the vision of Marxism or Marxism-Leninism. There are indeed in Marx many references consistent with *centralized* planning; while he also referred, of course, to control by 'associated producers', he can be shown to have been opposed, as Lenin was, to control by *sections* of the workers, since these would pursue sectional interests (until such time as sectional interests would wither away, and everyone was at one with everyone else, i.e. in my view cloud-cuckoo-land). The virtual elimination of the market mechanism, the apparent end of 'commodity production', seemed indeed to herald a rapid advance towards socialism. In the heady days of 1929–32 voices were heard claiming that planning had virtually eliminated economics (as a science of spontaneous exchange relations), and statistics too; the Central Statistical office was solemnly renamed the Central Office of National Economic Accounting (TsUNKhU; the word 'economic' was strictly not used, the Russian *khozyaistvo*, the *kh* in the above acronym, indicating management rather than economics). This theoretical extremism was paralleled by similar developments in other disciplines at the time.[20]

Some of these extremist attitudes were abandoned, together with the wilder flights of planners' fancies, possibly under the impact of the crisis (not too strong a word) of 1933. We know from published accounts that the first version of the *second* five-year plàn, covering the period 1933–7, was still fantastical; for example, the plan for coal for 1937 was set at an absurd 250 million tons. But when finally presented to the Seventeenth Party Congress in 1934, it had been drastically scaled down (e.g. the coal plan became 152 million tons), with both greater realism and more attention to the hard-pressed consumer. Efficiency and cost-consciousness also became accepted, indeed stressed, though not until the end of that decade was work begun on a textbook on political economy which, for various reasons, did not finally appear until 1954. But by then Stalin was dead, and within two years economists were beginning to ask fundamental questions (e.g. about the law of value and its role under socialism) which went beyond the inadequate and question-begging formulations proclaimed or authorized by Stalin.

Collectivization

Marx's attitude to the peasantry was, if not hostile, then surely dismissive. He spoke of 'the idiocy of rural life', and indeed this correctly reflected the facts around him. The bulk of the peasantry was illiterate, passive, superstitious. There seemed no future for property-owning smallholders. They were to be victims of capitalist farming, just as the petty-bourgeois shopkeepers and small manufacturers were to be ousted by monopoly-capitalism. It is significant that Marx omitted the 'self-employed' peasant from his definition of productive labour under capitalism, because in a 'pure' capitalist model he had ceased to exist. Individual peasants were to be replaced under capitalism by more efficient commercial farming, taking advantage of economies of scale. Indeed there are references in Marx to the use of 'labour armies' in agriculture after the revolution.

The first 'revisionists' cast doubt on all this. Bernstein, for instance, claimed that there were few economies of scale in agriculture, that the peasant would survive, and politically it did seem a little disingenuous to seek peasant votes on a programme that regarded the disappearance of the peasant as progressive. No wonder the German social democrats gained so little support in rural areas. But no one, not Marx, or Engels, or Kautsky, envisaged the use of force by socialists to expropriate the peasantry. The turning of the peasant into a landless labourer was seen as a tendency in capitalism, and men like Kautsky simply asserted that this was to be in the long run a progressive trend, and that it was not the task of socialists to arrest or reverse it by supporting peasant demands.

Russia, however, was an overwhelmingly peasant country. What were Russian Marxists to say about the peasantry in the context of socialist revolution, which could not succeed without peasant support?

Marx himself had doubts about the applicability of his doctrines to a semi-Asian country, in which traditional peasant communal institutions survived. This can be seen in the several rejected variants of his reply to the letter from Vera Zasulich, and the final version was ambiguous. Most Russian Marxists may not have known about Marx's reply – it was not published until 1924 – but in any case they ignored it. The communal institutions (the *mir*, or the *obshchina*) were indeed decaying. However, the consciousness of most Russian peasants was still pre-capitalist, pre-industrial. The effort of the tsar's prime minister, Stolypin, to create a property-owning peasantry was opposed by the bulk of the peasants themselves, as is shown by the fact that they undid much of the Stolypin reform during the turmoil of revolution, returning to communal tenure, with periodic redistribution, a ban on purchase and sale of land, and so on. The peasants' land hunger, that is, their desire to divide up the landlords' estates, was a revolutionary force, but once the land was divided the peasants' private-property instincts, which were still in an underdeveloped state, would surely grow stronger, and the interest in socialist revolution would disappear. Trotsky, in his theory of permanent revolution, foresaw that the proletarian revolution in backward Russia would be defeated 'the moment the peasants turned their backs on it'. Nor were the traditional communal institutions a way towards collective farming; while the revolution had the paradoxical effect of reviving their strength, they were *not* any sort of producers' co-operative; each household cultivated its own strips, owned its own livestock.

The Bolsheviks stood for nationalization, the Mensheviks for 'municipalization', of the land, but both saw no alternative to allowing the peasants effective control over land and produce. In the event the peasants made their own land 'reform'. The Bolsheviks had few members and little authority in the villages. They found it necessary in 1917 to allow the peasants to seize and redivide the land as they saw fit. This meant considerable variations in accordance with the balance of force in each village, but as a rule the solutions adopted led to a redivision of the land not only of the landlords but of the better-off peasants too. The net effect was to reduce inequality among peasants.

Inequalities did persist, however, especially in the aftermath of civil war, with grave shortages of implements and of horses. Some had them, others not. For these and other reasons (including the number of healthy males in a household, the propensity to drunkenness, enterprise, and so on), peasant stratification revived and became a major issue in the politics of the 1920s. Even before the revolution, Lenin saw hope in the support which landless labourers and 'the poorest peasants' would give to the proletarian revolution, while the middle peasants would vacillate and the richer ones, the so-called kulaks, would be class enemies. There were arguments in the 1920s about the kulak menace, whether they were extending their power dangerously and were in the position to hold the Soviet state to ransom by their control over marketable surpluses, or whether the kulaks could be seen as valuable producers who should be encouraged and, as Bukharin argued, who would gradually 'grow into' socialism through their links with the socialist urban and financial sectors.

It has been argued, notably by Theodore Shanin,[21] that this whole approach was erroneous, in that it under-estimated intergenerational mobility between the categories of poor, middle and rich peasant (they were, for instance, frequently relatives, or linked by marriage). Consequently there was more peasant solidarity than the dominant theories allowed for.

The basic problems facing the post-revolutionary leadership are probably well known to most readers and will only be briefly summarized here. The effect of the revolutionary land 'reform' was to break up large commercial landlord estates, and most of the consolidated holdings of the richer peasants also. The traditional attitudes of the peasant smallholders inclined them to producing largely for their own subsistence. The problem was exacerbated by unattractive prices. The net effect was a fall in marketings of farm produce to levels well below prewar. Yet industrial development would require much higher marketings, to feed the growing towns and for export.

This was seen by Preobrazhensky and others as the problem of 'primitive socialist accumulation'. Resources had to be transferred from the private sector (predominantly peasant) to the growing socialist urban sector, through some form of unequal exchange. While this was, in general terms, accepted as necessary, Preobrazhensky's reference to 'exploitation' of the peasantry caused protests, especially from Bukharin and his friends.

An immediate increase in marketings could be achieved by encouraging the most prosperous and efficient peasants to raise themselves above their neighbours, which in effect meant a pro-kulak policy. This logic was seen most clearly by Bukharin, who in 1925 produced his 'notorious' slogan 'get rich' (obogashchaites'). This was too much even for his then ally, Stalin. However, though Trotsky denounced the alleged pro-kulak policy of the majority, he too, in 1923, had advocated something similar: the peasant should 'get richer' (stal bogache).[22] For indeed, unless this was so, how could private peasant agriculture produce the needed surpluses over and above the village's own needs? The policy of relying on the 'middle peasant' while combating the kulak made no agricultural sense; a successful middle peasant became a kulak almost by definition. One could not achieve an increase in marketings by regarding every successful peasant as a class enemy to be combated.

The gradual increase in industrial investment which began in 1926, and speeded up as from 1928, made the problem acute. Shortages of consumers' goods, high free-market prices for food and relatively low official buying prices for grain combined to create a grain crisis in the winter of 1927–8. This led by stages to the decision to enforce all-round collectivization, and to eliminate the kulaks as a class by arrest and/or deportation. The consequences – massive loss of livestock, famine, acute hardship, bitter resentment – are too well known to require comment. This is not an economic history of the period. One question is, what had all this to do with Marxism, or how far did the events take place, or policies get adopted, because of Marxist or Marxist-Leninist doctrine? A second one is, what lessons can be drawn, and was collectivization in fact successful in achieving its objective?

It seems to me quite clear that forcible collectivization was contrary to Marxist doctrine and tradition. Nowhere in the works of Marx is it even hinted that the peasants ('petty-bourgeois' in interests and outlook), especially if constituting the majority of the population, should be suppressed by police measures. Marx foresaw their elimination by the forces of monopoly-capitalism, not the OGPU! Indeed, Engels warned against the use of coercion in respect of the peasantry. Lenin's attitude was more complex, but certainly in and after 1921 he strongly supported the *smychka* (link) with the peasants based on the market. As already mentioned, in one of his very last articles ('On co-operation'), he advocated an extremely cautious and gradualist approach; the peasants were to be attracted to collectivism by loose forms of voluntary co-operation, and by seeing the advantages to them of large-scale mechanization (Lenin had great faith in the propaganda power of tractors and electrification). Trotsky disagreed with Bukharin about the kulaks, but never advocated coercive collectivization, as distinct from 'curbing the exploitative proclivities of the kulaks'. Preobrazhensky considered that the regime faced contradictions which could only be resolved by the support of revolutions in the developed West, but, while sharing with the party as a whole a preference for collective as against individual agriculture, he did not envisage police measures as a solution.

Stalin knew all this and, when he launched his campaign, did so on false pretences (so to speak). Since coercion, other than against kulak class enemies, was obviously contrary to accepted doctrine, he claimed that the bulk of the peasants had joined the collective voluntarily, except where overzealous officials had distorted the party line. No doubt in some areas the poorest peasants joined in the campaigns to extirpate (and rob) kulaks and some may have joined collectives of their own free will. But it is surely by now an accepted fact that the majority of peasants were *coerced*. The necessity of *lying* was in a sense proof that what was being done did *not* conform to doctrine or ideology. Stalin also claimed that he was carrying out 'Lenin's co-operative plan', that is, that he was following the lines laid down by the dying Lenin in 1923. This too was false, as anyone re-reading Lenin's article can see for themselves.

Collectivization coincided with the first five-year plan. The needs of industrial investment were a major factor in the decision to force through collectivization as a solution of the food procurement problem. It also made impossible the provision of incentives which could sugar the pill. The peasants were not only forced into so-called collectives, but suffered material loss by doing so. The collectives were in practice *pseudo* co-operatives, the 'elected' management was in fact appointed by the party, and everything was subordinated to fulfilling the 'first commandment': delivery of produce to the state at low prices.

The net effects included not only heavy loss of livestock and a fall in production, but the discrediting of the idea of collective agriculture, by associating it with coercion, compulsory deliveries and impoverishment. The adverse effects persisted for a generation and more. Thirty years later a Soviet publicist was to deplore the fact that 'in order to kill the peasant's love of private property it proved necessary to kill his love of the land,' and in 1979 an article in *Pravda* referred bitterly to the indifference of the peasants to bringing in the harvest and ensuring fodder for collective livestock. So it is not only a question of history.

Was collectivization successful in mobilizing farm surpluses for industrialization? This is still a matter of some controversy. Michael Ellman[23] and James Millar[24] have argued, using some recently published Soviet data, that collectivization did *not* lead to any increase in off-farm sales, the larger quantity of grain and potatoes being more than offset by the steep decline in livestock products. At the same time, the need to replace slaughtered horses by tractors contributed to an increase in deliveries of industrial products to the villages. While the state procured produce at very low prices, some peasants made money by sales in the free market at very high prices. Ellman and Millar disagree about what conclusion should be drawn from these facts. Millar argues that this shows that collectivization was a counter-productive disaster. Ellman, on the contrary, considers that it succeeded – at very high cost, of course – in the objective of supplying basic foodstuffs to the growing towns. All agree that the *intention* of collectivization was to mobilize resources for industrial investment. It seems to follow that since net agricultural surpluses did not increase, the huge rise in investments was 'financed' by the urban sector, and that the working class made the major contribution.

My own view is a little different. One must, of course, agree that the state obtained less than it intended, from a lower agricultural output. *Given* the fall in production, collectivization and the associated coercion provided the needed foodstuffs, even though peasants starved as a result. Many millions of the less skilled workers in the 1930s were in fact recent ex-peasants, who left the villages (voluntarily or not) during the period of collectivization. Relative prices meant little at this time (i.e. in the period 1930–4), since prices did not reflect economic realities, and many goods were unavailable or strictly rationed. Thus a peasant who sold cabbages in the free market for, say, 100 roubles in 1933 and wished to buy a pair of trousers could not get any trousers (but, had he found a pair in a state store, they *would* have cost him 50 roubles . . .). In other words, at this period the 'exploitation' of the peasantry was not through prices, but through non-supply. Soviet statistics purporting to show an increase in consumers' goods production and deliveries are highly misleading; they ignore the virtual elimination of handicrafts (and pedlars) which had supplied a large proportion of rural needs.

This is not to deny that the urban working class also carried heavy burdens and suffered hardships at this period. They did. But actual starvation was in rural areas.

Collectivization was appalling in its effects. I recall hearing a Soviet scholar say in an open discussion that, far from being a model of socialism, it was a *tragedy*, which socialist countries should avoid if they could. It was implied that for the USSR it was an *unavoidable* tragedy. Was this so? If so, why? Given the need to industrialize, given the military aspect (isolation, external threat, the need to create the basis for an arms industry), was this crude and ill-prepared policy of forcible collectivization the only feasible line? Was there a 'Bukharinist' alternative? Would not a policy of higher taxation, possibly taking the form of a tax in kind, have been more effective? Was there not some scope for looser forms of co-operation, which took into account peasant habits and preferences? At least these are matters worth considering.

Finally, we must return to a question raised earlier. Can one *ever* justify a policy which treats the large majority of the population, the working peasantry, as an *object* of decision-making, its interests and desires regarded as almost an irrelevancy for a government which claimed to be a 'workers and peasants' government' (albeit with the proletariat nominally in a leading role)? Consider the implications for democracy, and for the leading role of the coercive organs. The rise and consolidation of Stalinism is closely related to collectivization.

The centralized 'command' model

As we have already seen, in the period of the first five-year plan, in the process of trying to fulfil extremely ambitious growth plans, the Soviet planning system became highly centralized. Output plans, with obligatory targets, laid down what was to be produced and for whom, and materials, machinery and other inputs became subject to a system of administrative allocation. The extreme tensions and confusions of the early 1930s are past history, but the essence of the system of directive or command planning is still with us. Therefore, though its rise can be attributed to the strains and stresses of ultra-rapid industrialization (and the priority of heavy industry) in a poor and underdeveloped country, its survival must compel us to look carefully at this model of planning, from the standpoint of its relationship to Marxist socialist theory.

In the early 1930s there was a short-lived return to the ideas of war-communism. Economic calculation was rejected, the spirit of the times being well reflected in the slogan 'there is no fortress the Bolsheviks cannot take'. Military terminology ('fronts', 'storming', 'bridgeheads', etc.) was in constant use. The large majority of the professional economists who had distinguished themselves in the 1920s were in prison or dead in the 1930s. Economics as such suffered a grievous blow, was almost abolished. No textbook on the subject was published between 1929 and 1954! One could say that economic calculation was (temporarily) rejected.

Of course, this was partly due to the general atmosphere of Stalinism. Repression hit other intellectual spheres too, affecting both Marxists and non-Marxists – history, philosophy, literature, law, and so on. Economics was particularly vulnerable at a time when major structural changes were being enforced by the political organs, for two reasons. One is that the political organs (and Stalin in particular) were not prepared to allow the emergence of any objective criteria by which official policies could be judged; the other is that economics does indeed lack adequate objective criteria for rational decision-making at times of rapid structural change, and there was a tendency for economists to favour caution at a time when caution gave rise to suspicion of a 'right-wing deviation'.

It has been argued, for instance in a recent book by N. Spulber,[25] that Marxist ideology is inherently inconsistent with, and tends to be opposed to, objective criteria and rationality in economics. This seems to me to be going too far. It implies that the now quite massive literature in the USSR and Eastern Europe on resource allocation and organization theory is non-Marxist or even anti-Marxist. But Spulber in his book is right to raise a fundamental question: did Marx and Lenin ever see clearly the economic implications of the socialism which was to supplant capitalism? Were not the principles they wished to apply mutually incompatible? It could be argued that the centralized Soviet-type planning system is the nearest *feasible* approximation to a model which specifically excludes 'commodity production' and the market, that it may be simply *impossible* to have a centrally planned and marketless economy without the bureaucracy (and alienation) which is its functionally inescapable concomitant.

There is also another kind of contradiction. Marx envisaged control by society, by the direct producers, over resources and over the allocation of labour, with decisions taken in the full knowledge of human needs. Costs would be calculated in hours of labour, and society would be able to decide by reference to use-values of alternative patterns of production, directly, without any monetary or value calculations. He *also* envisaged associations of free producers, with a real sense of effective control over the means of production and the product. But in a large and complex industrial economy, it is by no means clear how the 'free producers' can be deciding freely when there is no production for exchange. As several Marxist scholars have rightly pointed out, 'commodity production' is a consequence of the autonomy of production units. If this autonomy is eliminated, so as to incorporate them and their products in an all-inclusive plan determined by and for 'society', how are remote-control bureaucracy and alienation to be avoided, in what must then be a centralized system? Two hundred million people cannot meet together and decide anything. Their elected representatives (non-professional, part-time, rotating 'direct producers') can scarcely do more than vote on broad priorities. The idea that *managerial* decisions, or indeed micro-economic decisions generally, can be taken by the vote of a national assembly[26] of elected part-timers is surely a total fantasy ('by 315 votes to 180 it is decided that the Omsk bulldozer factory be supplied with 8,300 tons of sheet steel, by the Magnitogorsk steelworks . . .'?). If *any* 'free association' (or local commune) were to be given the right to take production decisions, then, to make a reality of them, it would have to be able to obtain the needed inputs, and for *this* to be possible it would need to negotiate with suppliers who, in turn, would have to be free to decide to produce this amount for this customer, and to obtain *their* inputs from *their* suppliers, and so on. This, as Soviet official authors have frequently pointed out, is the negation of central planning. In the USSR since about 1930 these transactions, and millions like them, are part of the current obligatory central plan, determined centrally, not by vote of elected assemblies, but by specialized officials.

In assessing the relationship between the Stalinist economic-political system and Marxism, we must bear in mind the importance of the specific circumstances of Soviet Russia. Backwardness, the pressure of very rapid industrialization and high rates of accumulation, isolation, military danger, the power of the 'Stalinist bureaucracy' and the lack of democratic political institutions must all be seen as part of the explanation of what occurred. But *part* only. It must not be supposed or assumed that in a more highly developed economy, with lower growth-rates, a better-educated people and a more democratic polity, the problems associated with centralized planning would be easier to handle. On the contrary, the greater complexity of a more highly industrialized society presents even greater operational difficulties than those faced in the USSR in the early 1930s. When there are literally millions of products, made by tens of thousands of industrial enterprises, the task of ensuring co-ordination and consistency becomes impossibly difficult.

It is essential for Marxists to re-examine, in the light of experience, the functional logic of a non-market economy. It is a centralizing logic. The sheer scale and complexity which centralization involves compels the creation of a vast planning-and-management hierarchy. It is sometimes said that the resultant weaknesses are due to the alienation of the workers (and of junior management too), the existence of conflict within the hierarchical structure, and so on. No doubt the alienation and the conflicts are real, and it is certainly the case that they result in the distortion of information flows and other negative phenomena familiar to analysts of the Soviet planning system. However, the alienation and the conflicts are an inescapable consequence of centralized planning itself, and the power that centralized planning puts into the hands of the central political organs is also part of the explanation of the power and privileges of the 'bureaucracy', and is also an obstacle to democratization of society. (Be it noted that democratization, even if achieved, in no way facilitates the task of ensuring the coherence of thousands of millions of interconnected production-and-allocation decisions!)

It used to be said – for instance, by Plekhanov and Bukharin – that economics would wither away under socialism. This is not only because under socialism as originally envisaged there would be no exchange or commodity-money categories, but also because the economic problems which beset all real societies would be eliminated *by definition*. Abundance could be held to imply universal satisfaction, and therefore no need for change. There would be no need to accumulate. There would be no need for incentives, since all would identify their individual interest with the interests of all of society, and all would be able to see what that interest was, with work a pleasure. Needs, and the best way to satisfy them, would be known *ex ante*. This is a socialist form of general equilibrium theory with perfect knowledge and perfect foresight and, I submit, as useless as such theories are when presented in bad textbooks by 'bourgeois' economists. The abuse of power by those in command was not seen as a problem, because under a real socialism it was thought that there would be no commanders – and therefore no thought was given to institutional or other checks on abuse of power by those who rose to positions of command.

It is a matter of opinion whether the socialism of Marx (or full communism) is conceivable in the future, given finite resource and various other constraints. Those who persist in believing in it would attach the label 'transitional' to any society which, following a successful revolution, was striving to 'build' socialism under conditions of scarcity and with the human material which actually exists (as distinct from the imagined New Man). In relation to such a society, Marxist economics has virtually nothing that is relevant to say. Its doctrines do not relate to any of the economic problems which must arise. If the 'law of value' operates only within a market economy, then the problems of valuation, of comparing costs and results, of how to use resources efficiently, are left without any answer or any usable methodology.

But, of course, the practical problems of planning require that some sort of methodology be devised. The leadership itself desired the reduction of waste, increased efficiency, higher labour productivity, technical progress. Even in Stalin's lifetime there was a cautious attempt to formulate investment criteria, as a guide for the planning organs in choosing between alternative means to given ends. After Stalin's death there was a gradual revival of theory, with sharp criticism of the bland and evasive formulations to be found in the textbook of political economy which was published in 1954 but which had been written with Stalin still alive. The applicability of the 'law of value' to a Soviet-type economy, which Stalin had excluded from transactions within the state sector, was re-examined at length. Input-output techniques and linear programming, and cybernetics, were no longer ignored or rejected, and their use and potential were discussed. Various quite radical proposals began to be aired, involving greater reliance on the market mechanism, with a reduction in the scope of administrative allocation of inputs. Planning methods came under scrutiny, and there were attempts to utilize organization and systems theories. It was recognized that there were stochastic and probabilistic elements in the planning process. A talented school of mathematically minded economists grappled with the task of defining a national economic optimum. They tackled on a high intellectual level the potential and limitations of mathematical tools. Professional economists have been drawn in to the planning process to a growing extent; thus for instance they serve on official committees, advise on problems of Siberian development, and so on.

Many of the proposals made by the more 'radical' economists have been rejected, and many reforms frustrated. The system has a powerful built-in defence mechanism against change. However, the need for efficiency, at a time of low population growth and many competing claims on limited resources, has stimulated a continued search for effective reform – but preferably one which will not upset the power structure and which will ensure the maintenance of existing priorities. The serious economic strains of recent years may compel Brezhnev's successors to take the risk of making major changes. This is not the place to discuss what they might be. But whatever they are, they will surely owe nothing to Marxian political economy, not because they wish to ignore it, but because it says nothing which relates to the problems they face. (Nor, let it be added, does Western 'mainstream' theory). It may be surmised that any meaningful reform which does not confine itself to reshuffling the functions of various central agencies *must* entail a greater degree of decentralization, which, in practice, will mean extending the role of contract and customer-supplier relationships, that is, commodity-money relations and the market. This is a simple consequence of the sheer physical impossibility of achieving by the 'traditional' methods of centralized planning the necessary co-ordination of multi-million micro-economic production-and-allocation decisions. Plan and market, as many recognize, are not alternatives, one of which must destroy the other. They *must* coexist. True, it will be an uneasy coexistence, generating conflicts and contradictions. But Marxists, of all people, should find it possible to accept that life with no conflict or contradictions is hardly likely to exist in the real world (and in any case it would be intolerably dull).

Notes: Chapter 5

1   K. Marx and F. Engels, *Sochineniya*, Vol. 14 (Moscow and Leningrad: 1931), pp. 315–16.

2   A. Katsenellenboigen, *Studies in Soviet Economic Planning* (White Plains, NY: Sharpe, 1978). p. 123. Katsenellenboigen emigrated from the USSR in 1975.

3   V. I. Lenin, 'State and revolution' in *Sochineniya*, Vol. 33 (Moscow: 5th edn, 1962), p. 101, and 'Can the Bolsheviks retain state power?', in ibid., Vol. 34, pp. 307–8 (my translation).
4   O. Neurath, *Vollsozialisierung* (1910).
5   E. Barone, 'The ministry of production in the collectivist state', in A. Nove and D. M. Nuti (eds), *Socialist Economics: Selected Readings* (Harmondsworth: Penguin, 1972), pp. 52–74.
6   Y. Gimpelson, *Voyenny kommunism* (Moscow: 1973).
7   L. Szamuely, *First Models of the Socialist Economic system* (Budapest: 1974; in English).
8   V. I. Lenin, *Lohinsky sbornik*, Vol. 11 (Moscow: 1929).
9   V. I. Lenin, *Collected Works*, Vol. 33 (Moscow: Progress Publishers, and London: Lawrence & Wishart, 1966), p. 27.
10 See Trotsky's speech to the 9th Party Congress and N. Bukharin's *Ekonomika perekhodnogo perioda* (Economics of the Transition Period) (Moscow: 1920).
11 See the Communist Manifesto.
12 H. G. Wells, *Russia in the Shadows* (London: Hodder & Stoughton, 1921), p. 137.
13 For instance by N. Davies in *White Eagle, Red Star: The Polish/Soviet War, 1919–20* (London: Macdonald, 1972).
14 N. Bukharin, *O likvidaforstve nashikh dnei* (Moscow: 1924).
15 R. Bahro, *Die Alternative* (Cologne: Europäische Verlagsanstalt, 1978), ch. 2.
16 A challenging view in this connection is that of R. B. Day, *Leon Trotsky and the Politics of Economic Isolation* (Cambridge: CUP, 1973).
17 Industrial prices in the autumn of 1923 were relatively *three times* as high as agricultural prices, compared with 1913. And even in 1913 the terms of trade between village and industry favoured industry, compared with Western Europe.
18 A not-very-good translation appeared in the volume edited by N. Spulber, *Foundations of Soviet Strategy for Economic Growth* (Bloomington, Ind.: Indiana University Press, 1964). A full account of Preobrazhensky's ideas may be found in D. Filtzer (ed)., *The Crisis of Soviet Industrialization* (White Plains, NY: Sharpe, 1979).
19 See J.-M. Collette, *Politique d'investissement et calcul économique: l'expérience soviétique* (Paris: Cujas, 1965).
20 See Sheila Fitzpatrick (ed.), *Cultural Revolution in Russia 1928–31* (Bloomington, Ind.: Indiana University Press, 1978).
21 Theodore Shanin, *The Awkward Class* (London: OUP, 1972).
22 See Trotsky's report to the 12th Party Congress, p. 322.
23 M. J. Ellman, 'Agricultural surplus and increase in investment: USSR 1928–32', *Economic Journal*, vol. 85, no. 340 (December 1975) pp. 844–63.
24 James R. Millar, 'Soviet rapid development and the agricultural surplus hypothesis', *Soviet Studies*, vol. 22, no. 1 (July 1970), pp. 77–93, and 'Mass collectivization and the contribution of Soviet agriculture to the first five-year plan: a review article', *Slavic Review*, vol. 33, no. 4 (December 1974), pp. 750–66.

25   N. Spulber, *Organizational Alternatives in Soviet-Type Economies* (Cambridge: CUP, 1979).
26   The religious fanatic would jib at the word 'national', although this makes things even worse for him. A *world* assembly?

6 Trotsky, collectivization and the five-year plan

This was first published in Francesca Gori (ed.), *Pensiero e azione politica di Lev Trockij*, Vol. 2 (Firenze: Olschki, 1982), pp. 389–404, which was the record of the proceedings of a conference on Trotsky held at Follonica, Italy, in October 1980. I had written a script in 1979 for a BBC programme on the occasion of the hundredth anniversary of Trotsky's birth. My reading of his works convinced me that most of those who call themselves Trotskyists have little understanding of what Trotsky really stood for while he was still a political force in Russia, or of the mixture of insights and blind spots which characterized his comments on Russian affairs when in exile. The tailpiece on 'bureaucracy' was added as a contribution to the discussion at the conference.

To have a correct appreciation of Trotsky's attitude to the policies which Stalin adopted at the end of the 1920s, it is necessary to examine his views of NEP. These have frequently been misunderstood, and indeed in retrospect Trotsky sometimes distorted the position he himself had adopted. It is widely believed (and was believed by this author too) that Trotsky was an advocate of policies inconsistent with the principles of NEP, that he opposed reliance on the market except as a temporary and hateful expedient, agreeing with Preobrazensky in seeing planning as in fundamental conflict with the market ('socialist accumulation versus the law of value'), that he wanted to launch an attack on the kulaks, that he favoured exploiting the peasantry to finance rapid industrialization. Mandel, in his recent book, attributes to him the following policy in 1923: 'a rise in real wages, the disappearance of mass unemployment, a general course towards accelerated industrialization, and an increased class-war in the countryside'.[1]

It is true that Trotsky's later writings could be quoted to support such an interpretation, but it runs totally counter to what Trotsky said and wrote at the time, that is, in the whole period 1921–5, before his expulsion from the leadership. It was also totally contrary to the practical possibilities of the period, and would have seemed like irresponsible demagogy in 1923. It should be recalled that the country was painfully recovering from total collapse, hunger, hyperinflation and chaos. It was Trotsky himself, precisely in 1923, who coined the term 'price scissors' to define the relationship between agricultural and industrial prices, which rose too grossly to the disadvantage of the peasants. It was Trotsky who therefore advocated a relative fall in the prices charged by state industry, based, of course, on reduction in its costs. He was also acutely aware of the deficiencies of total planning, which had been attempted in the period of war-communism, and when he spoke to the Fourth Congress of the Communist International in 1922 he emphasized the need for a long transition period in which there would have to be recourse to capitalist methods of calculation. Indeed, he said the following:

> in the course of the transitional epoch each enterprise and each set of enterprises must to a greater or lesser degree orient itself independently in the market and test itself through the market. It is necessary for each state-owned factory with its technical director to be subject not only to control from the top – by state organs – but also from below, through the market, which will remain the regulator of the state economy for a long time to come.

We shall see that this was quite consistent with what he wrote on the same subject ten years later. So it may be in certain respects that Trotsky was not at one with Preobrazensky, who did indeed see plan and market as irreconcilable opposites (which is not to say that Trotsky *liked* the market). This might help to explain the fact that Preobrazensky broke with Trotsky when Stalin made his left turn in 1928.

Trotsky had made the economic report on behalf of the Politbureau to the Twelfth Party Congress in 1923. This is where he spoke of the price scissors. While he also referred to 'the market devil', he insisted that it had to be used and tolerated. He naturally favoured the expansion of the socialist sector of the economy, as all the Bolsheviks did. But meanwhile he saw the necessity for stimulating peasant agriculture, and he quite specifically asserted that it is necessary that 'the peasant should become richer'. This is not very different from Bukharin's slogan of 1925, that the peasants should 'get rich'. Trotsky was also against taxing the kulak too heavily. True, he also urged that there should be a national plan, and criticized the Commissariat of Finance for excessive addiction to financial soundness. But there was very little room for manoeuvre in this still very weak economy, and there is no doubt that Trotsky supported currency stabilization and therefore balanced budgets. As for planning, one has only to read Trotsky's writings of the period to see that he did *not* regard it as the antithesis of the market. The following quotations should make this abundantly clear. In a letter to the Central Committee dated 24 October 1923, he speaks of 'overall guidance in planning, i.e. the systematic co-ordination of the fundamental sectors of the state economy in the process of adapting them to the present market'.[2] In his important pamphlet *The New Course*, written in 1923 and published in the following year, this is stated with even greater emphasis. Admitting that the existence of the market 'extraordinarily complicates' the task of planning, he went on:

> for the next period we shall have a planned economy allying itself more and more with the market and, as a result, adapting itself to the market in the course of its growth . . . By means of exact knowledge of market conditions and correct economic forecasts we must harmonize state industry with agriculture according to a definite plan . . . In the struggle for the domination of the market the planned economy is our principal weapon . . . We must adapt the Soviet state to the needs and strength of the peasantry, while preserving its character as a workers' state; we must adapt Soviet industry to the peasant market on the one hand and the taxable capacity of the peasant on the other . . . Only in this way shall we be able to avoid destroying the equilibrium of our Soviet state until the revolution will have destroyed the equilibrium in the capitalist states . . . What is needed is the effective adaptation of industry to the rural economy . . . The different parts of our state industry (coal, metals, machinery, cloth) do not match with each other. The present selling crisis is a harsh warning that the peasant market is giving us. The correct work of our state planning commission is the direct and rational way of approaching successfully the solution of the questions relating to the *smyčka* – not by suppressing the market but on the basis of the market.

Surely it hardly sounds as if Trotsky was against the market, or that he saw planning as inherently incompatible with the market, at this period. His argument was surely that lack of adequate financing and planned co-ordination was causing a failure of state industry to supply the market, and that this had a number of undesirable consequences, both economic and political.

It seems to me that Trotsky in the period 1921–5 did not have an economic policy prescription very different from that of Bukharin. In the words of Stephen Cohen, Trotsky was a kind of NEPist. There was in any case little room for manoeuvre within the constraints of NEP. As for Trotsky's denunciations of bureaucracy, these too could be paralleled by similar statements made at exactly this period by Bukharin. True, Bukharin's actions, especially in supporting Stalin, belied his words, but then Trotsky's actions were very authoritarian when he was the 'prophet armed'.

After 1925 Trotsky was openly in opposition and his attitudes changed. Also there was a change in the objective situation. Recovery had been rapid, the economy was less weak, the question of planning a process of industralization was, so to speak, placed naturally on the agenda. There was also the debate on the issue of socialism in one country, but I do not wish to go into this, which is of only marginal relevance to my main theme, since the desirability of industralization in the USSR was not in itself part of the dispute. It is also important to note that Trotsky's views should not be confused with that of his last-minute ally, Zinoviev. It was Zinoviev who in 1926–7 was particularly eloquent about the kulak danger and in denouncing socialism in one country. Richard Day has argued that the logic of Trotsky's theory of permanent revolution implied that a backward country could carry through a socialist revolution. In Day's view,

> the operative question was not whether Russia could build socialism in advance of the international revolution, but how to devise an optimum planning strategy, taking into account both the existing and the future international division of labour.[3]

While I do not entirely agree with Day, I think that part of the confusion is semantic. Trotsky might well have agreed that, in the absence of revolution in the West, it was possible to 'build' socialism but not to complete the building. Expressing it in terms of Russian grammar, one could use the imperfective but not the perfective aspects, *stroit*, not *postroit*. After his exile Trotsky became much more emphatic in denouncing the principle of socialism in one country and the kulak danger than he had been whilst still in Russia. What was certainly true was that after 1925 Trotsky was pressing for accelerated industrialization and criticizing the cautious plans put forward by some experts as far too modest. Stalin and Bukharin replied by attacking Trotsky's alleged adventurism and irresponsibility, and Trotsky repeatedly quoted with bitter sarcasm Stalin's quip that the country needed the Dnieper dam (which Trotsky had proposed in 1926) like a peasant who had no cow needed a gramophone.

However, even in an essay not primarily devoted to the subject, one must question the coherence of the Trotsky policy of the period. Trotsky did not propose the abandonment of NEP. Indeed, as we shall see, he attacked Stalin in 1932 for having abolished it. Yet within NEP even the modest increases in investments that did take place in 1926 led to acute strains and a goods famine. It was all very well for Trotsky to mock Bukharin's phrase about building socialist industry 'at the pace of a tortoise', but what was the alternative within the constraints of NEP? Trotsky's reply would have been that the goods famine had been caused by inadequate productive capacity, and more investment was needed. No doubt it was. But the regime was caught in a vicious circle; to invest much more required more savings and a temporary reduction of current consumption. It was certainly not possible to raise the large sums required by taxes levied solely on the rich. Trotsky and his friends advocated higher wages for workers and, by 1927, were also urging an offensive against the kulak. When the peasants reduced grain sales in 1927 in a bid to obtain higher prices, Trotsky and his friends attacked proposals for increasing these prices. It is true that by 1927 Bukharin's economic policies, designed to promote and preserve market equilibrium on which NEP rested, had run into serious difficulties. It was this fact which led to the crisis of NEP and to the split between Bukharin and Stalin, when Stalin adopted drastic remedies inconsistent with NEP. But what precisely was Trotsky's alternative?

In 1928, when the decisive change in policy occurred, Trotsky was exiled to Alma Ata, and early in the following year he was expelled to Turkey. While at first he was able to communicate with some of his exiled supporters, notably the intelligent Rakovsky, and received news from Russia, there is much he did not and could not know, and this should be borne in mind in judging his comments on the events of those years.

As already mentioned, a number of supporters broke with Trotsky when Stalin turned left. Presumably industrialization, collectivization, the attack on the kulaks, the break with Bukharin, were to their liking, though later they were again expelled and in due course executed. It is a reasonable hypothesis that their attitude to NEP and its implications was more negative than that of Trotsky. This hypothesis received support from what Trotsky wrote on the subject in 1932 and which will be cited later.

But what of Trotsky's own interpretation of Stalin's left turn? We see this from his contributions to *Byulleten' oppozitsii* that he was mistaken in a number of respects. One key mistake was his analysis of Stalin as a centrist, representing the bureaucracy, vacillating between left and right but tending to ally himself with the right, that is, with Bukharin, who was seen as the real enemy, representing the hostile bourgeois classes of kulaks and NEPmen. Trotsky knew that Bukharin and his friends had voted in the Politburo against Trotsky's expulsion, but he continued to assail Bukharin after his exile. He saw the so-called centrists as 'undertaking a leftward zig-zag, which in the process of struggle took them further leftwards than they wished'.[4] 'For a serious Marxist it is clear that the centrists' left turn was ensured exclusively by a struggle.'[5] Only the force of circumstances and pressure from the left had driven the 'centrists' away from their normal role as allies of the right. But they would and could backslide. Trotsky reprinted with evident approval Rakovsky's analysis written in exile:

the leadership had been compelled to appropriate for its own use many elements on the opposition's platform, was compelled to repeat after us that every concession to the kulaks or other hostile classes would lead to their strengthening . . . But all this is but words. Still faithful to its centrist position, which consists of uttering left phrases and committing right deeds, asserting in words the existence of a right danger, announcing that any concessions to the kulak must be eliminated, the party leadership in practice made concession after concession. Thus in June [1928] it raised grain prices.[6]

Trotsky and collectivization

This helps to explain Trotsky's initial misunderstanding of collectivization. He simply could not fit the actions of the Stalinists into his analysis of their class position. Indeed, is it the typical action of centrists and conservative bureaucrats to undertake a vast revolution from above? Yet even in 1932 Trotsky was still able to speak of 'Stalinism, the policy of a conservative bureaucracy'. Trotsky had viewed the grain procurement crisis of the winter of 1927–8 as a manifestation of kulak power, and regarded the belated and small price rise of mid-1928 as an intolerable concession to the kulaks. It follows that he could not have objected to the extraordinary measures taken by Stalin to collect grain. Indeed he and some of his correspondents alleged that, in the course of these measures, the kulak was still somehow favoured. When he first heard about collectivization, he first thought that the leadership had been taken unawares by the peasants' rush to join collectives, a rush due to the state's action in closing markets and enforcing compulsory deliveries. 'The gates of the market were locked. After waiting in fear outside them, the peasantry rushed into the only gates that were open, the collectivization gates.'[7] But immediately afterwards he expressed the view that 'the collective farm can become a new form of disguise for the kulak', apparently because collectivization was being undertaken on the basis of traditional peasant techniques. Even in November 1930 he wrote:

collective farms without the necessary industrial base will inevitably secrete kulaks. To call wholesale collectivization based on peasant tools socialist amounts to reviving the Bukharinist theory of the growing socialism of the kulaks, but in an administratively disguised and so more malignant form.[8]

Of course, collectivization as such was supported not only by Trotsky but by all Bolsheviks. Bukharin and his friends had voted for the collectivization resolution at the Fifteenth Party Congress in 1927. But two conditions had to be met. One was that it was to be voluntary. The other was that the material basis for large-scale mechanized agriculture had first to be created. It was Trotsky's belief that the first condition would follow from the second, that is, that the peasants would be convinced by the new techniques to abandon their traditional way of life. As more information reached him, he became increasingly critical of the way in which collectivization was being carried through, but his attitude remained somewhat ambivalent. Thus in answering questions put by the *New York Times*, he said that

> the successes in the sphere of industrialization and collectivization became possible only because the Stalinist bureaucracy came up against the resistance of its protege, the kulak, who refused to surrender grain to the state, and thus the bureaucracy were compelled to take over and carry out the policy of the left opposition.[9]

On the other hand in his letter to the Central Executive Committee in Moscow he stated that 'the opposition warned against the dangerous game of complete collectivization and the notion of liquidation of classes within the period of the first five-year plan'.[10] A few weeks later, attacking his former supporter Radek, he was more critical still, and showed himself a supporter of the NEP compromise.

> The creation of economic links between city and village was the task of the New Economic Policy . . . Nationalized industry must provide the peasantry with products in such quantity and at such prices as would entirely eliminate or reduce to a minimum in the relations between the state and the peasant sector the factor of extraeconomic force.

He then referred to the need to limit the exploiting activities of the kulaks and continued: 'on this foundation, on the foundation of a link between city and village acceptable to the peasant, economic construction could be advanced with confidence'. He went on to ask rhetorically: 'did the 100 per cent collectivization assure such a reciprocal relationship between city and village as to reduce extra economic force? This is the nub of the question.' He naturally answered 'no'.[11]

But the most systematic exposition of Trotsky's views in 1932 is to be found in 'The Soviet economy in danger' published in the *Militant* in New York in instalments at the end of that year. A few quotations will suffice.

> The headlong race to break records in collectivization without taking into account the economic and cultural potentialities of agri-

culture has led in fact to ruinous consequences. It destroyed the
incentive of the small commodity producer long before it was able to
replace it by other and much higher economic incentives. Administrative pressure which exhausts itself quickly in industry is absolutely powerless in the sphere of agriculture . . . The economic
foundation of the dictatorship of the proletariat can be considered
fully assured only from that moment when the state is not forced to
resort to administrative measures of compulsion against the
majority of the peasantry in order to obtain agricultural products;
that is when in return for machines, tools and objects for personal
use, the peasants voluntarily supply the state with the necessary
quantity of grain and raw materials. Only on this basis – along with
other necessary conditions national and international – can collectivization acquire a true socialist character.

He correctly noted that the price ratios between agricultural and
industrial products in 1932 appeared to have moved in favour of the
peasants, but this was not really so, because 'the availability of commodities does not correspond to the availability of money. In the language of
monetary circulation that is what is called inflation.'

The absence of commodities has pushed the peasant in the direction
of a strike: he does not want to part with his grain for money. Not
having become a matter of simple and profitable exchange for both
sides, the provision of foodstuffs and agricultural raw materials has
remained as before a political campaign, a militant drive, requiring
each time the mobilization of the state and party apparatus . . . If the
exchange between village and the city were advantageous, then the
peasants would have no cause whatever to hide their stocks, but if
the exchange is not advantageous, that is if it takes the form of
compulsory transfer, then all the collective farmers and the individual farmers as well will strive to hide their grain . . . Collectivization
becomes a viable factor only to the extent to which it involves the
personal interest of the members of the collective farms, by shaping
their mutual relations and the relations between the collective farms
and the outside world on the basis of commercial calculation. This
means that correct and economically sound collectivization at this
stage should lead not to the elimination of NEP but to a gradual
reorganization of its methods.[12]

What then was Trotsky's attitude in 1932, when he had had the possibility of examining the facts? He deplored the coercing of the peasants,
preferred voluntary exchange on terms acceptable to the peasantry to the
Stalinist system of compulsory deliveries, and although he regarded the

kulaks as a hostile class he did not approve of their liquidation by police measures. He envisaged collectives made up of willing members with modern equipment based on commercial calculation and market relations; in other words, his mind was still very largely within the assumptions of NEP. One is struck by a possible inconsistency: how could accelerated industrialization be undertaken, at the rate envisaged by Trotsky, let alone at Stalin's excessive pace, within the constraints set by market relations with an uncoerced peasantry?

Trotsky and the five-year plan

Naturally, Trotsky bitterly assailed the sudden turn towards extreme growth tempos and impossibly high investment targets.

> All arguments against super industrialization were suddenly rejected. The apparatus, working for years in the spirit of economic Menshevism, received orders to regard as heretical all that had previously been holy writ, and to turn into official figures those heresies which yesterday had been all Trotskyist. The apparatus – communists and specialists alike – were quite unprepared for this task. Attempts to resist or alternatively to seek explanations led to immediate and severe punishment. Planning officials accepted that it was better to *stand* for high tempos than to *sit* (in prison) for lower ones.[13]

Again and again he rightly criticized the unsound extremism of official policy, what he called 'prize gallop industrialization', which led to 'breaches of all economic and therefore also social equilibria'.[14]

It must be recalled that the period of the first five-year plan coincided with the years of the great depression in the West. Trotsky from time to time contrasted the rapid growth of the Soviet economy with the decline and mass unemployment which was developing in Western countries, seeing in this proof of the superiority of the socialist planning principle. For example:

> Grandiose enterprises have been created, new industries, entire branches of industry. The capacity of the proletariat organized into a state to direct the economy by new methods and to create material values in tempos previously unheard of has been demonstrated in life. All this has been achieved against the background of a decaying world capitalism. Socialism as a system for the first time demonstrated its title to historic victory, not on the pages of *Capital* but by

the Praxis of hydroelectric plants and blast furnaces . . . However, light-minded assertions to the effect that USSR has already entered into socialism are criminal.[15]

But Trotsky also placed great emphasis on excessive tempos, disproportions, poor quality, arbitrary planning, where orders drafted in remote offices are imposed on the masses, whose living standards were falling ('an increasingly inhuman load is being dumped on the shoulders of workers'). And yet in the same year, 1932, he was still able to assert: 'the Soviet regime means the rule of the proletariat, irrespective of how broad the stratum in whose hands the power is immediately concentrated'.[16] He also criticized the tendency towards autarky: 'modern productive forces cannot be confined to national limits by a resolution or an exorcism. Autarky is the ideal of Hitler and not of Marx or Lenin. Socialism and national states are mutually exclusive.'[17] Meanwhile 'dependence on the capitalist world is part of the automatic logic of economic growth'.[18]

Trotsky also re-emphasised at this period his view on the role of the market, money and commercial calculation as an essential counterweight to bureaucratic arbitrariness. Here are some of the things he wrote on the subject in November 1932:

if there existed a universal brain, registering simultaneously all the processes of nature in society, measuring their dynamics, forecasting the results of their interactions, then such a brain would no doubt concoct a faultless and complete state plan. True the bureaucracy sometimes considers that it has just such a brain. That is why it so easily frees itself from the supervision of the market and of Soviet democracy. The innumerable live participants in the economy, state collective and private, must make known their needs and their relative intensity not only through statistical compilations of planning commissions but directly to the pressure of demand and supply. The plan is checked and to a considerable extent realized through the market. The regulation of the market itself must base itself on the tendencies showing themselves in it. The drafts made in offices must prove their economic rationality through commercial calculation. The economy of the transition period is unthinkable without control by the rouble.[19]

He went on: 'only through the interaction of three elements: state planning, the market and Soviet democracy, can the economy be correctly controlled in the transition epoch'. The same ideas were expressed even more strongly in May 1933: 'the function of money in the Soviet economy can in a certain sense only now expand fully. The transition period as a whole sees not the reduction of commodity turnover but on the contrary its great expansion', because collectivization had reduced the extent of peasant self-sufficiency.

> Keeping stock of all the productive forces of society, the socialist state has the task of giving them the most productive distribution in use for society. The methods of economic and monetary calculation developed under capitalism are not rejected but are socialized. The construction of socialism is unthinkable without building into the planning system the personal interest of producer and consumer. And this interest can manifest itself only if in its service there is a tried and flexible tool, a stable currency. In particular a rise in labour productivity and improvements in quality or output are impossible to attain without an accurate measuring rod, freely penetrating to every nook and cranny of the economy, i.e. a stable monetary unit.[20]

Referring specifically to the conditions of 1932 and the extreme disproportions and shortages of the period, Trotsky recommended that the second five-year plan be postponed while these disproportions were corrected.

The following observations seem to be appropriate.

First, although Trotsky retained the belief in an ultimate communism in which commodity-money relations would wither away, he plainly believed in the necessity of the market throughout what he called the transitional epoch, seriously and for a long time. This contrasts with the typical attitudes of contemporary Trotskyist dogmatists, who insist that reliance on the market represents a step away from socialism and towards a restoration of capitalism. Trotsky's views on the limitations of central planning were refreshingly realistic. In particular he linked the market with Soviet democracy in the same sentence, and therefore might well have approved of those Soviet reformers who speak today about the need to 'vote with the rouble'.

Second, his criticisms of Stalin's policies were not dissimilar to Bukharin's, causing me yet again to put the question as to why these talented men so bitterly fought each other. Even in exile, his reaction to Bukharin's warnings about unsound and unbalanced plans was hostile. 'The rightists are as correct on questions of industrialization as the French social democrats are right in saying, contrary to Molotov, that there is no revolutionary situation in France.'[21] In other words, even an enemy can be right and still remain an enemy.

Third, one sees again how Trotsky's critique of Stalin's agricultural and industrial policies failed to connect with his analysis of the nature of Soviet society. What forces did his enemies represent? Was it still a workers' state, though with no rights for its workers? Was this Thermidor, Bonapartism, perhaps even oriental despotism? What was this bureaucracy which held power and to what did it owe its power? What sort of democracy, what sort of developmental planning, was in fact possible in a backward country isolated in a largely hostile world in which power was held by a disciplined party in the name of a passive working class? If Trotsky had won in 1925, how would he have ruled, planned, accumulated capital, dealt with the peasant problem? How could he have executed his policies other than through a bureaucracy? And how was it and why was it that Stalin shortly afterwards started killing so many bureaucrats? But such questions take us outside the area which is supposed to be covered by my essay.

A word on bureaucracy

Too many conference participants spoke of 'bureaucracy' with no attempt either to define or to analyse the concept, and the result was an unnecessary degree of mental confusion. Someone even wrote that 'the pressure of the bourgeoisie internally and externally *had created the bureaucracy*', or even that it was *'the organ of the world bourgeoisie'*.

Whom are we talking about?

Let me make a random list of the kind of persons whom Trotsky and others must have had in mind when they spoke of 'bureaucrats'.

(a) *Party* functionaries, e.g. local secretaries, central committee officials, dealing with finance, personnel, women, agriculture, police, political commissars, etc.

(b) *State* officials, working in various commissariats, plan bureaux, Vesencha, provincial Soviet administrations, etc.

(c) *Economic managers* at all levels.

(d) *Army* and GPU officers.

And so on.

Their existence was plainly essential. It is therefore inherently nonsensical to attribute the *existence* of a 'bureaucracy' to the world bourgeoisie, or for that matter to backwardness – unless, that is, one defines bureaucracy as having nothing to do with function, in other words uses it as a kind of empty pejorative.

The more planning there is, the more officials are needed to administer production and allocation and to co-ordinate the various sectors, replacing the 'spontaneous' interrelationships of the market mechanism. This too is surely self-evident. So is the fact that those who allocate and distribute acquire power and influence. There plainly had to be a stratum of persons working in offices and endowed with authority over other people and over material and financial resources.

In the Russia of the 1920s there were several reasons why the 'bureaucrats' (functionaries, officials) were in a particularly strong position *vis-à-vis* the rest of society.

One is indeed connected with backwardness. The majority of the people were peasants. Many workers were passive or indifferent. The party leadership felt itself to be operating in a 'petty-bourgeois swamp'. To appeal to 'democracy' *outside* the party was not out of the question; only the *party* dictatorship was seen as ensuring the basis of so-called proletarian power and of a future march towards socialism. The party had to dominate all 'representative' institutions: the soviets, the trade unions and also the press. Though Trotsky did protest against the regime *within* the party, neither he nor any other Bolshevik leaders envisaged at this time any political or other public institutions free of party control. Indeed he spoke to the Thirteenth Congress about 'exaggerations' in the area of *party* democracy becoming 'a channel for petty-bourgeois influences'.

Second, the party (as well as Trotsky) was opposed to managers being responsible to elected workers' councils. Lenin and his followers (with a few exceptions) favoured one-man management (*edinonachalie*). The potential 'workers' control' counterweight was absent. Indeed, Trotsky was even more emphatic than Lenin about the need to subordinate even workers' democracy (let alone the peasant majority) to party dictatorship. Here he is at the Eleventh Congress:

> The 'workers' opposition' puts forward dangerous slogans which fetishize the principles of democracy. Elections from within the working class were put above the party, as if the party had no right to defend its dictatorship even when this dictatorship was temporarily at odds with [*stalkivalas'*] the passing feelings of workers' democracy . . . It is essential to have a sense of – so to speak – the revolutionary-historical primacy [*pervorodstvo*] of the party, which is obliged to hold on to its dictatorship, despite the temporary waverings of the masses . . . and even of the workers.

Rejecting the workers' opposition demands for power to factory committees, he even more revealingly stated:

> Formally speaking this is indeed the clearest line of workers' democracy. But we are against it. Why? For a basic reason, to preserve the party's dictatorship, and for subordinate reasons: management would be inefficient . . .

Note that efficiency considerations were for him secondary, party dictatorship was primary. But how was it to operate without bureaucracy?

Third, the generally low level of culture affected the style of the new officialdom. The proletarian origins of many functionaries in no way ensured an easy relationship between them and the rank-and-file of workers or peasants. Both Bukharin and (in his justly famous letter) Rakovsky pointed to the fact that ex-worker officials could and did become detached from the working class, and indeed could become a privileged caste actively hostile to workers' rights.

Is my argument an example of 'bourgeois' myopia, in total contradiction to the outlook of Trotsky? Well, shall we say 'not total', for here is Trotsky himself:

> The state apparatus is the most important source of bureaucratism. On the one hand it absorbs an enormous quantity of the most active party elements and teaches the most capable of them the methods of administration of people and things, instead of the political leadership of the masses. On the other hand, it largely preoccupies the attention of the party apparatus, over which it exercises influence by its methods of administration. That in large measure is the source of bureaucratism of the apparatus, which threatens to separate the party from the masses . . . It is unworthy of a Marxist to consider that bureaucratism is only the aggregate of the bad habits of office-holders. Bureaucratism is a social phenomenon, in that it is a definite system of administration of people and things. Its profound causes lie in the heterogeneity of society, the differences between the daily and fundamental interests of various groups of the population . . .
>
> In other words bureaucratism in the state and party apparatus is the expression of the most vexatious tendencies inherent in our situation.
>
> Bureaucratism is engendered . . . by functions that the party exercises through the medium of the state apparatus of administration, economic management, military command and education.[22]

This was in December 1923. Admittedly Trotsky (and his supporters) developed other theories too. However, Rakovsky (in 1928) quite specifically stressed that the danger would have existed even if there were no hostile capitalist environment, that bureaucracy arises when 'a certain part of [the working-class] turns into agents of authority [agentov vlasti]'.[23]

I do not entirely agree with the above, but it is clearly serious and relates to the real situation, not to empty slogans.

So, to sum up.

(1)   A functional bureaucracy was inescapably necessary, as indeed it is in any society today.

(2)   To attribute it to external causes is simply absurd. Nor was its *existence* due to backwardness.

(3)   Bureaucrats exercise authority in various spheres, and this brings dangers of abuse of power, excesses of privilege, disregard for the views and interests of the rank-and-file, and so on. To reduce the opportunities for abuse one needs genuinely free democratic institutions and a free press.

(4)   In the circumstances of the time, institutions which could act 'from below' to limit bureaucratic abuses were absent or ineffective. (They remain absent today.)

(5)   Stalin doubtless used the self-interest of the 'bureaucracy' in his rise to power, but eventually killed a high proportion of the bureaucrats.

(6)   The question as to whether a socialist society *could* exist without functionaries, without a division between rulers and ruled, under conditions of material abundance, is in the present context irrelevant; no one in his right mind would assert that such a society could have existed in the USSR in the period I have been discussing.

Notes: Chapter 6

1   E. Mandel, *Trotsky: A Study in the Dynamic of his Thought* (London: New Left Books, 1979), p. 82.
2   L. Trotsky, *The Challenge of the Left Opposition* (New York: Pathfinder Press, 1975), p. 59.
3   R. B. Day, *Leon Trotsky and the Politics of Economic Isolation* (Cambridge: CUP, 1973), p. 4.
4   *Byulleten' oppositsii* (hereafter *BO*), 1929, nos 1–2, p. 9.
5   *BO*, 1929, nos 3–4, p. 33.
6   ibid., p. 13.
7   *BO*, 1930, no. 9, p. 4.
8   *BO*, 1930, nos 17–18, p. 25.
9   *Writings of Leon Trotsky 1932* (New York: Pathfinder Press, 1973) (hereafter *WLT*), p. 48.
10   ibid., p. 60.
11   ibid., p. 89.
12   ibid., pp. 270–5.
13   *BO*, 1929, no. 7, p. 3.
14   *BO*, 1930, no. 10, p. 16.
15   *WLT*, 1932, p. 260.
16   ibid., p. 183.
17   ibid., p. 232.
18   ibid., p. 266.
19   *BO*, 1932, no. 31, p. 8.
20   *BO*, 1933, no. 34, pp. 5–6.

21 *BO*, 1932, no. 31, p. 10.
22 L. Trotsky, *The New Course*, quoted from *The Challenge of the Left Opposition*, op. cit., pp. 92–3.
23 *BO*, 1929, no. 6, pp. 14–20.

7 Soviet economics and Soviet economists: some random observations

This paper was presented to the World Congress of Slavists and Sovietologists at Garmisch (Germany) in 1980, and appeared in French ('L'économie soviétique et les économistes soviétiques, quelques observations', *Revue d'études comparatives est-ouest*, June 1981, pp. 121–45). It refers to only a small portion of the original and challenging ideas put forward by Soviet economists in the past decade or so. In particular it fails to do justice to the large and intelligent school of mathematical economists who have developed 'SOFE' (System of Optimally Functioning Economy), which has been analysed at length in a published dissertation by Dr Pekka Sutela of Helsinki: *Socialism: Planning and Optimality* (Helsinki: Societas Scientarum Fennica, 1984).

Introduction

There are several things which this essay cannot be, and does not pretend to do. A full survey of the activities of the Soviet economics profession, even if confined to the last ten years, would require a long period of research and a dissertation of book length. I cannot pretend to have read more than a fraction of the vast published literature. So this essay simply represents some comments about some of the economists whose work struck me as being of particular interest. I have divided them and their work into categories, but these are – as the Russians say – *unslovnye*, and in any case they overlap. Thus Aganbegyan, whom I have categorized as 'practical', is also a mathematical economist of note and has ideas on reform; Petrakov, classed as a 'reform-theorist', is also no mean mathematician, and so on.

I have also omitted obvious names, of those of the older generation whose main contribution dates back beyond the 1960s, and/or who are very well known to everybody. Hence there will be hardly any references to Kantorovich, Fedorenko, Konyus, or Khachaturov. Nor will I attempt an analysis of the work of such important (but dead) economists as

Nemchinov, Novozhilov and Strumilin, though the influence on the younger generation of (especially) Novozhilov has been substantial and surely very beneficial.

The ideas and theories put forward are those of the Soviet economists concerned. My own critical comments will be kept to a minimum.

So, on to some Soviet economists and their work.

Reform theorists

Three economists appear to me to be interesting and important, though of course, there are a whole number of others. These are Petrakov, Karagedov and Kazakevich. The last two are based in Novosibirsk, while Petrakov is on the staff of TsEMI in Moscow.

Nikolai Yakovlevich Petrakov has a long list of publications, including

Khozyaistvennaya reforma: plan i ekonomicheskaya samostoyatel'most' (Moscow, 1971).
Sotsialistecheskiye printsipy khozyaistvovaniya (Moscow, 1970).
Kiberneticheskiye problemy upravleniya ekonomikoi (Moscow, 1974)

and a large number of articles, especially in *Ekonomika i matematicheskiye metody* (hereinafter *EMM*), some of which will be listed later.

For many years Petrakov has been arguing for a clearer theoretical conception of the role of prices in the context of effective decentralization of micro-economic decision-making. He has advocated major reforms for twenty years; his earlier works included the little book *Rentabel'nost' i tsena* (1964). His arguments have developed substantially in scope and depth, due not only to the relative failure of the 1965 'reform' but also to his consciousness of the limitations of the applicability of mathematical modelling to the complexities of real-life economies.

He notes the inherent weakness of price 'theories' based on cost-plus, and the theoretical and practical futility of the long arguments as to 'cost plus what' (i.e. cost plus a percentage of cost, a percentage of the wage, or a percentage of total capital assets). How can such prices be used for economic calculation at any level? In this respect, he regards the 'price-of-production' approach as least objectionable, in that it does take capital cost into account. But all suffer from *zatratnaya kontseptsiya tseny* (the cost conception of price). 'It was silently assumed that all the output, howsoever priced, will be sold, that prices would affect neither the volume of requirements nor the structure of consumption. If the user is indifferent to the level of prices, if user-enterprises do not care at what prices they buy, or if they will be compelled to buy by administrative order, regardless of their khozraschyot interests', then why bother with price theory? But prices are being used, and should be used more in economic calculation, and prices based on cost deny 'any influence of the user on price. The theoretical assumption of the disposal [*realizatsiya*] of all the output . . . is the equivalent of assuming the absolute monopoly of the producer', with no choice for the user (*Khozyaistvennaya reforma*, pp. 34–6). Recognition of the limitation of cost-plus have led many economists to list a large number of relevant 'price formation factors', ranging from the quality of the labour and capital assets to the social significance of the output. Petrakov points out that the theories concerned gave no indication of what weights should be assigned to these ill-assorted and ill-defined factors. He again returns to the simple proposition: *will the goods sell* at that price, will there be a surplus or a deficit? It depends on *supply and demand*. Prices which ignore this must be misleading, to planners and managers alike.

Petrakov's model of a micro-economic plan is essentially based upon contracts between producers and users, with the centre determining payments into the budget in the form of 'long-term norms', related to the use by the enterprise of various resources (labour, scarce materials, equipment, and so on). The current output plan would be the responsibility of management, which would then have no reason to strive for a low plan. A progressive profits tax would avoid excessive differentiation. Prices should be much more flexible. Petrakov points out that the huge task of revising millions of prices is impossibly clumsy, and so implies that most prices should be subject to negotiation, but does not spell this out clearly. He does, however, quite clearly advocate going fully over to 'trade in means of production'. An enterprise desirous of paying for an input ('and even paying extra') expects to use it to advantage, 'Whereas under conditions of material-technical supply what is dominant is the system of direct indents [*zayavki*] for allocated goods [*fondy*]'. Price has no real meaning here. Items in deficit are distributed between the most important users. What is an 'important' user? This is left to the decisions of the planner who allocates, but this is an ambiguous and misleading concept (ibid., pp. 47–8). Petrakov also advocates the fullest use of bank credits for financing investments, which should 'cure' the disease of trying to obtain grants from the budget, while encouraging economic use of funds for modernizing existing factories. Enterprises should be encouraged to keep unused profits in bank deposits and receive, say, 4 per cent interest on these deposits. Then, given that there is capital charge of 6 per cent, they would not undertake new investments unless they expected a rate of return of 10 per cent or more.

Petrakov is deeply interested in the cybernetic approach to the planning system. 'The socialist economy is regarded by the theory of optimal planning as a consciously optimized cybernetic system of colossal complexity' (ibid., p. 56). This leads him to discuss criteria for an optimal plan, and so the problem of utility, use-values, under conditions of 'tremendous differentiation of means of satisfying (ever-changing) needs'. Valuation (*otsenka*) must be related to the level of supply in relation to effective demand. He reminds us of Strumilin's notion, put forward in 1920, that, as a rough approximation, if supply of a good increases in geometric progression, use-value rises in arithmetic progression.[1] In some form, use-value must be compared. In Petrakov's conception, this is done in aggregated form at the centre, but in micro-economic detail this can only be the result of the interaction on a *khozraschyot* (or market) basis of thousands of production units in close links with the distribution system and the users. The production units will in general take decisions to which *marginal* analysis will be applicable, since these 'micro' decisions will be incremental in character. Essential to any cybernetic system is feedback (*obratnaya svyaz*). The degree to which a given decision to produce any item actually satisfies need can only be seen *ex post*, when it is 'realized' (i.e. sold), and 'therefore the process of realization in the economic system must be such that the economic situation of the producer must be directly and wholly dependent on the extent to which he satisfied the user'. This must be through the price mechanism (ibid., p. 71).

Management could not and should not be wholly independent but Petrakov sees the centre as essentially setting the parameters, levying fixed charges (e.g. for use of natural resources) and making rules, and also fixing prices of key materials and products, while allowing micro-decisions to be taken 'automatically'. The greater autonomy of producers, the greater the feedback, and if this causes 'irritation' to the central organs, then this 'inconvenience' is a means of increasing economic effectiveness of the system. Plans, aims and objectives are in need of constant checking and correcting.

The prices advocated by Petrakov would correspond to those of an optimal plan, with due regard to conditions of supply, use-value, relative scarcity of means, opportunity-cost. Will these be inconsistent with Marxian value theory? But surely, he claims, Marx recognized that prices fluctuate under the influence of supply and demand. 'If on the basis of Marx's value theory we have prices radically different from objectively determined valuations (i.e. optimal plan prices), this would mean that these (i.e. 'Marxian') prices would not be equilibrium prices' (ibid., p. 85). And surely comparisons of use-value, valuation by users, enters into, does not contradict, the labour theory of value. He cites Engels, who criticized Ricardo for defining value only in terms of the effort required to produce: 'value is the relationship of production costs to use-value'. Marx, it is true, treated use-value as merely a precondition, but this, according to Petrakov, was because at that stage he abstracted from consumption. Marx emphasized social need in chapter 10 of Volume 3 of *Das Kapital*, when he discussed production in relation to the needs of society (ibid., pp. 92–3). It is *not* just a matter of counting the quantity of labour-power used. 'Socially necessary labour is labour valued (measured) by its social results, i.e. the extent to which it satisfies social need' (ibid., p. 100). He also notes that those who identify marginal price with the highest-cost producer silently assume the law of diminishing marginal productivity; there are circumstances in which an extra unit of output could come from producers with below-average costs.

Petrakov has been a prolific contributor to journals. A list of titles of recent articles gives some idea of the scope of his work: 'The question of the economic-mathematical management model taking uncertainty into account' (with V. Rotar', *EMM*, 1978, no. 3); 'Complex programmes in the system of economic management' (with E. Rudneva, *EMM*, 1978, no. 4); 'On one approach to the stabilization of economic growth', examining possible connections between scale and complexity and growth rates (*EMM*, 1979, no. 6), in which the discussants included Fedorenko, Boyarsky, Danilov-Danilyan, Maiminas, Bagrinovsky, Makarov, Fayerman, as well as Petrakov, making fascinating reading.

Petrakov may be criticized for being silent on certain matters. Thus he does not mention the issue of self-management, or anything to do with the rights of subordinates *within* his (undefined) production unit. One also wishes he was clearer in analysing what sort of micro-economic decisions *can* be efficiently decentralized; surely there is a difference between, say, electricity or oil on the one hand and trousers and onions on the other. Nor does he spell out how much price control, or price freedom, he is advocating. But he is clearly a most intelligent economist with a mind of his own.

Raimond Gareginovich Karagedov is the author of what, in my opinion, is the best-written economics textbook to appear in Russia for many a long year: *Khozraschyot, effektivnost' i pribyl'* (Novosibirsk, 1979). In his preface to this book, Aganbegyan makes it clear that the author prefers 'the wide use of commodity-relations', that he does not overlook the necessity of centralizing major economic decision, but that the centralized plans can be most effectively realized through the initiative and interest of production units. 'The author does not conceal his sympathy with the economic mechanism introduced by the Hungarian economic reform of 1968, which did not envisage any specifically addressed [*adresnykh*] plan targets for enterprises' (pp. 6–7).

Karagedov's great strength lies in the fact that he sees both the vital importance of prices and profits *and* their limitations. Social and psychological factors, 'human relations', analysis of behaviour of *homo economicus* are also seen as vital. Thus one cannot ignore the conflict between payment by (economic) results and payment related to quantity and (technical) quality of work. It is necessary to be aware of 'the limit of permissible departure from the principle of payment according to work'. He takes a realistic view of Hungarian experience in this and other respects. He repeatedly stressed that the reform he is advocating does not *replace* the national economic plan, but is related to the methods of its implementation (with, of course, some feedback; the micro-economic initiatives and responses at lower levels must have some effect on the central plan). The attempt to ensure micro-economic coherence and conformity to user requirements by central orders cannot succeed because of the scale of the task. It is essential to use indirect, financial, 'economic' means to stimulate initiative and enterprise.

What, he asks, is the basic cause of the need for *khozraschyot?* The autonomy, separateness, of production units. What is the cause of this? Will they cease to be separate under communism? Karagedov stresses the importance not only of technological and purely economic factors but also 'administrability' (*upravlyayemost'*) and the sociological 'dysfunctional effect' of 'excessive centralization' and the resultant human frustrations. Decentralization of decision-making must be based on a system of valuations and stimuli which link as far as possible the interests of the production unit with those of society as a whole. The present system fails to function effectively in these respects.

Is it then simply a matter of using the profit motive more consistently? It is by no means so simple. Karagedov launches into a long and fascinating analysis of 'economic effectiveness and profitability in non-Marxist literature'. In 140 pages he presents an account of relevant Western theory from Adam Smith and Ricardo to Marshall, Pareto, Pigou, Schumpeter, Joan Robinson, Arrow and Simon. General equilibrium, welfare economics, behavioural theories of the firm, monopolistic competition, are discussed sensibly, clearly, briefly, with refreshingly undogmatic critical remarks. The index shows 15 entries for Samuelson, 10 for Pareto, 8 each for Walras, Hicks and Baumol (6 for Engels). In my view these 140 pages represent a remarkable *tour de force*, showing deep knowledge of Western economics and extremely wide reading.

Karagedov shows how Western concepts of efficiency and profitability have evolved. What was the cause and nature of profits? Reward for abstinence or 'waiting', for the productivity of capital, entrepreneurship, risk-taking? What of the concept of zero profit in equilibrium, and its relationship with the notions of profit maximization and of 'satisficing'? The original and challenging ideas of Shackle are quoted too; limitations of information, expectations under non-actuarial uncertainty, organizational structure, all affect the decisions of real firms in the real world. For the first time (to my knowledge) in Soviet writings due attention is paid to external effects. Out of all this Karagedov draws some reasonable conclusions: abstract schema of general equilibrium are far removed from any reality, and there are many Western economists who cast doubt on the relationship between profitability of the separate firm and efficiency, welfare, and so on. So when he returns in the third part of his book to the Soviet economy, having (with the help of a quotation from Morishima) established that socialist profits are inherently different from capitalist profits, he is able to use Western theories as part of his argument. He makes the distinction, very important in the Soviet context, between *productivity* and *effectiveness*, the former related to *volume*, the latter to the *degree of usefulness* of what is produced. Many Soviet economists are shown to neglect this distinction, so that it seems not to matter *what* is produced so long as the volume (gross or net) of output increases. He subjects to devastating criticism the 'criterion of effectiveness' recommended in an Academy research document; this is based on the ratio of net output to the size of the labour force. Thus suppose one compares two variants, differing only in the fact that the investments required for the second variant are double the first, *and* the first is completed quicker. If all that is considered is net output and the size of the labour force, they would appear to be equally 'efficient'! The recommended criterion could indeed lead to even more bizarre results (pp. 240–2).

Karagedov, like Petrakov, naturally rejects prices and valuations based only on cost or effort. They must reflect also 'conditions of consumption' and demand. 'Production serves the satisfaction of the wants of society . . . The consumer can influence production only if prices respond to demand. Then the economic mechanism is operative, which corrects the structure of production and brings it closer to the structure of consumption' (p. 246). Profitability (or surplus product) related to cost-plus prices would be a misleading criterion. But in any event, overall one should prefer higher net product to higher profit; the higher the net product, the more there is to divide. If one can achieve a given level of national income with a lower rate of reinvested profits, this would surely be preferable. If it is possible to increase wages, this should not be seen as a reduction in effectiveness!

The above arguments about maximizing net product rather than the surplus (or profits) are unanswerable at macro level. But what of what Karagedov calls the 'local' or micro level? Here the criterion of profitability is much more defensible. In a formal decomposition model, in equilibrium, profit-maximizing management operating with optimal-plan prices will act similarly to entrepreneurs in perfect competitive markets (with zero profitability). But, as Karagedov correctly points out, such a model is based on unreal assumptions; externalities, ecological questions, uncertainty, imperfect knowledge, indivisibilities, are all ignored. Furthermore it is assumed that the objective function is known, which in fact it is not and possibly cannot be. Given the grave doubts expressed as to whether capitalist corporations meaningfully strive to maximize profits, is it reasonable to assume that socialist managers would or should consider only profit as *the* criterion? Karagedov quotes both Western and Soviet work about the motivations of managers and officials, which are evidently far more complex. Shackle is quoted too: 'the natural condition of an efficient economy is not a static optimum, the best utilization of *given* resources, but growth, continuously improving utilization of constantly increasing resources'.[2] He criticizes some Soviet models, for instance, that put forward by Pugachev, which use prices which fail to take into account changes in demand conditions, as well as other factors mentioned above.

Karagedov goes on to analyse the important contributions of Kantoro-vich and Novozhilov. While showing his own deep appreciation for their contributions, he puts forward some serious criticism. Thus Novozhi-lov's concept of profit (net product minus wages and rental and capital charges) is shown to be inconsistent with a model in which profits would tend to zero under an optimal plan. Profits would then emerge as a reward for coping with the unplanned, the unexpected. Suppose (argues Karage-dov) some new technique is devised which reduces costs and leads to a positive net profit. This could only arise if the authors of the optimal plan were unaware of the technique, in which case the plan was not optimal (pp. 270–1). But he praises Novozhilov for (*inter alia*) showing that Marxist economics is capable of handling allocation of scarce resources and using marginal concepts (p. 275).

He also shows the inadequacy of some well-recommended investment criteria. Thus if the average rate of return is used as a *minimum* cut-off rate, then this leads logically to a continuous rise in the average, and so also in the minimum cut-off rate (pp. 287–8). He notes that there could be confusion between national economic effectiveness and 'local' profitabi-lity of investments in those cases in which an enterprise may be subject to high fixed charges (for instance if low-cost oil-wells pay a high rental charge, this may reduce their profits to average levels, but plainly it would be advantageous to invest where costs are lowest!). He returns to using as the criterion the increase in the net product, i.e. national income, but 'this can be measured only in prices which react to changes in the structure of production and consumption', i.e. flexible current prices. Profit, or the surplus, is one guide to choice of means, but since the ratio between the surplus product and the necessary product (or between investment and consumption) is largely predetermined by planners, it is not really a (macro) variable, especially if the aim is to increase consumption. But this cannot be an ideal measure, as there *is* no ideal measure, a proposition backed by a quotation from Oscar Morgenstern's excellent book (which, by the way, appeared in Russian in 1968). Inevitably there must be some qualitative, subjective judgements, and, of course, social desiderata which do not have a monetary measure.

In his conclusion, Karagedov returns to the important distinctions between macro (or central planners') and micro (or managerial) criteria. He draws a suggestive parallel: criteria applicable to an enterprise are by no means applicable to sub-units of that enterprise. The essential difference

between the macro and micro level in this connection is seen by Karagedov to relate to the fact that, for the enterprise, wages are given, and so
greater efficiency (e.g. lower costs) finds its expression in higher profits,
so that profit-based criteria are most apposite at this level; whereas an
increase in total net output (national income) would enable the central
authorities to increase personal incomes and/or accumulation, in proportions which they can decide. Profitability, while of course not a perfect
micro criterion, emerges as a reward for 'creative activity and enterprise'
at enterprise level (p. 331). Zero profit in the model arises from the fact
that, on the formal assumptions underlying it, there would in fact be no
choices for management to make. (This analysis he reinforces with a
quotation from Koopmans.)

Karagedov insists on the importance of centralized planning, which
must determine 'the major economic decisions . . . the rates of growth,
basic directions and optimal developmental proportions in the long term.
These cannot emerge spontaneously as a result of the actions of autonomous profit-oriented enterprises . . . In determining the basic economic
proportions, the centre thereby limits the role of commodity-money relations as a regulator, and of profits too. Its regulatory and optimizing
functions manifest themselves within these proportions' (p. 334). He then
criticizes the concept of 'market socialism', which he defines as *total*
enterprise autonomy motivated *only* by profit, and attacks 'the naïve
idealization of the market'. The market provides short-term rather than
long-term information; it reflects disproportions after they have arisen.
Arrow is quoted (his 'Social choice and individual values') to show the
inapplicability of the market mechanism where one is concerned with
social consensus and social action. He also cites with approval the Hungarian economist Csikos-Nagy to support the proposition that one can have
effective central planning without necessarily issuing specific instructions
on current output and, while rejecting the naïve market-worshippers (and
the overconfident mathematical programmers), he ends by strongly supporting commodity-money relations and rational prices, within sensibly
defined limits. The above sketch of his ideas does not do them justice. His
book should be read.

David Moiseyevich Kazakevich is another of the Novosibirsk team. He
is known to me only by his book, *Ocherki teorii sotsialisticheskoi ekonomiki*
(Novosibirsk, 1980). His book lays greater stress on Marxist political
economy as such than do either Petrakov or Karagedov. He quotes hardly
any Western authors, and the index shows 39 entries for Lenin. Yet his
practical conclusions differ little from the two 'reform-theorists' mentioned above. The book seems to be addressed to readers who had been
brought up on standard Soviet textbooks. By intelligent selection of
quotations from the founding fathers, he is able to show that the problems
can be analysed, and solutions expounded, without being 'anti-Marxist'

or 'bourgeois'. I remembered a discussion I once had in Moscow (*not* with Kazakevich). When I suggested that the prices advocated by an economist might be difficult to justify in terms of theory, he replied: 'If we can devise a rational price system and get it accepted, I can assure you that these prices *will* conform to the Marxian theory of value!'

This raises the general question of the applicability of Marxian economic theory to the Soviet-type system, the meaning in this context of the law of value. This is a very difficult subject, and Kazakevich cannot resolve satisfactorily the many theoretical problems which necessarily arise. But he makes a good and stimulating attempt, quoting and analysing many other Soviet economists in the process. One naturally understands his anxiety (shared by Kantorovich, Novozhilov and many others) to show that the requirements of efficient calculation (or the calculus of efficiency) are not inconsistent with the labour theory of value.

Kazakevich criticizes those who wish to confine mathematics to a mere method of calculation (as if the qualitative aspects of problems are unaffected by mathematical analysis) *and* the opposite extreme, that is, those who suppose the algorithms of mathematical programming can be a plan-programme.

He tackles the difficult question of defining the 'basic economic law' of socialism in the USSR. While this is intelligently done, he can hardly overcome the problem of separating objective 'laws' from the conscious decisions of the authorities, and of distinguishing between antagonistic and non-antagonistic contradictions. Among these latter he refers to that between general and partial interests, but then rather lamely settles for the contradiction between ever-growing needs and the means of satisfying them. He then refers to the 'law of proportional development', using this to stress the importance of proportionality and balance (e.g. between sectors, regions, investment and consumption, and so on). In his discussion of long-term planning, he naturally (and rightly) stresses the vital role of the central political-economic organs.

He advocates planning by fifteen 'sector-complexes', which are at present divided between many ministries. These range from energy and chemicals to defence industries and housing, and he considers that they must be closely related to *territorial* production complexes. Regional planning is a weak point at present; existing *oblast'* boundaries are unsuitable, and regional plans are often no more than the sum total of sectoral plans relating to the area.

An optimal plan is one which maximizes social welfare. How can this be measured? Kazakevich praises Novozhilov's attempts to approach the problem: an iterative procedure in which one seeks to minimize costs (especially but not solely labour inputs) to achieve a given volume of output, increasing this volume in each iteration until resources are fully utilized. Other criteria are also discussed. Kazakevich (like Karagedov) holds that criteria applicable at different levels can differ, and he cites some research on this, carried out at TsEMI in Moscow and also in Novosibirsk (e.g. by Granberg, Aganbegyan, Pugachev) on regional and sectoral plans.

Why do commodity-money relations exist in the USSR? Kazakevich rests his case primarily on *scarcity* of means. He quotes Granberg with approval: within, say, a fifteen-year plan perspective, both non-reproducible and reproducible resources are limited, which implies *opportunity-cost*. Real national economic cost can only coincide with average cost on the assumption that scarce (limited) resources are not used. He notes the importance of the work of Novozhilov and Kantorovich in seeking a basis for *valuations* which reflect these facts. Social need and utility must be taken into account. Therefore 'socially necessary labour expenditures, determining the value of a good, emerge as a result of comparing the increment of utility and the increment of national economic cost incurred in its production' (p. 138). Kazakevich agrees with the other 'reformers' that decentralization to production units with a degree of autonomy is essential, since the innumerable incremental decisions about what and how to produce cannot be effectively handled at the centre, and producers' autonomy implies production for exchange and therefore commodity-money relations with the valuations appropriate to them. Nemchinov and Novozhilov are quoted in support of the proposition that labour socially necessary for production must relate (be equal) to labour necessary in given conditions of consumption. Kazakevich defends valuations of this sort against the accusation that, by emphasizing relative scarcity, they no longer have a cost basis and reflect 'bourgeois theories of marginal utility'. No, he insists, expenditure of live and embodied labour remains the basis, but one must also take into account such other factors as relative scarcity, the degree of satisfaction of wants, and so on. He criticizes such economists as Boyarsky and Kronrod, who insist that socially necessary labour relates only to conditions of production, regardless (it seems) of the usefulness of what is produced, and who therefore regard any sort of optimal–plan prices, which *must* reflect scarcity of resources, as either bourgeois or unrelated to value theory.

Kazakevich's price theory is fundamentally similar to that of Petrakov and Karagedov. One of his examples concerns modern equipment. If it is sold cheap 'to encourage its use', then its production may be unprofitable, while the number of users will exceed the number of machines, making administrative allocation necessary, with inevitable misallocation. He too advocates *trade* in means of production. Prices should not be based on static optimization assumptions, but should include 'dynamic and proba-bilistic' factors which (Kazakevich agrees) have not yet been elaborated. He discusses the meaning of marginal cost pricing: he agrees with the talented mathematical economist Volkonsky that what matters in perspective planning is *not* the highest cost (*zamykayushchiye zatraty*) but the cost of expanding output (*prirostnye zatraty*); pricing should take into account the average cost of increasing output in the next few years – of oil, for example. He also stresses the importance of rental or fixed charges for natural resources.

Kazakevich criticizes agricultural procurement prices for failing to reflect marginal costs. Differential rent is levied not on land, as it should be, but on the product, through regional price differentiation, which is theoretically wrong and practically clumsy. In discussing distribution he seems to accept Marx's assertion that purchase-and-sale create no value, and that therefore the resources devoted to collecting money and paying cashiers in shops are part of the 'surplus product created in the productive sphere', while packing, unpacking, showing goods to customers, are 'productive'; but then he evades the statistical problem by saying that costs in distribution cannot be so distinguished.

He has interesting chapters on money and finance, here again basing his argument on copious quotations from Marx and Lenin. He regards it as very important that production be adequate to meet demand at established prices: 'though inflation as a class phenomenon described in Marxist-Leninist literature cannot exist under socialism, the socialist national economy is not guaranteed against over supply of paper money' (p. 189). He follows other reformers by urging the much wider use of credits in the financing of investments, with a higher interest rate.

He criticizes those who identify socialist planning with administrative 'obligatory' centralization, so that the use of indirect 'economic' methods then appears to be a movement away from socialism. Administrative and economic methods coexist, in proportions which depend on circumstances. In wartime, understandably, resources are tightly controlled. It would be odd if methods typically used in periods of critical shortage were identified with socialism.

Kazakevich then seeks to draw up a list of the elements of a centrally determined plan:

norms of effectiveness of utilization of investment resources;
capital charges, interest payments, differential rent, payroll tax, etc.
   (with some regional differences);
amortization rates;
wage and salary rates;
profits tax, and norms for incentive funds.

Some prices would also be fixed centrally, but he does not say how many or by whom.

Payroll tax would penalize hoarding of labour and speed up the introduction of labour-saving processes. He notes that today's labour shortages are due primarily to wasteful and irrational use of labour-time.

There would then be 'independent planning of the volume of output, sales, details of the product mix, the number and categories of the workforce, costs, and the utilization of retained profits' (p. 218). Costs should be correctly redefined, to include rental payments, interest, and so on. He is opposed to the very existence of turnover tax, and the two levels of prices that accompany it. He cites data I had not previously encountered for 1975, to show that of the total revenue under this head, light industry provided 25 per cent, food industry 14 per cent and wines and spirits 32.5 per cent, while 28 per cent was paid by heavy industry (p. 235). Kazakevich believes that prices should fully reflect social cost, that is, that various charges paid by enterprises to the budget (profit tax, rents, payroll tax, and so on) should be high enough to allow most of turnover tax to be eliminated. Of course some items, such a vodka and tobacco, could be subject to excise duty.

Kazakevich, in common with other reformers, stresses the importance of measuring not just the quantity of output but its usefulness, its *poleznyi effekt*. Apart from the need to economize labour, materials, energy, it is essential to save investment resources by making it easier and more advantageous to modernize existing enterprises, rather than apply to the state budget for funds to build new ones. Current and capital expenditures are at present planned quite separately. It is also essential to modernize the processes of capital repairs; this now employs far too high a proportion of machine-tools and of the labour force.

Kazakevich discusses intelligently the question of the rates of growth of department I and department II, noting that technical progress can result in economies in fixed capital and materials, and not just of labour. He also makes the observation, unusual in Soviet publications, that low rents often benefit citizens who are better off, that it may be socially fairer to raise rents, and to use the resultant saving in subsidies to increase family allowances (pp. 336–7).

He ends by looking forward towards communism, on which he has little that is new to say. Ultimately, 'if non-commodity valuations do replace monetary ones, then this will only be when socialist commodity relations develop fully and exhaust their usefulness' (p. 363). For all practical purposes, Kazakevich is clearly for extending the use of market relations. But, as already mentioned, he and the others are remarkably vague about how prices are to be determined in practice (all 12 million of them), and has not a word to say about the role of the labour force in any kind of decision-making. None the less, his book deserves careful study as an example of thinking about efficiency, reform and their theoretical implications.

Analysts of current practice

A great many Soviet economists consider various ways of improving the existing system, without actually advocating new models or new theories, though some doubtless have major reforms in mind.

An example of such a first-class analyst is Viktor Petrovich Krasovsky. His specialism is investment. His work includes some written jointly with another talented economist, Kvasha, who died a few years ago. He has edited a number of books and symposia, and contributed extensively to these and to learned journals.

In an article in *EKO*[3] (1975, no. 5), he goes systematically through the various stages of the investment process, beginning with the project-makers (*proyektnye organizatsii*), the criteria they use, the criteria by which their performance is judged, the lack of contact with those who will ultimately operate the new factory and/or equipment, and with technological innovation. The documents they produce are 'measured now not in sheets or volumes . . . but in wagon-loads', yet they are often late and incomplete. One is reminded that investment projects are no better than those who draft them, that choice can only be between projects which have in fact been prepared, and also that the incentives and success indicators applicable to project-makers affect what they propose.

In the same article, and in other publications, he has much to say concerning the subsequent stages of capital construction. There are long delays, which mean that even if the machines chosen at the project-making stage are up to date when chosen, they are likely to be obsolete when the plant is completed ten or more years later. He has much to say also on the notorious *raspyleniye svedstv*, construction delays, tendency to underestimate costs, imbalances between plans and the means of fulfilling them, and so on. In a hard-hitting article, he takes issue with the official price index for machinery and construction (*Voprosy ekonomiki*, 1980, no. 1). The price index is quite wrong; costs do not fall, they rise. Thus the investment cost of producing one ton of steel averaged 431.3 roubles in 1965–70, 586.1 roubles in 1971–5 and 760.5 roubles in 1976–80. He analyses at length the causes. Thus new machines tended to be much dearer than the old, and the construction industry systematically tried to increase its costs, for instance, by using dearer materials, since 'the dearer the materials used, the easier it is to fulfil the plan for construction and installation work, and obtain a higher wages fund and a higher profit, which was calculated as a percentage of costs . . . At the same time the volume of project-making work was measured by the scale [value] of construction work . . . which stimulated the project-makers to provide for higher expenditures' (p. 110).

Krasovsky in the same article had must to say about the misleading methods sometimes used to calculate the 'rate of return' (*fondo-otdacha*) of investments; thus if the 'output' is taken to be school places, hospital beds, or square metres of housing, improvements to equipment and quality are often bound to appear as the 'worsening' of *fondo-otdacha*. Similarly, if the given investments are intended not to increase output but (for example) to reduce the amount of heavy physical labour, the conventional methodology would also yield misleading results.

A year earlier (*Voprosy ekonomiki*, 1979, no. 1), and also in his contribution to the book he edited (*Investitsionnye protsessy narodnokhozyaistvennykh kompleksov* (Moscow, 1975), Krasovsky had much to say about complementarities and indivisibilities, matters usually neglected in Western work on investment criteria, but which are in fact of vital theoretical and practical importance. The Soviet economic administration is divided between ministries, sectors. Yet any major investment programme is likely to involve the interaction and co-operation of several sectors. Obviously investment criteria, to make sense, must relate to the programme or project as a whole, and cannot be meaningfully split into separate bits. The choices *within* a complex must be made with the impact on the complex in mind. But where there are a large number of participants in a major project, co-ordination becomes very difficult. Tasks must be carried out in the right sequence. Each major complex should have a clear co-ordinator-chief. Krasovsky advocates methods (e.g. network analysis) which would reduce delays and interrelate more closely the various segments of the investment project. Criteria to be used would relate to minimizing time, within a given investment budget, or minimizing the budget within a given time. He introduces the notion 'coefficient of complementarity' to measure (and emphasize) the ratio of indirect to direct investment requirements, since under-estimates of indirect investments can lead to serious delays and bottlenecks. He notes the need to study the experience of the Volga automobile plant (Tolyatti), and the big programmes of development in Siberia. Planning organs must reorganize their work accordingly. In the *Voprosy ekonomiki* (1979, no. 1) article Krasovsky subjects the project-making stage to yet more vigorous criticism. Not only are these programmes very large and costly, but their output plan is expressed as a percentage of the total investment cost, the projects they draft are an undifferentiated package, not divided into tasks arranged in sequence, and it is not clear from them who is responsible for what. It is plainly essential for somebody to determine interlinked plans for carrying through complex investment tasks, and not divide them between different ministries and departments, and this must include proper consideration of 'the time factor'; there are delays at each stage, from project-making and construction to a very long 'start-up' period (*osvoyeniye*), which goes on sometimes for many years. Sometimes the delay in bringing a plant into operation is due to lack of minor but essential complementary items.

Krasovksy is continuing to point to weaknesses in investment practice, and seeks to relate formal investment criteria to the tasks of actually planning major investments. He does not relate these explicitly to any optimizing macro model, though he is evidently interested in the use of mathematical programming at the level of a complex investment 'package'.

Abel Gezevich Aganbegyan is the director of the Institute of Economics of the Siberian branch of the Academy of Sciences, and also editor of *EKO* and of a number of valuable research studies, these being concerned in the main with mathematical programming and optimization, the problems of regional planning with special reference to Siberia, and the powers and functions of management. He thus straddles several of the categories into which I have tried to divide this essay.

Aganbegyan's ideas on programming found clear expression in a volume, *Problemy narodnokhozyaistvennogo optimuma*, which he edited in 1969. In his own contribution, he sees the economy as a 'highly complex system of technical-economic and social-economic links', with 100 million people producing about 10 million varieties of products in over 300,000 production units of all kinds, in dynamic and changing circumstances. Stochastic elements exist, owing to changing demand, unpredictable forms of technical progress, human behaviour (e.g. migration, changes in employment), climate, developments abroad, and so on. The factor of uncertainty tends to become more important. Aganbegyan discusses possible optimization models, for example, of interregional flows and intersectoral balance, eliminating some of the more ambitious schemes as impracticable in really existing circumstances. Issues discussed include aggregation and disaggregation by commodities, the need to plan by complexes or sectors, the choice between trying to maximize output (or satisfaction of requirements) within given constraints, or to achieve a given output or satisfaction while minimizing costs. Of course, some constraints and parameters can be varied, some are 'stronger' than others. Aganbegyan's work in this field is closely linked with such able economists as Granberg, Bagrinovsky and Val'tukh.

He was co-responsible for the appearance of a first-rate analysis of the problems of Siberian development, *Razvitiye narodnogo khozyaistva Sibiri* (Novosibirsk, 1978), though this contains no contribution from him. His concern for practical difficulties comes through in a powerful, indeed devastating, article which *Pravda* published (7 December 1979). This pointed to the very serious consequences of lack of coherent regional planning: appalling transport bottlenecks, with each ministry building north–south links to the already overloaded Trans-Siberian railway; underdevelopment of the Siberian building materials industry, necessitating costly transportation over thousands of miles of bulky materials; lack of local refining capacity in the oil and gas regions, to which refined petrol has to be brought in cans; failure to complete the necessary housing and amenities, resulting in excessive labour turnover. In other articles he has pointed to the need to overcome departmental-ministerial boundaries. Putting a case similar to that of Krasovsky, he states that complex programmes, which contain many indivisibilities and complementarities, suffer from being split up between enterprises under different ministries. This is particularly damaging in Siberia, where most of the social overhead capital has to be built up from nothing. This problem has led to many discussions at Novosibirsk on the subject of Territorial Production Administrations and their relationship with the existing ministerial structure.

Aganbegyan has also played a leading role in research on the powers of enterprise directors, collecting and analysing their views on the limitations of these powers. His report on the results of this research appeared in *Pravda* (12 November 1973). The many limitations and frustrations arising from the exercise of the power of ministries were well and clearly presented.

He also pubished a vigorous article (*EKO*, 1976, no. 3) on the importance of evaluating performance by reference to *results*, the need to adapt production to the needs of the users. His examples range from failure to adapt lorries, and also bulldozers, to the conditions of Siberia, to the non-provision of co-ordinated transport services and of repair facilities. 'The factory which made [the machine] has no connection with repairs of its own product. The user must organize this himself. It is not surprising that repairs are among the least effective sectors in the economy' (p. 9). He also observes that plans for the production of gas pipe, which are in tons and metres, stand in the way of production of high-quality pipe capable of withstanding high pressures, and this causes loss for the economy. He is clearly very much concerned with organizational structure and plan indicators, and it is no accident that he wrote a friendly introduction to the book by 'reformer' Karagedov, which has been discussed above.

Not least of the services of Aganbegyan to economics is his editorship of *EKO*, surely the brightest and (along with *EMM*) the best of the economics periodicals in the USSR.

Among the other 'practicals', brief mention should be made of Efim Manevich, who has for many years been analysing questions of labour and wages. A good sample of his work is his article in *EKO*, 1978, no. 2, on labour shortage. It is, in his view, caused by the powerful incentives to management to keep extra workers, for the same reason as they hoard materials, and also because some workers would be liable to be mobilized for agricultural work, and for the 'storming' that would be necessary at the end of a plan period. The pay of management rises if the numbers working under them increases, as this determines the 'category' of the enterprise. Further, the deductions from profit to various incentive funds are expressed as a percentage of the wages fund, and thus could decline if numbers employed decline. If these disincentives to save labour were removed, and various auxiliary tasks properly mechanized, substantial economies would be possible. The author praises the Shchekino method, but notes great distortions in its application (he cites some instances of ministerial behaviour totally inconsistent with the method, which were bound to make it ineffective).

Space and time compel me to limit myself to one more talented 'practical', Oleg Rybakov, a specialist on foreign trade. His work, especially his contribution to *Planovoye khozyaistvo* (1974, no. 12, and 1976, no. 2) and also his book, *Ekonomicheskaya effektivnost' sotrudnichestva SSSR s sotsialisticheskimi stranami* (1975), show him to be well aware of sophisticated foreign trade and international specialization criteria, and also the obstacles to their use (e.g. the existing domestic and foreign trade pricing, exchange-rates, and so on). Those interested may be referred to the above-listed sources. Also of importance in this field is the work of Oleg Bogomolov. But enough is enough.

Political economists

These discuss the present Soviet system ('mature socialism') in its relations to Marxist political economy and the transition to communism. It is widely believed that Soviet theoreticians are discouraged from looking ahead to the communist stage, but in recent years such matters have been discussed by a number of writers. Those to be mentioned below are only a modest selection.

Pashkov, Glezerman, Kozlov and Cherkovets edited a volume entitled *Metodologicheskie problemy issledovaniya ekonomiki razvitogo sotsializma* (Moscow, 1976) and Pashkov, Val'tukh, Cherkovets and Kurovsky were responsible for *Potrebitel'naya stoimost' produktov truda pri sotsializmo* (Moscow, 1978). These in the main represent a moderately conservative position, with criticisms of the claims of certain reformers, and of Kantorovich and Novozhilov, to be consistent with the labour theory of value, but some contributions are lively and challenging. While the category of social utility is recognised as vitally important, even so original an economist as Shatalin states that this category 'expresses the real practice of conscious choice between plan alternatives', presumably by state organs, emphasizing social rather than individual valuation. Val'tukh and Komin are deeply concerned to avoid being committed to the concept of marginal utility, and the latter attacks Petrakov for his emphasis on prices which balance demand and supply, defending the view that value under socialism is based essentially not on results but on a quantity of (socially necessary) labour. But the bulk of the 1976 volume is concerned with defining

'mature socialism' and its place in historic development, with contributions on the impact of scientific-technical revolution on production
relations (by Kaspustin), 'the dialectics of change of class structure' (by
Stepanyan) and 'the problem of fully overcoming class differences' (by
Venzher). Venzher quite explicitly raises the point that if we now have
mature socialism, it follows that there are 'new possibilities in solving
social-economic problems of further movement towards communism'
(p. 210), by removing all remaining human inequalities.

There is also a volume edited by Cherkovets, *Osnovnoi ekonomicheski
zakon sotsializma* (Moscow, 1978). There are intellectually adequate
chapters on 'the interrelationship of effectiveness, proportionality and welfare under mature socialism', which tackle seriously the issue of criteria
and of optimal proportions. Cherkovets and his fellow authors discuss and
argue about alternative interpretations. There is a section dealing with
planning methods and the objective need for *khozrazchyot*, and the final
chapters tackle the transition to communism, and 'the process of dialectical withering away of some economic forms which exist under socialism',
including the 'contradictory' evolution' of commodity-money relations,
which must both develop and gradually vanish. Vanish how? The author
frankly does not know: 'real development in the future will indicate more
concrete ways of resolving this problem' (p. 344). What is advocated is the
fullest and most rational use of the market mechanism ('supply, demand,
price'), until the time when technical progress will have reached such a
level that 'productivity will not depend on the individual qualities of the
worker' and there will be no more distinction between concrete and
abstract labour. 'Masses of concrete labour will be assigned *a priori* in a
planned manner in accordance with social requirements' (p. 347). How? It
seems clear that he has no idea, but it will happen one day.

On a higher level is Richard Kosolapov, in *Sotsializm: k voprosam teorii*
(Moscow, 1979). After a somewhat routine critique of revisionist interpretations of class struggle in the West (notably that of Marcuse), Kosolapov tackles with skill such difficult questions as 'the new nature of
commodities and their organic connection with the nature of socialism'.
He begins by 'the abstraction of "pure" socialism'. Rejecting the 'state
capitalism' interpretation of Soviet reality, he refuses to accept that the
worker *buys* commodities in a shop with his wage. 'The "sale" by the
state of consumer goods to the worker is in essence an issue of his share in
the social product . . .' (p. 234). He could only *buy* if he sold, but he does
not *sell* his labour-power (to whom, if the state is not a capitalist?). The
goods he buys 'belong' to society, and so partly to him too. Otherwise
labour-power must also be seen as a 'commodity'. To understand all this,
argues Kosolapov, one must depart from the simplifying abstractions of
'pure' socialism. Reality is extremely complex. Stalin's formulation on the
law of value under socialism was only partly wrong. Consumer goods do

cease to be collectively owned when they pass into individual ownership, but since there is no separate group of property-owners, this does not constitute commodity exchange. The product of labour has no *exchange-value*, he argues. What happens to 'value' when all means of production are socialized? Quoting both the 'Critique of the Gotha Programme' and Volume III of *Kapital*, Kosolapov notes that Marx envisaged the need for 'the regulation of labour time and the distribution of the social product', and the need also for 'social accounting', and concludes that under socialism 'there is no commodity and no value' and that 'commodity and value exist' (p. 219). He argues that *exchange* between autonomous producers does not take place, nor 'value' emerge in exchange between private producers. But the *form* (not, it seems the content) remains, because *money* is used, since one cannot (yet?) calculate in hours of labour. Value has acquired a new content and so ceased to be value (p. 225). Socialist goods are *formal'nyi, uslovnyi tovar* (formal, conventional commodities). Other economists are wrong, he holds; of course economic calculation is essential, but this will be bookkeeping appearance, not essence. Nor does it matter that workers might feel that they are hired by the state-appointed boss (he quotes a letter to that effect on p 271). What matters is the objective situation; the worker is objectively a sort of co-boss (*khozyain*).

Kosolapov also discusses class structure and its prospective abolition, raising cautiously some potentially quite explosive issues, such as the difference between 'classless' and 'socially homogeneous', and the existence of 'non-class difference' between people and strata; but his own picture of the 'leading' role of the working class in Soviet society is idyllic, to say the least. He discusses skilfully the distinction between productive and unproductive labour, the nature and future of the intelligentsia (of course 'not a class'), the nature of freedom and coercion, centralization and even (briefly) dangers of a 'cult of personality'. A long chapter is entitled 'Some general problems of the first phase of communism', with some attempt at definitions; there is to be abundance, the disappearance of the need for incentives, and so on. Socialism is not a social-economic formation in itself, it is a stage in the process of building communism.

I would not suppose that Kosolapov is on an exceptionally high intellectual level, but he is worth citing as one of the better examples of the efforts which some political economists are making to think about transition to communism.

Mathematical economists and systems theorists

The USSR can justly boast of the quality of its mathematicians. The journal of TsEMI, *Ekonomika i matematicheskie metody* (*EMM*), is on a high intellectual and theoretical level – so high indeed that it frequently surpasses my regrettably inadequate knowledge of mathematical techniques. Such outstanding scholars as Belkin, Pugachov, Volkonsky, Dadayan, Shatalin, Lurie, are just a few in a long list of names. As has already been noted, Aganbegyan and Petrakov are also active in this field. I would like to drawn attention briefly to two less well known figures: Maiminas and Chernyak.

Efrem Zalmanovich Maiminas is a product of the University of Vilnius and of Moscow (where his supervisor was Nemchinov). A good example of his quality is the book *Protsessy planirovaniya v ekonomike: informatsionnyi aspekt* (2nd edn, Moscow, 1971). He is particularly interested in information flows in relation to decision-making structures, 'economic cybernetics, the systems approach'. Economic-mathematical models are frequently inapplicable in isolation. He shows himself well aware of relevant Western literature; his bibliography includes Ashby, Arrow, Beer, Cyert, Hitch, Koopmans, Marschak, von Neumann, Morgenstern, Shubik and Simon. He has much to say about language, economic life as part of the social system, incentives, self-regulation, plan criteria, the collection and analysis of information, the 'multi-step hierarchical nature' of the economic system. He follows Novozhilov in finding ways of reconciling effort (labour utilized) with result, within the Marxian theory of value.

He discusses the contradictions that arise out of the complexity and interrelationships of the elements that make up the economic system. This, on the one hand, requires centralized decision-making, since at lower levels it is impossible to grasp the interdependencies. On the other hand, this can move decision-making far above the level of the actual production units and the producers, and this, and also the vast scale of the system, argues for decentralization. An optimum system of information flows, control and regulation must be devised.

Several chapters are devoted to an analysis of 'planning acts', their nature, the stages by which the necessary information is assembled, consideration of alternatives, and so on. He discusses and formalizes such matters as risk and uncertainty, forecasting, the human attitudes and interests of the decision-maker, and so on. He puts forward (pp. 206–7) an interesting kind of 'separation-of-powers' analysis. Given that human beings are fallible and influenced by their situation, the three stages of information collection, the drafting of alternative proposals and the actual decision should be divided so that the decision-maker receives information and proposals which are not affected by possible bias of the decision-maker. Maiminas refers to games theory and coalitions, and points out that the preferences of persons and institutions taking part must also be taken into account.

Information flows are analysed intelligently and realistically. Again, a basic problem is sheer scale. He cites a calculation that shows that in Soviet industry at all levels every year there are 120–170 *milliard* 'indicators' (*pokazateli*), of which 12–17 milliard are above enterprise level, 2·7–3·6 milliard at all-union level (70 per cent of them concerned with material-technical supply). Gosplan, in formulating the plan, handles millions of figures. Information is frequently imperfect, for a number of reasons which he discusses; the 'language' may be ambiguous or incorrectly understood, the information may be deliberately withheld or falsified, and so on. The interest of the information-provider is an important factor. Maiminas classifies and analyses various forms of information and their handling.

All this is linked with the planning process. Maiminas discusses criteria for evaluating planning systems, their cost, flexibility, punctuality (plans must be ready in time), coherence, and so on. He ends by considering the potential of automated systems of control (ASU). He is clearly an intelligent explorer of the area that he calls 'economic cybernetics'.

Yuri Ilyich Chernyak, whom Maiminas cites approvingly, has expressed his interesting ideas on systems theory in *Sistemnyi analis v upravlenii ekonomikoi* (Moscow, 1975). In his words, 'system analysis is the methodology of researching into underlying nature and relationships by means of analysing institutions as purposeful systems and the interrelationships between objectives and the means of their realization'. Systems analysis was developed in America 'at the request of the military', but can be adapted to Soviet conditions. He appreciates that the full deployment of systems analysis is itself costly, and is only justified by the importance and complexity of the problems to be handled. If routine methods are reasonably effective, they should be used, 'unless routine *is* the problem'. He is naturally concerned with language, information flows, decision-making processes and hierarchy. But perhaps the easiest way to present his idea is to reproduce the 'sequence of stages' in systems analysis (a summary of his pp. 46–8).

I   *Analysis of the problem*
     Does the problem exist?
     Its precise formulation
     Analysis of its logical structure
     The evolution of the problem (in past and in future)
     Its external links (with other problems)
     Is the problem in principle resolvable?
II   *Determination of the system*
     Specification of the task
     The position of the observer
     Definition of the object
     Its decomposibility

Defining sub-systems
Defining the environment
III   *Analysis of the structure of the system*
IV   *Formulation of aims and criteria*
Aims and demands from above (*nadsistemy*)
Aims and constraints of the environment
Formulation of the overall aim
Determination of criteria
Decomposition of aims and criteria by sub-systems
Composition of the overall aim out of criteria of sub-systems
V   *Decomposition of aim, identification of resource requirements*
VI   *Availability of resources and processes*
VII   *Forecast and analysis of future conditions*
VIII   *Evaluation of aims and means*
IX   *Selection of variants*
X   *Diagnosis of the existing system* (and how to improve it)
XI   *Drafting a complex development programme*
Measures, projects, programmes
Sequence of aims and tasks
Determination of spheres of activity and responsibility
Plan of action, within resource and time constraints
XII   *Organization necessary for achieving the objectives*

Chernyak's other books include *Informatsiya i upravlenie* (Moscow, 1975), and *Analiz i sintez sistem v ekonomike* (Moscow, 1970). He is co-author of work on 'economic semiotics', the use and impact of language of communication.

Conclusion

There is really no conclusion, except to say that, despite many constraints, Soviet economics is still very much alive. The high professional level of the mathematical economists is beyond doubt. Also of importance is the fact that some of the best brains in the profession are trying to tackle the challenging problem of how various techniques and models can be applied to the real world. But, of course, it does not mean that they *will* be applied. The price reform now in process of execution ignores totally the arguments on prices of such as Petrakov and Kazakevich (as can be seen, for instance, in the article on prices by Glushkov, the chairman of the Prices Committee, in *Planovoye khazvaistvo*, 1980, no. 6). This should remind us of the strength of tradition and routine. But we should not exclude the possibility that economic failures will bring nearer the day when the talented reforming members of the economic profession will get a sympathetic hearing.

Notes: Chapter 7

1 I discuss Strumilin's arguments in Chapter 4, above.
2 G. L. S. Shackle, *The Years of High Theory: Invention and Tradition in Economic Thought, 1926–1936* (Cambridge: CUP, 1967); retranslated from R. Karagedov's translation.
3 *Ekonomika i organizatsiya promyshlennogo proizvodstva*, the house-journal of the Economics Institute of the Siberian Academy.

PART THREE

The contemporary Soviet economy

8 *The Soviet economy: problems and prospects*

First published in *New Left Review*, no. 119 (January–February 1980), pp. 3–19, this essay was intended to continue a long-running argument with the 'New Left' as to the nature and causes of, and possible remedies for, the Soviet Union's economic difficulties. Since the time at which it was written (1979), the deceleration of growth has continued; the actual rate is significantly below even the modest percentages currently being claimed, and this has been reflected in a downward amendment of anticipated growth. Table 8.1 shows serious shortfalls in coal and steel, and oil output began to decline in 1984–5. The new and younger leadership has shown itself well aware of the existence of the problems referred to in this paper, and Gorbachev's speeches are full of determination to find remedies. It is much too soon to say whether they will in fact be found. The statistical tables have been updated.

It has become customary on both right and far left to stress the weaknesses of the Soviet economy. The French book market is well stocked with works such as Emmanuel Todd's *La Chute finale*, picturing the USSR as a land where nothing works and everything disintegrates. Senator Jackson's advisers tell him that it is in a state of crisis so acute that the United States can demand major political concessions in exchange for its grain and technology. A variety of neo-Marxist critics point to extremes of inefficiency and waste. Indeed, a catalogue of blunders and distortions can be assembled without difficulty from the pages of the Soviet press. Shortages, corruption and confusion seem endemic, while growth has slowed. But the West too faces acute problems, with zero growth, inflation, unemployment, and the prospect of major disruptions through strikes and also in the world trading system. It is legitimate to ask, are they in a worse mess than we are? Have they not some 'systemic' advantages as well as weaknesses? Have the latter perhaps been exaggerated? Could they be corrected without major political-social convulsions? Is the Soviet system, relatively speaking, an example of stability in an increasingly unstable world? Finally, what light, if any, can Soviet experience shed on the theory or practice of economics under socialism?

But the correct assessment of Soviet strength or weakness does not, or should not, depend on political attitudes. If, as may well be the case, my analysis is erroneous, this would be partly because evidence is mixed or inadequate, but also because the answer depends on the *weight* which one attaches to those elements of strength and weakness which we identify. There is also the vexed question of political stability; it is probably difficult even for the KGB, let alone an outsider, to assess the intensity of discontent, and we should never forget that there are wide gaps in our information. Thus if by any chance there were a strike of metal-workers in Krasnoyarsk at this moment, we may be reasonably sure that it would not be reported in either the Moscow or the local press (which does not, of course, mean that there *is* a strike in Krasnoyarsk at this moment).

Priorities and planability

Let us now try to define the areas of strength and weakness. In my view, there are two factors involved: the *degree of priority*, and what could be called *planability*. Both relate to the basic problem of any centrally planned economy: the unmanageably huge number of interrelated decisions to be taken. With market forces absent or severely limited, and with prices unrelated (in theory *and* practice) to demand, scarcity, or need, considerations of profitability can only play a subordinate role in decision-making. The centre plans quantitatively whenever possible. The task of management at all levels is plan fulfilment. Thousands of enterprises produce millions of products, 12 million if fully disaggregated, according to *Voprosy ekonomiki*.[1] The uninitiated seldom appreciate how many varieties there are: a thousand kinds of ball and roller bearings alone, to cite just one example. Each product relates to some distinct use or user, requires a different input of materials and components. According to the logic of the centralized planning model, the central organs know what society needs, and can issue and enforce plan-*orders* to ensure that these needs are effectively and efficiently met. This requires multi-million instructions as to what to produce, to whom deliveries should be made, from whom inputs should be received, and when. All this must be made to cohere with plans for labour, wages, profits, investment financing, material utilization norms, quality and productivity for each of many thousands of productive units. In practice this task can never be completed, plans are repeatedly altered in the period of their currency, supplies and output targets fail to match, there are numerous instances of imbalance and incoherence. This is due not to the lack of commitment of officials, or to stupidity, but to the fact that the magnitude of the task far surpasses the possibility of fulfilling it. The 'centre' is inevitably divided into ministries and departments, and these, together (or in conflict) with local interest groups, distort or conceal information and compete for limited investment resources.

However, the system is effective in the imposition of centrally determined priorities. When there is shortage (of materials, rail wagons, labour, or whatever), the central party-state apparatus ensures that what it regards as most important gets what it needs. Thus the defence industries appear to be reasonably efficient, as are the steel, oil and electricity generating industries. Electricity can also serve as a good example of 'planability'. It presents no product-mix problems (kWh are kWh are kWh), power stations on a grid can be centrally controlled from a single control panel, and the information about need, now and in the future, is best assessed at the centre (and not only in Soviet-type economies). In the planning of fuel and energy the USSR does well. A long view can be taken of this high-priority sector, and the necessary investments accordingly determined. Our own market-oriented economies accommodate themselves badly to supply shortages, for instance of oil. The USSR has responded to its own energy problem by massive efforts to develop oil and gas in Siberia, efforts which have achieved marked success in the face of formidable natural obstacles. The USSR's irrational prices matter little when decisions are taken which relate to energy supply in, say, 1990; none of us know what will be the prices and costs in 1990, and we must proceed on best estimates of future demand and supply largely in quantitative terms, which the Soviet central planners can estimate at least as well as, probably better than, any Western capitalist oilman. Furthermore, action can be taken without having to bother with the pressure groups, lobbyists, or the need to win the next election.

Further 'pluses' for the Soviet system are the absence of serious unemployment – in fact labour is frequently short – and the relative stability of wages and prices, made possible by a centrally imposed incomes policy (with no independent trade unions); though, as we shall see, there is some partially concealed inflation. These 'pluses' are accompanied by formidable deficiencies, which, it is important to appreciate, are also the consequence of the system, and so might be regarded as a *cost* of the advantages listed above. This is one reason why reform proposals designed to overcome these deficiencies have met with strong opposition, from the beneficiaries of the existing arrangements.

The first and most obvious point is that priorities, to be effective, must relate only to a relatively small part of the totality. Therefore most activities are non-priority, and, under conditions of over-full utilization of resources ('taut planning'), they frequently run into trouble: failures in deliveries of materials, long delays in construction of new plant, lack of co-ordination between output and inputs, poor quality, and so on. The central authorities, of course, desire that output should match requirements, that user demand by studied, that buildings be completed on time, that technical progress be encouraged and productivity raised, and repeatedly issue decrees to that effect. But, outside of the top-priority sectors, there is great difficulty not merely in enforcement but in meaningfully defining these doubtless excellent objectives. Let me illustrate. Over-worked planners have to aggregate, that is, issue plans for such categories as 'footwear', 'spare parts for farm machinery' or 'window-glass', not having either the time or the information to enable them to instruct a given factory to make and deliver two hundred brown shoes of a given size and quality, or piston-rings, or glass of a particular specification. Plan instructions are therefore, so to speak, non-specific, defining an aggregate total, which may be in tons, roubles, square metres, or whatever. *This* instruction is clear and binding, and so enterprises produce not what the user actually requires, but that assortment which adds up to required aggregate quantity. This long-standing disease has been the subject of innumerable critical articles in the Soviet press. One consequence among many is the unintentional stimulation of waste of materials: if the plan is in tons, the heavier the goods the better; if in rouble-value, then the dearer the inputs the better, provided this finds its reflection in the officially approved prices. Conversely, initiatives leading to less heavy or expensive materials threaten plan-fulfilment in tons or roubles.

Bureaucracy replaces the market

One reason for the persistence of these distortions is that those who 'commit' them are supervised by officials (ministerial or party) who are themselves directly interested in plan-fulfilment. So much so that, as numerous reports testify, these officials alter plans upwards or downwards, adjusting them during the period of their currency to the expected performance of their subordinate managers, so as to report that there are no failures. But in any case plan-fulfilment targets are bound to cause distortions, howsoever defined, so long as there is a multiplicity of types, designs and weights of the given product. Thus when window-glass was planned in tons it was too thick and heavy; so they shifted the plan 'indicator' to square metres, whereupon it became too thin. Common sense tells us that glass should be thick or thin according to the circumstances of its use, but such detail is not and *cannot* be within the cognizance of the central planning organs. Aggregation is a 'must', if next year's plan is to be drafted before the end of the century.

The greater the multiplicity of possible alternative products and methods, the less is the 'planability' of the given sector. One sees this in agriculture, where land can be used for many purposes and there is a wide variety of natural conditions and weather hazards. Agricultural mechanization suffers greatly from poor-quality machines, the notorious lack of spare parts, and what Soviet critics (from Brezhnev down) call *nekomplek-stnost'*, that is, lack of essential complementary equipment, which causes bottlenecks. Another example of *nekomplekstnost'* was illustrated in a

Krokodil cartoon. A passenger in a train points to mountains and asks: 'Have we reached the Caucasus?' The train-conductor replies: 'No, these are nitrogenous fertilizers, over there is potash; the Caucasus we get to tomorrow.' We see here how achievements in one sector (fertilizer output has risen impressively) are partly negated by failure in a related sector (which is the responsibility of a different ministry); thus there are insufficient bags, means of transportation, machines, for actually getting the fertilizer to the farms and spreading it on the fields, so it piles up at railway sidings.

If management is rewarded primarily for plan-fulfilment (i.e. obeying orders), it is plain that it is interested in easy-to-fulfil plans, and so there is concealment of productive possibilities, and also over-application for inputs and hoarding of materials and labour. There is also an unintentional 'built-in' disincentive to innovate. All innovation carries with it some risk, and requires changes in plans. But risk is not rewarded, and long before the advantages of the proposed innovation become apparent, the manager may be transferred or demoted because he has not fulfilled the current plan. Emphasis is indeed given to technological innovation, but in practice its diffusion depends on the initiatives of thousands of managers, and it often suffers the same fate as well-intentioned orders to economize materials, which conflict with the overriding need to fulfil current aggregate plans.

Plans are 'taut' because designed to stimulate effort, to achieve growth, to combat tendencies to routine and inertia, that is, to act as a substitute for competition. Planners should, in theory, express in their orders the needs of society. However, experience shows how difficult it is in practice to *define* what is needed, and to identify how best to provide it, in operationally meaningful detail. In its functioning, the system is unresponsive to user needs, is wasteful of resources, is not geared to innovation. It is bureaucratic not primarily (as some imagine) because of the self-interest of bureaucrats, but because the overwhelmingly difficult task of co-ordination, inherent in central planning, requires a complex bureaucratic structure of ministries and departments. Bureaucrats replace the market-mechanism. (This happens also *within* large Western corporations, since their internal interrelationships are *administered*.)

Is alienation the problem?

A view held by some on the left is that Soviet planning is not planning at all. How can it be 'real' planning, when these distortions occur and when the outcome frequently fails to conform with the intentions of the planners themselves? This is more than a matter of terminology, for underlying this view is the belief that there could now exist a 'real' socialist democratic planning system which would dispense simultaneously with market, bureaucracy and hierarchy, based upon some undefined form of mass democracy. Those who hold this view are usually quite unaware of the complexities of the modern industrial structure, with its innumerable complementarities and interdependencies. It is not clear where, in this process, is the place for political democracy as an alternative to both market and bureaucracy. Democratic procedures are indeed essential, but these cannot be meaningfully applied to multiple-millions of micro-economic decisions; an elected assembly can vote on broad priorities (e.g. more for primary education, or housing, or developing a region), but hardly on whether 3 tons of constructional steel should be allocated to this or that building site, or that production of red dyestuffs be increased by 3 per cent.

It is sometimes argued by Marxist 'fundamentalists' that the basic problem lies in alienation, in the conflicts of interest between workers, management and centre; all would be well if they all identified with a common interest. These conflicts do indeed exist (and between different branches of the centre also). Yet this line of thought contains or implies several fallacies. One is that a more positive or co-operative attitude on the part of those concerned could resolve the essence of the problem. It is doubtless true that human attitudes affect the *quality* with which work of all kinds is done. But this does not of itself even begin the task of coping with multiple millions of complex interrelationships. The essential point is not one of whether workers or managers or planners wish to do the right thing, but one of discovering what the right thing to do is, and then acquiring or ensuring the means to do it. Action requires the presence of three elements: *information, motivation* and *means*. If any one of these is absent, decisions cannot be taken or implemented. Motivation alone is, quite evidently, not enough. Many well-meant efforts are frustrated because the required resources are allocated by several remote plan offices. It is also not appreciated that the marketless planning model is of necessity centralized (how can a purely local body decide what society needs and how best to provide it?), and it is precisely the vast and complex scale of operations of central planning which is a major cause of this very alienation. 'Unless one is prepared to accept that the structure of regula-tion in interconnected production is objectively hierarchical, then the whole problem of socialist democracy can only be raised in an agitational way', wrote Bahro, without, unfortunately, drawing from this the con-clusions that suggest themselves. Finally, it is implied that a society can or could exist in which there would be no conflict between sectors, and between sectors and centre, not to mention individuals, over the allocation of resources. This essentially utopian part of the Marxist tradition rests, and can only rest, on a vision of abundance. There must surely be conflict, as any materialist would have to admit, unless there is plenty for *all*, that is, when the concept of opportunity-cost, of choice between mutually exclusive alternatives, loses its meaning. Economics would then have withered away, along with the state. Let us leave aside the question of whether it is a valid or useful vision of a remote future. It is clearly not a state of affairs relevant to what was, is, or could have been, in the Soviet Union. May I add that this is not to deny that the spread of democracy and the reduction or privilege in the USSR would make a difference to the Soviet economy, or to the now somewhat cynically negative attitude of many workers to their work; merely that it is self-delusion to suppose that this would solve the basic problems of micro-economic planning.

Workers' self-management, that is, some version of the Yugoslav model, is quite another matter. But of course this rests squarely on the basis of market-oriented enterprise autonomy. Needless to say, this too causes its own difficulties, in terms of both efficiency and doctrine. But the beginning of wisdom in these matters is to appreciate that there are no solutions which, along with their positive elements, do not have some negative aspects. It is therefore my contention that the Soviet economy is planned centrally, and that the defects and distortions which are noted (and rightly noted) by its critics are inherent in centralized planning itself.

Balance sheet of Soviet economic performance

So, after this (in my view necessary) detour, let us return to the present state of the Soviet economy. The following points appear to be uncontroversial, and probably figure prominently on the agenda of the Politbureau.

1 Statistics clearly show a slowdown in growth, and the current five-year plan will *not* be fulfilled in a number of important sectors and overall. Growth does continue but, when allowance is made for certain kinds of statistical exaggeration, perhaps at 3–3½ per cent per annum, rather than the claimed 4–4½ per cent or so.[2]

2 To the heavy cost of armaments (which would rise even if SALT had been ratified by the US Senate) must be added the cost of agriculture. Close to a third of total investments are now devoted either directly to agriculture or to the sectors of industry which serve it. The rate of return to those investments is small. Far from being a source of revenue, agriculture has become a net burden on the rest of the economy. The subsidy to livestock raising now amounts to 23,000 million roubles annually; say, £15,000 million, at the not-too-unrealistic official rate of exchange. [Note added in 1985: it has doubled since.]

3 It has been (rightly) decided to invest massively in Siberia, to ensure essential supplies of fuel and materials. For obvious reasons it is expensive to invest in these inhospitable and remote regions, and workers must be

offered good wages and amenities, otherwise they refuse to go or to stay (forced labour being no longer of economic significance). In the long run the riches of Siberia will be a major 'plus'. In the shorter run Siberia absorbs resources on a huge scale, and there could be a serious energy bottleneck in the next few years. Official sources stress the need to economize fuel.

4   There is a shortage of labour, due in part to demographic factors; a low birth-rate, except in formerly Moslem areas, has brought the rate of increase in the total labour-force close to zero. Virtually all growth must now be based upon higher productivity. But there are also plenty of instances of overmanning and inefficient use of labour (inadequate mechanization, geographical maldistribution, and so on). Agriculture is short of labour at peak periods, requiring mobilization of millions of urban workers and soldiers to help with the harvest. Redeployment of labour, difficult to achieve without compulsion, is a 'must'. Experiments designed to achieve this (e.g. the so-called Shchekino experiment)[3] have made little difference.

5   Also essential are the more efficient use of investment resources, and more rapid diffusion of technical progress. There is a chronic tendency to start too many projects, which then cannot be completed for lack of necessary materials and labour. Orders are then issued to complete only the most important projects, which causes the others to remain unfinished for a decade or so, leading to bottlenecks through the non-delivery of complementary materials, components, and so on. Brezhnev declared that this is to be a 'quinquennium of effectiveness and quality'. Effectiveness in the use of investment resources; quality not only of machinery and technology but also, he insisted, of consumers' goods, with much greater influence of the user and his (or her) requirements on what is produced and distributed. Progress in these respects has been much too slow.

6   Finally, there is a serious problem of poor distribution, of imbalances between demand and supply, affecting both the allocation of inputs to industry *and* the citizen as a purchaser of goods and services. Shortages are endemic. There are queues. Such items as meat, and also many manufactured goods, are unobtainable for long periods. All this gives rise to many negative phenomena commonly associated with a seller's market: indifference to the customer's requirements, petty and not-so-petty corruption, hoarding, and so on. It is widely believed that shortages have grown worse in recent years. This is *not* due to a reduction in supply; on the contrary, consumption has been rising. But incomes have been rising faster, and there has been a reluctance to increase retail prices. For example, meat prices have remained unaltered for eighteen years, while average money wages have risen by close to 70 per cent. No wonder there is a meat shortage! Recent increase in certain prices (coffee and petrol last

year, restaurant meals, furniture, jewellery, and so on, this year) will not be sufficient to cope with this chronic 'concealed inflation'. Prices in the peasant free market have been rising.

7 There are also problems connected with foreign trade. In years of large grain imports the USSR runs a larger deficit than can be covered by gold sales. Some of its allies (especially Poland) are in a much more vulnerable position, with very large debts to the West. Comecon integration progresses slowly, since both the USSR and the other countries concerned must increase their exports to the West so as to cover their needs for hard-currency imports.

It seems desirable, indeed necessary, to quote some statistics, but this is less simple than it sounds. For reasons already given, aggregate statistics tend to overstate the growth rate. How misleading can be even some 'sectoral' statistics may be illustrated from a *Pravda* article: when a plant making pipe produced cheaper, better-quality pipe weighing 25 per cent less, the statistical 'effect' was a reduction in both the 'volume' of output and in labour productivity.[4] This explains the reluctance of management to adopt more economical variants, but also shows the imperfections of measurement. Perhaps Table 8.1, which relates to physical output of some important products, can be used to illustrate both the shortfall in plan-fulfilment *and* the fact that growth continues, albeit at a slower rate.

It is not disputed that the rate of increase in the productivity of labour and the yield on capital investment have been falling, as has the level of profitability. Industrial and construction costs have edged upwards, and new machinery in particular is often much dearer, and not much more productive, than the models it replaces.

In agriculture the record year 1978 has been followed by the much less satisfactory 1979 (the difference is attributable to weather conditions). The much greater degree of mechanization and 'chemicalization' lays a greater burden on the planning of industrial supplies, and rising costs are a measure of inadequacies in this direction. At least equally important is labour morale: peasants seem to be unwilling to work harder at the peak harvest periods, and this, as well as incomplete mechanization, causes a massive 'import' of labour from the cities (and the army) every autumn. Collective and state farms are too large, and interference with their managements by party officials further complicates their task. The huge investments made in agriculture have had some effect; both output and productivity have been rising, but at a slow rate. Meanwhile the relative cheapness of foodstuffs (compared with industrial consumers' goods) ensures that demand exceeds supply, resulting in chronic shortages in many parts of the country.

It is instructive to contrast the Brezhnev period with the Khrushchev era. Krhushchev – and the performance of the economy under his rule – contained some very contradictory elements. Some of his actions had

Table 8.1 Soviet economic performance

	1965	1970	1975	1980 (plan)*	1980	1984	1985 (plan)*
Electricity (milliard kWh)	507	741	1,039	1,380	1,295	1,493	1,575
Coal (million tons)	578	624	701	800	745	712	785
Oil (million tons)	243	353	491	640	606	613	632
Gas (milliard m³)	128	198	289	435	435	587	620
Steel (million tons)	91	116	141	168	157	154	—
Fertilizer (nutrient, million tons)	7·4	13·1	22·0	33·5	24·8	30·8	36·5
Chemical fibres (gross)	0·40	0·62	0·95	1·49	1·35	1·40	1·60
Cement (gross)	72	95	122	144	134	130	141
Fabrics (all, million m²)	7,320	8,640	10,100	12,800	11,400	11,800	12,700

*The five-year plan targets, set five years earlier.

positive results. Thus in 1953–8 his agricultural policies constrasted with Stalin's earlier neglect and led to a quick rise in output, over 50 per cent in five years. However, in the next five years growth virtually ceased, and his numerous 'campaigns' and reorganizations caused much confusion. In industry he rightly gave priority to oil, gas, chemicals, all previously neglected, but again his methods led to confusion, resentment, disorganization. Brezhnev brought greater predictability and stability; there have been no 'harebrained schemes', no massive reorganizations, and there has been more reliance on expert advice. But the ageing leadership has now slipped towards immobility. Instead of Khruschev's admittedly unsound ideas about introducing communism by instalments at specified dates (after having 'overtaken America'), we now have the present state of affairs defined as 'mature socialism' (sometimes as 'real socialism' – shades of Bahro's *real existierende Sozialismus!*), which surely reflects a greater degree of complacency, not necessarily shared by citizens queuing for sausage! Urgent problems still await solution.

The scope for administrative reform

Does all this constitute a crisis? In one sense, I think we can call it such. A system of centralized planning originally designed under Stalin for ultrarapid industrialization of a backward country is now increasingly an obstacle to efficiency, no longer able to cope with the problems and complexities of a modern industrial economy. But then is the West able to cope with them? What could they learn from us? What paths are there to the reform of their system which will not carry with them dangers of accelerating inflation, instability, unpredictable social-political consequences? Conversely, can the existing system be so improved and streamlined as to eliminate some of the worst inefficiencies and distortions, while preserving the elements of strength? How far is the political leadership committed to resisting major changes? The party-state machine derives very considerable advantages from the present system; it provides them with a function and enhances their power and influence (replacing the invisible hand with the visible hand, *their* hand). Power over allocation is used to divert scarce goods and services for their own use, through a network of special shops, hospitals, villas, and so on. These and similar arguments lead some critics to the conclusion that 'the party' will block all changes and that no change is possible without prior political convulsions, which would shake or overthrow the dominance of the party.

There is clearly a strong case to be made along these lines. But it should be recalled that the party leaders want not only privilege, control and stability, they want results. They may indeed be conservative septuagenarians, but they know and say, with Brezhnev, that the scientific-technical revolution requires fundamental changes in methods of planning and management.[5] It adversely affects Soviet power in the world if grain has to be massively imported from America, if Soviet technology lags behind, if growth rates fall, if plans are unbalanced and resources wasted. When citizens react angrily to goods shortages, this is bad also for internal security. It worries the leadership that, with the existing system of incentives, waste often 'pays', indeed shows up in statistics as increased output and productivity. There is here a theoretical as well as a practical weakness: 'the greater the total expenditure of labour and materials, the greater the [apparent] productivity. Use-values are not counted.'[6] Corrective action is seen to be essential.

But what corrective action? Here opinions differ widely. Brezhnev and his comrades appear to be seeking greater efficiency through a mixture of exhortation, computerization and re-organization. Industrial enterprises are being merged into associations or corporations (*obyedineniya*), thereby reducing the number of units to be planned and facilitating specialization. There is a drive to form 'agro-industrial complexes' in rural areas. Planners are instructed to pay more attention to ensuring coherence of plans, managers are ordered to carry out their delivery obligations, various experiments are undertaken to reduce waste (tighter utilization norms, measurement of plan fulfilment in terms of net output, bonus schemes to encourage labour productivity and discourage the hoarding of labour by management, and so on). Efforts are made to reward quality. The Mathematical Economics institute, under Fedorenko, and other research institutes, have been seeking to adapt computers and programming techniques to the needs of centralized planning.

On 29 July 1979, *Pravda* published a decree on economic reform. Commentaries referred to many of the weaknesses which are mentioned in this essay, and which the reform is designed to overcome. The key changes are as follows.

(a) Construction enterprises are to be judged in relation to buildings completed, not by work done and money spent.
(b) Long-term plans are to be more closely integrated with current (annual) plans, at the centre and in industries.
(c) The use of 'normed net product', instead of gross value of output or of sales, is to eliminate the inducement to use dear material inputs.
(d) More use is to be made of long-term agreements between firms.
(e) There will be greater emphasis on the fulfilment of contractual delivery obligations.
(f) Obligatory plan instructions will cover also the introduction of new technology, the size of the labour force, quality indicators, material utilization norms, in some cases also cost reduction, reduction in

number of unskilled workers, labour productivity targets, output targets in physical terms, profits, etc.

(g) New measures are also intended to ensure a closer link between industrial-sector and territorial-regional planning, and between the plans for investments and the material means of implementing them.

It is too soon* to judge the effect of these proposals, since they have yet to be worked out in detail, let alone implemented, but I take leave to doubt whether these measures are on the right lines. No doubt some improvements are possible; thus for instance it has long been necessary to eliminate the interest of construction organizations in using dear materials and delaying completions. But already one can see two major weaknesses in the 'reform'. The first and most important is the multiplicity of plan indicators. This not only puts an even greater burden on the planning organs, but virtually guarantees inconsistencies and anomalies. One has only to look at the above list. Second, the 'normed net output' indicator is far more complicated than might appear. Let me illustrate with an example. Suppose an industrial association or enterprise makes fifteen different products. To calculate the net output of each, one has to subtract material inputs, but some of these will be common overheads. It will also be necessary to allocate to each its share of profit, and this will be done by arbitrarily assuming that each product is equally profitable which, at the given prices, will not be the case. Consequently, there will be a contradiction between real profitability and the notional 'net-product' calculation, and probably also between both and the duty of fulfilling *quantitative* plan targets. Millions of extra calculations will need to be made to determine 'normed net product'. Not only this; in an article commenting on the reform, the authoritative D. Valovoi warns that if the growth in volume of output (and therefore also of labour productivity) were still measured in terms of gross value of output, this would introduce yet another contradiction, so he advocates measuring growth in terms of net output, 'as is done in developed capitalist countries'.[7] So there is no clarity yet on this point, though the text of the decree[8] does speak of planned growth of *net* product. In addition, the proposals envisage retaining gross value of sales as a plan indicator for ministries. If this is done, the ministries will exert pressure on their subordinates to avoid producing too cheaply, for familiar reasons. Surely the cure may be worse than the disease?

Improvements are doubtless possible. However, if my analysis of the basic causes of inefficiency is correct, these measures will make little difference. The essential problem is the impossible scale of centralized micro-economic planning, the fact that subordinate units adjust their actions to·the plan targets laid down from above, and not to the needs of

*i.e. in 1981.

other enterprises or to the revealed preferences of the citizens. Of course, Brezhnev and Kosygin agree, indeed repeatedly assert, that production should be for use, that user demand must be taken fully into account, that resources should be used economically. The question is, how can the complex and clumsy bureaucracy – complex and clumsy because of the enormous task it has to perform – achieve the required flexibility? How can it preserve the system of 'directive planning' (Kosygin's definition) *and* stimulate initiative and innovation? How can plans be made internally consistent when the task of co-ordination exceeds the capacity of humans and computers alike? *A propos* the latter, a wise Hungarian economist, Maria Augustinovics, once remarked that one reason for the limited application of computerized programming is that even the most inflexible and hidebound bureaucrat is infinitely more flexible than any computerized programme.

The market solution

The alternative must be in the direction of decentralization, and (*pace* Bahro) this can only be based on negotiated contracts between producer and customer (plus trade as an intermediary).[9] The relevant model is that of the Hungarian economic reform of 1968. (Hungarian reality has moved some way from the original model.) Its basis was that enterprises were no longer to be handed compulsory output plans from above; they were to make their own plans in negotiation with customers, while being free to purchase the inputs they required. The abandonment of centrally determined current output plans and of administered allocation of inputs are two sides of the same medal. The compulsory output plan is integrally linked to the supply plan; the output of most enterprises is some other enterprise's input; and the first step in making up the annual plan in the USSR is the collection of information about the needs of productive enterprises for materials, components, and so on. Central *directive* planning would be confined to major investments, with the 'micro-economy' steered largely by economic means (taxes, subsidies, etc.).

However, any reform on these lines is necessarily based on production for exchange and not production for use, that is, it relies to a considerable degree on the market mechanism. This upsets both the 'fundamentalists' and the neo-Stalinists. Did not Marx and Engels see socialism and commodity production as incompatible? Did not Stalin in his last work advocate a continued reduction in the area in which commodity exchange and 'the law of value' operated? But what is the effective alternative to a reform which, in effect, allows production units to negotiate freely with each other as suppliers and as customers? The Bettelheims and Sweezys seek solutions in slogans, such as 'the mass line', or in counterposing monetary calculation to plans based on 'socially useful effect' (and this without telling us how it should be measured or whose task it is to do the measuring, or how to ensure that decisions are implemented). Nor do they explain how there can be 'control by the direct producers', that is, meaningful workers' participation in economic decision-making, unless decisions about production are taken *at the level of the production unit*; it is this which makes the Yugoslav model rely on the market.

There is a real dilemma here for sincere socialists, a dilemma which must be squarely faced, not evaded. Let us take as an example the fact that a market, if it is to function, requires some degree of competition. For many socialists this is offensive; they counterpose it to socialist co-operation, and indeed it does appear to contradict the notion of workers' solidarity. However, the total absence of competition implies the tying of customer to supplier by the plan; this situation exists in the USSR, and is a cause of much dissatisfaction, since the customer (for instance, the manager of a state factory, or retail store) cannot go elsewhere if the quality of the goods or services provided is poor, or another supplier is better. But if one *can* go elsewhere, albeit to another state or co-operative supplier, that already implies competition, that is, the possibility that one producer can gain from satisfying the customer better than another, which in turn implies that an unsuccessful producer would be penalized. Unless one makes the assumption that under an imaginary 'real' socialism productive units will never give cause for dissatisfaction, there must, of course, be some sort of penalty or corrective action. In the USSR this is imposed or taken by bureaucratic superiors, in the form of reprimand, transfer, demotion, denial of plan-fulfilment bonuses. But experience strongly suggests that none of these is as effective as the provision of *economic* carrots and sticks, linked with *economic* criteria for success or failure. Market and competition require spare capacity, and this raises the spectre of unemployment, whereas the USSR takes pride in ensuring full utilization of resources. Unemployment must, of course, be minimized, but how are efficiency and flexibility to be achieved without spare capacity?

In conceiving a democratic socialism, one ought surely to envisage groups of people (a local community, say, or a factory or farm) being able freely to decide to acquire various goods, for use in either production or consumption. Two methods only are known by which they could do so. They could be *free to buy them*, from the supplier that suits their needs best, or they would have *to apply for permission* to obtain them. Assuming that these goods have alternative uses, a hierarchical superior would have to consider wherever *this* use for them should be authorized. The 'fundamentalist' escapes from this dilemma by identifying socialism with abundance, that is, with the existence of ample supplies for all purposes on which any group could draw (and this in a world where over half the population is on the margin of subsistence). The bureaucrat considers that it is his (occasionally her) responsibility to allocate scarce goods in accordance with

politically determined priorities. Both are hostile to the market in principle. But at least the bureaucrat's view relates to the real world, as well as
being in his/her interest.

The market and competition carry with them certain costs and dangers;
few doubt this. It would be necessary to avoid excessive income inequalities (but not at the cost of eliminating incentives), and it would also be
essential to keep a major role for central planners in the taking of major
investment decisions. It is also important to appreciate that certain areas,
such as the energy sector, could and should remain under centralized
operational control. (Who would 'decentralize' Electricité de France or the
Central Electricity Generating Board? Not even Sir Keith Joseph.) The
question of the level at which decision-making is best located is a complex
question, by no means solely economic, and one which surely calls for a
wide variety of different solutions, depending on the sector and the type of
decision. It is certainly absurd to imply that decentralization plus the
market mechanism represent a panacea, and do not give rise to difficulties,
both economic and political-social. But it is also hard to avoid the conclusion that no solution can be devised which does not involve the market
mechanism in some form.

Be all this as it may, the Soviet leadership has shown every sign of being
determined to reject the 'market' solution. It is unlikely that Brezhnev's
successors will be different in this respect. There is too much at stake: the
position and role of petty officialdom at all levels, the priority of the
'military-industrial complex', the (understandable) fear of instability and
of the unpredictable side-effects of major reform of a mechanism which
has, in its principles, changed little over the last forty-five years or so. Nor
can one discern any pressure from below in this direction. True, the
workers would like goods of better quality to be available, not to stand in
queues, and so on, but the market's logic is usually not understood: as also
in this country, people want higher wages *and* lower prices, oppose
redundancies even if their skills are urgently wanted elsewhere, and blame
the resultant shortages on speculators, bosses, bureaucrats, or whoever. It
is a fact that in Eastern Europe opponents of reform can and do appeal to
the workers' residual sense of identifying socialism and justice with *opposition* to market forces. Paradoxically, this has the effect of reinforcing the
privileges of high officialdom, in so far as these take the form of privileged
allocation of goods unavailable to the ordinary citizen; they arise from the
fact that demand and supply do *not* balance. It is surely quite incorrect for
Bettelheim to argue that the 'new bourgeoisie' favours market-type
reforms! The *present* system serves their personal material interest best. As
for managers, some do indeed want more income and more power, but
some prefer the situation which Hegedus has called 'organized irresponsibility' to the disciplines imposed by a market, to which they are not
accustomed and where they might fail.

Problems and prospects

Where is the Soviet economy heading if no major reforms are in fact adopted? To repeat a point made earlier, there is no catastrophe imminent, the system is not in chaos, the quality of its planning and of its production are not in decline. Indeed, quality is actually improving. So, to take another example, is agricultural output, allowing for year-by-year weather variations, though at a very high cost. Exclusive emphasis upon chaos and waste, the image of production of unsaleable rubbish is misleading, especially if constrasted with the past, when the Soviet system was *more* wasteful, *more* inefficient, *less* productive. People have *not* become worse off. What has happened is the persistence of the second-rate and a failure to keep pace with the needs of technical progress, the growing complexity of industry, the rising demands and aspirations of the masses, with incomes (demand) outpacing supply. Resources are still often used wastefully. But even if growth stays at the modest levels of 3 per cent per annum over the next few years (which seems to me a reasonable forecast to make), this may contrast favourably with Western economies, reeling under renewed blows from OPEC and driven to beggar-my-neighbour trade policies (and anxious to sell technology to the USSR on favourable credit terms). Even 3 per cent is better than zero.

Is there then no danger to their system, no crisis? This would be going too far, so let me end by trying to identify what appears to be a basic source of potential economic (and therefore social-political) instability. This is the increasing gap between *rising expectations* and slowly changing reality. There is also the alarming and growing gap between the cash and savings in the hands of the population and the supply of goods, especially foodstuffs. Given the absence of a (legal) professional trading class and the inefficiency of the official distribution network, shortages can and do cause real hardship in some areas. There is also a wide gap between the complacent optimism of the media and the experience of ordinary citizens, reflected in the following Moscow joke: 'If you wish to find enough food to fill your refrigerator plug it into the radio.' Most observers concur that ideological commitment, in the name of which earlier generations of young people suffered privations to 'build socialism', has long disappeared. Mass terror is no more. Work discipline is weak, with many reports of absenteeism, slackness, drunkenness, pilfering. Stability, the isolation of the few active dissidents, depends on giving people grounds for hope of better material conditions; the huge rise in savings bank deposits is due not only to the gap between purchasing power and the value of goods available in the shops, but also to saving up for the much-hoped-for car, co-operative flat, or a colour TV set. If the gap between hopes and reality becomes too wide (and if in addition the car and TV set are out of action for lack of spares, and repairs to the flat cannot be made without large bribes), this could cause trouble. This trouble can be exacerbated by the government's obstinate refusal to raise prices to reflect actual supply-and-demand conditions. This not only increases the already-strong tendencies towards corruption, but inevitably causes grave shortages in some towns, distribution being on a 'hierarchical' basis, with Moscow at the top. (This has given rise to a cynical jest: 'We are said to have reached the stage of mature socialism. What is the dividing line between mature socialism and the lower kind?' Answer: 'The Moscow circular highway.') Under these conditions, though there are in fact more goods available, people feel more frustrated than ever in their efforts to find the goods they want. Discontent can be enhanced by travellers' tales; not only the glittering 'consumerism' of the West, but the much greater choice and apparent abundance of Czechoslovakia and Hungary, give rise to irritation and impatience.

Engineers, technologists, teachers, doctors, office staffs of most kinds, have another source of discontent. They have lost ground in the 'wages league', and many earn less than skilled workers. Much 'class analysis' of Soviet society suffers from a strange anti-intellectual bias, from a tendency to counterpose the interests of the workers and the intellectuals, treating the latter as if they were allies of the party-state elite. Yet far from being privileged, the mass 'intellectual' professions are poorly paid, with none of the privileges of high officialdom. Doctors, teachers, middle-grade qualified engineers, most office staff, earn less than bus-drivers. It is true, sadly, that there is a wide gulf of mutual incomprehension between them and the workers (and indeed also between the workers and the peasants); the regime can appeal to the anti-intellectual prejudices of the masses, and in the past has frequently done so. It is odd that some of that regime's 'new left' critics should help in this task.

This brings me back to the 3 per cent growth rate. Given the demands of the army and Siberia, given also the urgent claims of the Central Asian republics with their rapidly rising (but immobile) populations, *and* the ever-increasing demands of agriculture, plus the need to improve rural amenities to prevent an exodus of skilled labour, there is little room for manoeuvre, little to spare for improving living standards of workers or intellectuals – unless there is a substantial gain in efficiency and productivity. But is this possible without the sort of reforms which the party leadership is reluctant to contemplate?

On a recent visit to China, I was asked (in Shanghai): 'Would you regard the Soviet system as socialist, and, if not, what would you regard as socialist?' A difficult question indeed, especially its second part, and complicated by China's own recent experiences. They are seeking a way which is neither that of the convulsions of 'cultural revolution', with its downgrading of efficiency and productivity (surely fatal in a backward and very poor country), nor the continuation of the Soviet centralized model, large elements of which have survived earlier attempts at reform.

They too are looking for some new economic structure, which will combine plan and market, centralization of basic decisions and the stimulation of local initiative, managerial responsibility with workers' participation, material incentives and an egalitarian ideology. The least we can do is appreciate how difficult is the task, in China or anywhere else, of devising a 'working model' of a socialist economy, and how small is the relevance in this connection of the theoretical legacy of Marx.

Notes: Chapter 8

1 *Voprosy ekonomiki*, 1977, no. 12, p. 5.
2 The exaggeration arises mainly from the tendency to conceal price increases (for example, managers introducing 'new' and dearer products which are allegedly better and are not, while withdrawing cheaper models); this affects the output index through the price index which is used to calculate it. There is also false reporting, but this could also take the form of concealment of output as well as exaggerating it.
3 The idea was to allow wages economized by reduction of overmanning to be shared by the remaining employees, but the scheme has been much watered down.
4 *Pravda*, 3 September 1979.
5 In his speech to the 25th Party Congress.
6 D. Valovoi's three articles in Pravda, 11, 12 and 13 November 1978, make this and many other points of a highly critical nature.
7 *Pravda*, 3 September 1979.
8 *Ekonomicheskaya gazeta*, 1979, no. 32, supplement.
9 Bahro is an opponent of large-scale units and centralization, but unrealistically advocates small units which would be largely self-sufficient; see his *The Alternative in Eastern Europe* (London: New Left Books, 1978).

9 Soviet agriculture in the 1980s

This was first published in A. Brown and M. C. Kaser (eds), *Soviet Policy for the 1980s* (London: St Antony's/Macmillan, 1982), pp. 170–85. The statistical tables have been updated. They show a very substantial shortfall in relation to the plans for 1981–5, due in considerable part, it must be stressed, to persistently below-average weather conditions. The original paper included an addendum incorporating the changes decreed up to 1983. Since then Gorbachev has become General Secretary, and it is clearly significant that it was he, in his capacity as the Politbureau member in charge of agriculture, who finally gave the leadership's blessing to the autonomous workgroups system, now usually referred to under the designation *kollektivnyi podryad*, or 'collective contract'. Extensive published criticism was concentrated on the ineffectiveness of the RAPOs (regional agro-industrial associations), and the many difficulties encountered by the introduction of the *kollektivnyi podryad*, as well as those caused by the still inadequate supply system. Further changes seem to be imminent, in view of the high priority given by the top leadership to progress with the 'food programme' and the very high cost to the state of agricultural operations (the subsidy bill now exceeds 40 milliard roubles).

No one doubts that agriculture is a weak sector of the Soviet economy. There are serious shortages of food, especially livestock products. The leadership is conscious of the urgency of the need for higher production and greater efficiency. Brezhnev, in November 1980, described the food supply situation as even more serious than the energy, metal and transport bottlenecks, and these are serious enough.

The statistics (see Table 9.1) show some progress. Over the longer period the progress appears to be quite impressive. Indeed, gross agricultural production in 1980 exceeded that of 1960 by over 50 per cent, which can hardly be described as a disaster. What, then, is the nature of the trouble, what are the causes of the malaise, what remedies are proposed, and what are the prospects? It is to these questions that this essay will be devoted.

The fact that agriculture is failing to provide the products demanded by the consumer is, naturally, a function not only of output but also of price.

Table 9.1 Soviet agricultural plans and performance (five-year averages)

	1966–70	1971–5	1976–80 Plan	1976–80 Actual	(1980)	1981–5 Plan[b]	1981	1982	1984
Gross agricultural output (value, milliard roubles)	100·40	113·70	131·80	123·70	121·20	139·80	120·70	127·40	135·00
Grain (million tons)[a]	167·60	181·60	215·00	205·00	189·10	240·50	(150·00)	(180·00)	(180·00?)
Cotton (million tons)	6·89	7·67	9·00	8·93	9·96	9·25	9·60	9·30	8·60
Sunflower seed (million tons)	6·39	5·97	—	5·32	4·65	6·80	4·60	5·30	4·50
Sugar-beet (million tons)	81·10	76·00	96·50	88·40	79·60	101·50	60·60	71·00	85·30
Potatoes (million tons)	94·80	89·80	—	82·60	67·00	—	72·00	78·00	85·30
Meat (million tons)	11·60	14·00	15·30	14·80	15·10	17·25[c]	15·20	15·20	16·70
Milk (million tons)	80·60	87·40	95·00	92·60	90·70	98·00[c]	88·50	90·10	97·60

Sources: Narodnoye khozyaistvo SSSR, 1979, pp. 219–20, proceedings of the 26th Party Congress, and *Pravda*, 26 January 1985.

Notes:
[a] The grain figures after 1980 are rough estimates, in the absence of official data.
[b] Average for the five years.
[c] Plan for 1985.

Retail prices of staple foodstuffs have remained unchanged since 1962. Average money wages have risen since then by about 70 per cent. Allowing for the enlarged labour force and the (larger) growth of incomes of collectivized peasants, one can see that total money incomes must have approximately doubled. Agricultural production, especially of livestock products, while considerably higher, could not and cannot keep pace with increased demand due to the higher money incomes. The prices paid to the farms have been greatly raised. The gap between these and the low retail price is covered by an immense subsidy, which by 1970 must have reached 24 milliard roubles, or upwards of $30,000 million at the official exchange rate, the highest food-and-agriculture subsidy known in history.[1] [By 1985 the subsidy was touching 50 milliard roubles.] The attempt to build up livestock herds to try to meet this demand and the resultant rise in requirements of fodder grain explain why the USSR has a grain deficit despite the fact that grain harvests are considerably higher than they were twenty years ago (when virtually no grain was imported).

Soviet harvest yields, and the productivity of livestock and of labour, while certainly well above the levels of 1960, are still very low by international standards, even in comparison with other communist countries. One should, of course, whenever possible compare like with like. Thus Soviet soil and climate conditions are much less favourable than those of the United States, or of Hungary, say. But when all allowance is made, performance is poor, and the fact that it is now much better than it was in 1960 merely proves how bad it was in 1960 (when it was well above the abysmal levels which prevailed in the last years of Stalin's rule).

Agriculture under Stalin suffered from acute neglect. Underinvestment and low incomes could readily explain poor performance. Under Khrushchev there was a basic change of policy. Prices were raised, investment and incomes increased, the priority of agriculture was enhanced. After an initial spurt in output (it rose by almost 50 per cent in 1953–8), Khrushchev's erratic policies and 'campaigning' methods brought the upward movement to a temporary halt. This, and bad weather in 1963, contributed to his fall. Brezhnev criticized his predecessor's methods at the March plenum of 1965, but continued his policies, minus the excesses. Prices paid to farms were raised several times, without a corresponding increase in retail prices, investments in agriculture rose relatively and absolutely, incomes of peasants continued to increase faster than urban incomes (though from very low levels), the fertilizer programme was pressed forward, efforts were made to expand the supply of tractors and other machinery. Investments in land improvements, cowsheds and infrastructure have all been rising. Agriculture now absorbs vast recources.. No longer can it be said that it is 'exploited' for the benefit of industry. On the contrary, agriculture has become a kind of ball-and-chain, a burden for the rest of the economy. There is not only the huge subsidy already referred to, itself in part the consequence of high costs of production. Investments in agriculture, the larger part of which are budget-financed, absorb about 27 per cent of total investments, an unusually high percentage for an industrialized country. To this must be added the investments in those industries which serve agriculture (tractors, fertilizer, etc.). Labour is much better paid, both in state and in collective farms, and the increase in incomes far exceeds the gains in productivity, which naturally means that costs are rising.

Why has agriculture not done better? What prevents it from achieving its goals? Apart, of course, from the problems created by climate, which is indeed an important handicap.

All the causes which I will now list are discussed in various ways in Soviet published sources, or figure in speeches by Brezhnev and by other leaders. Of course, there could be disagreements about the relative importance of these various factors, and also about remedies. But it is hard to imagine that any serious Soviet scholar would disagree strongly with the analysis that follows.

First on the list are problems connected with labour. These are of various kinds. There is the migration out of agriculture of skilled men and women, in search of a better life in towns, a tendency which exists in East and West alike, but seems to be particularly serious in the USSR, because of the very wide disparities in rural and urban life-styles. This in turn is due to the remoteness and primitiveness of many villages, with their unpaved tracks which turn to deep mud, and the still inadequate educational opportunities – it is hard to recruit teachers for the 'uncultured' backwoods. The effect of all this is to create acute shortages of skilled labour, necessary for the operation and (especially) repairs and maintenance of machinery. The authorities are well aware of the importance of these facts, and plan a substantial improvement in village amenities, shops and housing.

At least equally important is the problem of labour incentives in the excessively large farms, which often have around 500 members or employees, scattered in several villages and engaged in a multitude of activities, cultivating numerous crops and keeping every kind of farm animal. A sort of diseconomy of scale (or alienation, if one prefers the word) then develops. The peasants do not feel responsible for the final outcome, and indeed there is often little visible connection between the quality of their work and the harvest. A frequently cited example relates to tractormen engaged in ploughing. They are paid on piece-rates, measured in terms of hectares ploughed, and receive bonuses for economizing fuel and avoiding breakages. All these indicators 'benefit' from ploughing as shallow as possible. The resultant losses in the harvest cannot be ascribed to the individuals concerned. So the fact that the tractor-drivers are well paid in no way ensures that they perform their work efficiently.

This lack of responsibility also contributes to labour shortages at peak times. Farmers the world over work very long hours to cope with the harvest rush. In the USSR, however, many do not bother. 'We will sow, God will send rain, then people will come from towns to gather in the harvest', this is how the attitude was described by a Soviet economist in private conversation. This, as well as gaps in mechanization, cause the mobilization every year of millions of townspeople and part of the army for work on the harvest. A particularly vivid letter to his fellow villagers by Fyodor Abramov, reproaching them for their indifference, and the neglect of essential tasks, was printed in *Pravda*, 17 November 1979:

'When was it known that able-bodied *muzhiki* go away at the time of the harvest? . . . The old pride in a well-ploughed field, in a well-sown crop, in well-looked-after livestock, is vanishing. Love for the land, for work, even self-respect, is disappearing. Is this not a cause of absenteeism, lateness, drunkenness . . .? We have indifference, passivity, fear of upsetting one's fellow villagers. And with all this the hope for the strict and fair boss, who will arrive from somewhere and impose order. Almost like the Nekrasov poem: 'the master will come and will judge' (*vot priyedet barin, barin nas rassudit*).

His cry from the heart produced a lively correspondence. This is no trivial matter. In agriculture more than anywhere the attitude of those who work to what they do is decisive. The effect is highlighted in a remarkable calculation by the labour economist E. Manevich: the numbers mobilized to help with the harvest increased 2·4 times between 1970 and 1979, and exceeded 15 million persons![2]

Then there is the damage done by the excess numbers of *orders from above,* of imposed plans and detailed instructions. Compulsory delivery quotas can stand in the way of specialization, lead to loss when certain crops and livestock which the plans require are unsuitable for the circumstances of the particular farm. But this is only a small part of the story. Ample evidence exists of systematic petty interference. Orders are given about what should be sown, in what quantity, when. Sowing campaigns, machinery repairs campaigns, harvest campaigns, are supervised by party and state officials, which countermand decisions by farm managers and the advice of the agronomists. Criticisms of these practices appear frequently. Thus: 'Too many compulsory indicators are imposed from above . . . Particularly frequent is the prescription of areas to be sown. The agronomist . . . in practice cannot decide himself what to sow, exact figures are imposed on him, and he is ordered strictly to carry out these orders . . . Thus our farm was forbidden to reduce the area under potatoes' (and so on; *Pravda*, 30 March 1981). 'Although the party has long ago condemned the practice of giving detailed orders [*administvirovaniye*], this "style" has not disappeared. From the *raion* and *oblast* come orders: extend the area of this crop, cut the area of another. Thus the *oblast* agricultural department calls in our specialist and orders him to double the area sown to maize this spring. But where can we find the hectares, without ruining our crop rotation?' (*Pravda*, 26 March 1981). 'Why regulate our everyday activities? What field to sow on Friday and which on Saturday, where to have clean fallow and where not, surely this is a matter for the *kolkhoz* specialists . . . Yet up till now the party secretary is apt to tell the *kolkhoz* chairman where and what to plough' (*Pravda*, 11 May 1981). In the same issue, a decision by the *kolkhoz* management committee to allow the chairman to go on sick leave was reversed by the *rai-ispolkom* and the party secretary. Not even such a decision as this is left to the farm management. Another source states that, in his area, one cannot slaughter a head of cattle without the written persmission of party and state officials (*Pravda*, 16 January 1980).

Why? The absurdity of such practices are evident, the irresponsibility they cause is obvious. In the days when state purchase prices were extremely low, it was clearly in the interests of the *kolkhoz* management and of the peasants to avoid fulfilling state plans, and so it was 'rational' for party and state organs to supervise closely every task, including routine tasks, of a sort which any industrial manager would be entrusted to carry out. (To fulfil industrial plans was and is in the material interests of executants.) However, prices paid to farms are now much higher. Why, then, cannot management of *kolkhozy* and *sovkhozy* be trusted to do their job? Old habits? Instinctive distrust of peasants?

It must be added that the way in which farm management's perform-ance is evaluated can produce perverse results, as is graphically shown in yet another critical article in *Pravda*, 'Reward for being backward' (*Poosh-chreniye za otstavaniye*, 9 March 1980). Not only are those farms who succeed in persuading the planners to give them an 'easy' plan rewarded for plan over-fulfilment, but there is a serious fault in the price system. A 50 per cent bonus is paid for deliveries over the compulsory quota, or in excess of the amount delivered to the state in previous years. But suppose there is a drought, then the harvest is lower. 'In some countries this is taken into account, and prices are higher in a drought year. With us it is the other way round. A centner of grain in a favourable year, when its cost is lower, is paid the higher bonus price, while the (average) price is lower in a drought year' (ibid.).

Among the reasons often given in the press for high costs in agriculture are not only those connected with labour, but also of machinery. New machines often cost disproportionately more than old ones. Machines are administratively allocated, and the ones actually needed to cope with local conditions are often unavailable. A vast literature deals with what is called *nekomleksnost'*, that is to say the absence of complementary equipment, which reduces the effectiveness of the available machines and contributes to labour bottlenecks. Many complaints relate to lack of what is called *malaya mekhanizatsiya*, for example, equipment for loading, unloading, materials handling, mowing. Plans for simple one-man-operated grass-cutters, urgently needed for haymaking in farms and for individual peasant use, remain unavailable despite decisions to produce them. Quality of many kinds of equipment is poor. One reason given why women are little used as tractor drivers is that the design of the tractors makes the work heavy, dirty and unpleasant (M. Fyodorova, *Voprosy ekonomiki*, 1975, no. 12, p. 57), and the lack of mechanized work for women is a source of discontent, especially as most village girls now receive a ten-year education. Shortage of spare parts is notorious. Equipment requiring electric power (especially milking machines) cannot be used effectively because of frequent power cuts. (*Pravda*, 23 January 1981, provided vivid examples of the effects on cows and on milk output in west Siberia.) Specific items of equipment which farms seek to order, through the intermediary supply organization Sel'khoztekhnika, often cannot be or are not provided. What is provided is apt to arrive in separate parts, somehow to be assembled in farms' own workshops.

All this reflects the inadequacies of industrial planning, the lack of effective co-ordination and balance, the lack of influence of the customer over what is produced and allocated. One further example among many is fertilizer. Its output has greatly increased, which is, of course, highly desirable. But there is a shortage of bags, storage space, means of transport, machines to spread it on the fields. So much of it piles up at railheads and on farms, and is wasted. Many cartoons in *Krokodil* and elsewhere relate to this theme. One which appeared in May 1981 showed a pile of fertilizer in the open in a *kolkhoz*. A visitor remarks: 'If an inspector sees this, out in the rain, there will be trouble.' To which a local man replies: 'What inspector would reach us on *these* roads!' But more about roads in a moment.

Why so few grass-cutters? Are they not simple to make, and cheap? Answer: *because* they are simple to make and cheap, and are thus not a significant part of the value of output for plan-fulfilment purposes (*Pravda*, 4 May 1981). ('For mini-technique, mini-interst.')

A highly critical article by I. Suslov (*Voprosy ekonomiki*, 1982, no. 12) noted the disorganizing effects of the multiplicity of 'service' agencies – such as Selkhoztekhnika and Selkhozkhimiya (the latter providing ferti-lizer, spreading pesticides, etc.) – which try to fulfil their own quantitative plans instead of aiming at maximizing the final output of agriculture. This, and the greater dependence on industiral inputs, has, in Suslov's view, made *khozraschyot* meaningless, because agricultural performance depends so little on managerial decisions within agriculture itself. He pointed to the worsening financial results, due to escalating costs, and they have indeed escalated, as the figures in Table 9.2 show all too clearly.

Table 9.2 *Agricultural Costs (roubles)*

	1970	1980	1970	1980
	kolkhozy		sovkhozy	
Grain (excl. maize) (per ton)	50	76	53	84
Cotton (per ton)	404	478	362	508
Sugar-beet (per ton)	22	31	29	42
Potatoes (per ton)	62	120	76	139
Beef (live weight) (per ton)	1,166	2,177	1,277	2,344
Pork (live weight) (per ton)	1,194	2,018	1,111	1,726
Milk (per ton)	177	287	189	308
Eggs (per thousand)	73	87	64	64

Sources: *Narodnoye khozyaistvo SSSR*, 1970, p. 387 and 1980, pp. 259, 276.
Note: The one exception, eggs, is due evidently to the much more widespread use of factory farming (battery hens).

So, despite very large investments, the return is low, and some processes remain undermechanized. The shortage of spare parts has been the subject of speeches, articles and cartoons for fifty years, and seems incurable. One reason is the large number of breakages, due to poor maintenance and the appalling roads.

This brings one to problems of *roads and transport*. Hard-surface roads are few. Although there is a sizeable programme for highway construction, there are hardly any byways. Unpaved tracks between the farms and the outside world, and between units of the same farm, turn to deep mud in autumn and spring, and mud turns into deep ruts when it dries. Industrial supplies and consumers' goods can be held up for weeks on end, and farms face grave problems in getting produce out. The state of the roads wears out tractors and lorries prematurely. Several Soviet economists, for instance Khachaturov, have been pointing out for years that 'roadlessness' (*bezdorozhye*) causes very heavy economic loss. But there is the difficulty caused by lack of stones and quarries on the great Russian plain, which inhibits local efforts to make hard-surface roads and adds to the cost of building. (Invading German armies were known to improvise a hard surface by tying logs together and laying them over the mud.)

Matters are not helped by lack of specialized forms of transport, especially lorries adapted to their tasks. Thus grain is all too often carried to elevators on open lorries, and some of it blows away. Critics also point to many other related 'lacks': storage space is short for grain, vegetables and fruit; there are not enough elevators; there is an underprovision of storage in wholesale and retail trade. There is a long-notorious shortage of packaging materials of all kinds. The effect is and can only be losses, so that part of the produce of the peasantry never reaches its users. This is well known and much commented on by Soviet critics. *Pravda* in 1980 ran a long series of articles about the reasons for lack of vegetables and fruit in urban shops (apart from the reasons mentioned above, there is also lack of incentives for the trading network to handle perishables). The tenth five-year plan (1976–80) contained a decision to build grain elevators to a capacity of a further 30 million tons, but the plan was greatly underfulfilled, and another *Pravda* article (16 May 1981) deplored the use of money supposedly devoted to elevator building for other purposes; yet 'just in the central areas of Russia, for lack of shelter, about 18 million tons of wheat remain in the open in autumn, unprotected from rain and snow'. The authors said that losses under these conditions were supposed to be 1 per cent, 'but, so to speak, this is only so theoretically'. It is to cope with this complex of inadequacies that it has been decided to plan the entire 'agro-industrial complex' as one interrelated whole, paying particular attention to infrastructure, packaging, distribution, and so on. No one doubts that a great deal remains to be done.

Another and quite different bottleneck item is *fodder for livestock*. The shortage of fodder grain, and the resultant level of imports, has been commented on already. But one must stress that one cause for the high demand for grain and grain concentrates is lack of other kinds of fodder. Yields of hay are low, there are not enough root crops. The net effect is that Soviet livestock eats much more grain, per unit of livestock or of meat, than its American or West European equivalents, and the diet is unbalanced. There are plans to increase greatly various chemical additives, and recent decrees have sought to encourage haymaking by allowing the peasants who do the work to keep a big proportion for their own live-stock. One handicap, already mentioned, is lack of small haymaking equipment, capable of being used in small meadows, on grass verges, and so on. It is quite clear that shortage of fodder is causing serious problems for the livestock industry. The American boycott had only modest effects; Soviet imports from Argentina, Canada and Australia rose sharply in 1980. None the less, meat and milk production is stagnating, and the key to progress is (rightly) seen as a substantial rise in production of all kinds of fodder in the Soviet Union itself.

Last on the list of problems (and high on the list of remedies) is the private plot. Official policies towards the little household allotment of land and to privately owned livestock have altered frequently since col-lectivization, alternating between encouragement and obstruction. Thus Khrushchev in 1953 strongly criticized the policies of Stalin's last years, greatly reduced taxes, eliminated compulsory deliveries of private pro-duce, sought to provide incentives for higher production. Yet in *his* last years there were again restrictions, criticized in turn by Brezhnev in the March 1965 plenum held after Khrushchev's fall. Now again many critics point to obstructions of many kinds and the need to overcome them. Thus some markets refuse to allow the sale of produce brought from other *oblasti* (*Pravda*, 16 May 1980), some farm managements refuse to provide pasture for private cows (ibid.). Why, asks another critic, is hardly any equipment, or tools, provided for individual cultivators? (*Pravda*, 4 May 1981). 'Over many years there developed a negative attitude to the requirements of private auxiliary enterprises' (ibid.), and so on. As we shall see, the present attitude is positive, and measures are being taken to stimulate private production, especially livestock. However, one other problem must be mentioned. Peasants are now much better paid for work for the *kolkhoz* or *sovkhoz*. To look after cows and pigs is troublesome, to take produce to urban markets is costly in time and effort. As a result, sales in urban markets have shown little increase in volume, despite much higher prices, and one cause of shortage in urban areas has been the higher consumption of meat and other products in the villages. Young people prefer leisure to milking cows.

These, then, are the basic problems of Soviet agriculture. The authorities realize that they are interconnected, that a 'complex' approach is essential. Thus there is clearly no point in expanding fertilizer production if it outruns the means of storing, transporting and spreading it. Investments in modern livestock farms make no sense unless there is more to feed the animals on. The large investments currently being made in land improvements (*melioratsiya*) in central and north-west Russia will yield a poor return unless the mechanization, labour incentives and infrastructure are radically improved.

What, then, can be done? What is being done? What, finally, should be done?

Official policy lays stress on the need for still higher investments, on re-organization based on 'agro-industrial complexes', that is, essentially on better and more comprehensive planning. Missing from policy statements and the speeches at the party congress was any emphasis on the need to devolve authority and responsibility to the farms themselves, though, as already noted, occasional articles do criticize excessive interference from above. In fact such intereference cannot diminish so long as party decrees repeatedly urge the party and state authorities to ensure that various tasks are carried out, that machines are repaired, seeds made ready, the harvest completed, and such decrees continue to appear. The ideas underlying the concept of the agro-industrial complex are sound. However, their imposition as a campaign of re-organization could surely result in still further bureaucratization, a diminution of the autonomy of farm management. These developments should be carefully watched.

A potentially positive reform would be the widespread introduction of the autonomous work-team (*beznaryadnoye zveno*). The idea was already the subject of experiment and discussion fifteen years ago. Its essence is simple. An area of land is handed over to a small group (say, five to ten people) for the cultivation of a given crop or crops, together with the necessary equipment. They are allowed to organize their own work, without having work-schedules imposed on them (hence *beznaryadnoye*), and are paid by results. This saves supervisory labour, and also ensures that it will not seem advantageous to gain on piece-rates by ploughing too shallow; everyone is interested in the size of the harvest. Experiments were described as successful, but they were halted for a number of years, partly (one imagines) because such a tendency seems contrary to the established practice of planning large units and exercising tight control, partly because of genuine organizational and social difficulties; not all the work, and not all the workers, are suitable for such work-teams, and payment by results is apt to give rise to very large income disparities within the same *kolkhoz* and *sovkhoz*, which causes friction.

Despite these complications, the idea has re-emerged in the official press. *Pravda* has published articles extolling this form or organization of labour; for instance, on 25 November 1979, 14 July 1980, 26 March 1981, 25 May 1981 (this last one refers to a small *beznaryadnaya brigada*, but the principle is the same). Official decrees, speeches at party congresses, do not advocate the introduction of this method, but neither do they condemn it. It appears that it is being quietly adopted in some areas, but is still regarded as controversial and experimental. Its advantages are being publicly extolled, and it certainly does overcome the psychological diseconomies of scale, by identifying a small team with a specific area of land or a number of livestock. Unequal payment between *zvenya* (or between those in these teams and those not) can be, and in some reported cases is, accompanied by equal pay for all within the given *zveno*, justified by the fact that they share the work among themselves by their own decisions with the minimum of individual specialization. Here is a typical passage from a typical article:

> We try to interest our personnel morally and materially in their work, to stimulate the achievement of good final results. We give preference to the autonomous (*beznaryadnoi*) system of organizing and paying labour. We allocate fields and equipment to *zvenya*. Now it is no longer necessary to remind people what they have to do and when. The peasants appreciate this. Labour turnover has dropped . . . (P. Kravchenko, chairman of a *kolkhoz* in the Kharkov *oblast'*, *Pravda*, 25 March 1981).

So maybe this method will be adopted, because, despite its disadvantages, despite the fact that it contradicts the established habits of issuing orders to and through large-scale units, it works well. The authorities are by now very deeply concerned with the inadequacies of agriculture, and committed to putting them right as fast as possible. However, the matter was not mentioned at all at the Twenty-Sixth Party Congress. As long ago as 25 December 1979 *Pravda* published an article in which the author asked the Ministry of Agriculture to express its view on this kind of *zveno*. As far as I am aware, there is still no official 'line' on the subject (but see the addendum to this chapter).

The urgent need for more food undoubtedly underlies the much more positive policy towards private plots and livestock, which even a *Pravda* editorial (10 June 1981) does not hesitate to call the 'individual sector' (*individual'nyi sektor*). In speeches such as that of Brezhnev to the Twenty-Sixth Party Congress, in numerous articles, in editorials, such as the one cited above, restrictions and obstruction are criticized, and the need to encourage private production and marketing is emphasized. The point is made that to expand meat or vegetable production on private plots improves feeding of peasants and of townspeople, and is much less costly than a similar increase on state and collective farms. Published criticism refers to such obstacles as difficulty in acquiring piglets, calves, chicks, the unwillingness of some state and collective farms to provide pasture, the problem of fodder supply, the lack of interest on the part of co-operative trade to purchase private produce, which causes unnecessary journeys to markets by those willing to sell. Incredibly, one source reports that the co-operatives are forbidden, by a decree adopted in 1975, to pay cash directly to peasants selling private produce. The sellers have to travel specially to the *raion* centre and stand in a queue for payment (*Pravda*, 16 May 1980). It is also noted that some households are unwilling to bother with private livestock, and prefer to travel to the nearest town to buy eggs, ham, and so on. Land which could grow crops is too often denied to individuals even though it is not in use. All this, it is insisted, must now change. There is to be encouragement for peasants to produce more, and also a drive to provide allotments in the suburbs for townspeople. Industrial enterprises are urged to set up more auxiliary farms. These already provide produce for canteens and for sale to employees, and such activities are to be expanded.

Measures to expand private production which receive favourable press comment include using farm machinery to plough and cultivate household allotments (*Pravda*, 31 July 1980), and of course to ensure regular supplies of fodder and access to pasture (16 May 1980, 29 April 1981, the editorial of 10 June 1981, and many others). Publicity has been given to the idea, adopted long ago in Hungary, under which the peasant households undertake to fatten pigs or other animals and then sell them to either the farm or the state procurement agencies, and are provided with fodder at an agreed low price. It then makes little difference who actually owns the animals. In some quoted instances they are fattened by the households on behalf of *kolkhoz* owners, in others the piglets, say, are sold to the peasant and then sold back. The above-cited *Pravda* editorial points out that peasant-owned livestock sold for meat to the *kolkhoz* can be delivered to the state as a *kolkhoz* product and so benefit from the bonus price for overquota deliveries. The need is seen to make such deals attractive to peasants, some of whom may prefer not to bother to expand their private activities, now that they are much better paid for state and collective work (and there is not much to buy for the extra money in village shops). Provision has also been made for the retention for private animals of part of the hay cut on collective and state meadows, as part of providing incentives for expanding haymaking. Articles appear urging the provision of small mechanized equipment suitable for the small allotments, ranging from motor mowers to scooters with sidecars or trailers (4 May 1981, etc.).

An important and informative article by G. Shmelev appeared in *Voprosy ekonomiki*, 1981, no. 5, and it is hardly accidental that he works in the Institute which studies other socialist countries, and shows himself particularly well-informed on the flexible ways in which private and co-operative activities are encouraged, and interrelated, in Hungary. He quotes many figures not previously published. Thus the average size of the private plot is 0·31 hectares in *kolkhozy*, 0·17 hectares for workers and employees in rural areas (0·21 hectares in *sovkhozy*), and Shmelev notes that *kolkhoznik* plots and livestock are substantially below the permitted maxima. In 1979 private plots accounted for 26·5 per cent of total agricultural production. (This is higher than the amount I had calculated and published in *The Soviet Economic System*, but the reason is plainly that I had used figures in 1965 prices, while Shmelev's are in 1973 prices; as livestock products account for two-thirds of the value of private output, and prices for livestock products have been substantially raised, this has the effect of increasing the share of private produce in the total.) Shmelev mentions approvingly the decree of 5 January 1981 which encourages private livestock raising and the fattening of collective livestock in private households; more land on which to grow fodder crops will be provided to the peasants. He urges the extension of such arrangements also to vegetables, fruit, flowers. He strongly advocates positive and vigorous encouragement of private plot production, and deplores the fact that good decrees are being implemented too slowly.

Is this a genuinely new policy, or is it a 'repeat' of a temporary pro-private-plot cycle, to be followed by obstruction and restrictions? We cannot yet tell, but my feeling is that it is something qualitatively different, that the authorities have learnt a lesson from the serious shortages that now exist. Private livestock raising may well tend gradually to decline as and when sufficient supplies are available from collective and state farms. Until then, it is important to stimulate it, to make it genuinely profitable, so as to cope with shortages at maximum speed and at minimum cost. The basic snag is the overall shortage of fodder. If there is not enough even for socialized livestock, will the local authorities in fact carry out the obligation to supply private cows, pigs, and so on? We shall see. Meanwhile let us note that the correct policy is being followed, at least in this instance, at least for the time being.

However, the other measures being taken are much less promising. Agro-industrial complexes, schemes for linking *sovkhozy* and *kolkhozy*, and perhaps gradually merging the two kinds of farm, all add to bureaucratic complexities. It remains as difficult as ever to get the desired equipment and spares through Sel'khoztekhnika, which has been over-charging for the use of its own workshops and tends to hoard necessary spare parts and means of transportation. There are complaints too about yet another body, Sel'khozkhimiya, which is supposed to spread fertilizer, herbicides and lime, on the fields, but whose rewards and plans are not linked with the size of the harvest (*Pravda*, 30 March 1981). As already mentioned, the habits of giving orders from above persist, and an examin-ation of any recent agricultural decree shows that the local party officials are repeatedly instructed to ensure that various measures are carried out, thus ensuring the continuance of interference, and of its negative effects. Better plans imposed from above, more discipline and tighter norms seem to be traditional and persistent methods by which greater efficiency is to be realized. Surely such methods are unlikely to succeed. (I once saw among a list of norms imposed from above a utilization norm for wire to be used for tying together bales of hay!)

What, then, is needed? Surely, more than anything else, greater free-dom of decision by those on the spot, on the farms. I recall once being told by a Soviet farm official, shortly after the abolition of the machine tractor stations (MTSs), that this measure was a mistake. I was surprised, and asked why he thought that this apparently sensible decision was erroneous. He replied: 'Before 1958 *kolkhozy* were forbidden to buy tractors. After 1958 *kolkhozy* were forbidden *not* to buy tractors. The correct decision was to allow those who wish to buy to do so, and those who lacked workshops and maintenance personnel to hire them, i.e. to *let them choose*. After all, some American farmers hire combine-harvesters, for instance, others own them.' There is much wisdom in this. The greatest enemy of agriculture is what the Russians call *shablon*, the impo-sition of some standardized decision or pattern on a vast variety of local conditions. The late Naum Jasny used to say that what was most needed was *samotyok*; the word suggests uncontrolled spontaneity, and in the eyes of Soviet officialdom has a pejorative meaning.

A decree reported in *Pravda* (14 July 1981) does go some way towards recognizing this, since it specifically instructs officials to stop excessive interference; plans imposed from above should determine delivery obliga-tions for several years ahead, and farms should be free of petty tutelage. This has been said before, with little effect, and we shall see if old habits will persist.

The same decree introduced a change in the price system, the effect of which is not yet clear. Until 1981, 50 per cent extra was paid to farms for deliveries in excess of the plan. It has now been decided to 'incorporate' this bonus into the basic price, and then to pay 50 per cent extra for deliveries in excess of the average previously sold. Whether this is an increase depends on how the previous bonus has been 'incorporated' in the basic price; is the latter to be 10 per cent higher? So far we do not know. It could mean yet another increase in the already extremely high level of subsidies.

In my view the basic principles of effective reform in Soviet-type agriculture are those which underlie the relative success of Hungarian farming. Their essentials are the following. First, much greater freedom to choose what to produce, whether to specialize, what livestock to raise; there are neither compulsory delivery quotas nor any imposed plan indicators. This means that state purchase prices must be so fixed as to persuade the producers to choose the desired pattern of production. Second, in the place of administered allocation of inputs there is (more or less) free trade; farms can buy equipment, tractors and chemicals, from wholesalers or producers. This makes a great difference. Third, farms management can make flexible work arrangements within the farm, to interest the peasants in their work; these include the Hungarian version of the autonomous work-team. Fourth, farms undertake a variety of non-agricultural sidelines, ranging from building and decorating to small-scale manufacture and various services (e.g. motor vehicle repairs), which add to revenues and provide off-peak employment. Fifth, the private sector has been encouraged, to good effect, and with great flexibility. Thus there is no limit to the number of private animals, the owners can make contracts with their farm, or with the state food industry, or take meat to market, and can purchase fodder as required. Finally, the Hungarian authorities have dared to increase retail prices of food, to a level at which supply and demand is in approximate balance.

There is clear evidence in Soviet publications that the Hungarian experience has been carefully studied. Indeed, some of the recent proposals to encourage peasant housholds to fatten livestock may have been directly derived from such study. However, at present the chances of the Soviet leaders adopting the whole Hungarian 'package' are very remote. It runs quite counter to their attitudes and policies. Equally strong arguments for major micro-economic decentralization, and the greater use of the market mechanism, in other spheres of the economy have been put forward and rejected. In Hungary they have been accepted in principle and at least partially put into practice. It is for this reason that Hungarian farms can freely purchase their inputs; the reform has eliminated administered allocation of inputs in industry too. There is no sign either that the Soviet authorities are contemplating a change in the principles of price-fixing, or that they will face the necessity to increase retail prices of food (for political reasons that one understands).

So what will happen, in the absence of a major reform of the system? Large-scale investments in agriculture will surely have some limited effect. Table 9.1 shows that the plan for 1985 is not very ambitious, but it rests on some rather optimistic assumptions, especially in grain output, and it may be confidently predicted that it will not be fulfilled. Some increase over present levels of production is none the less likely. Given the expected rise in personal incomes, it seems clear that the already-existing shortages of many foodstuffs will persist. The outlook it not catastrophic, but neither is it at all hopeful. And much, as usual, will depend on luck with the weather.

What are the implications of the above analysis for foreign trade? Will the Soviet Union continue to be one of the world's largest importers of grain? After all, in 1913 Russia was among the world's largest exporters of grain! There is no doubt that the Soviet leadership is unhappy at this dependence on imports, and the long-term aim is to achieve self-sufficiency, which is represented by emulating the United States in producing one ton of grain per capita. As also in the United States, the major part of this grain would be eaten by animals.

This brings one to the key issue, one that will in fact determine the level of Soviet grain requirements and imports in the next decade: the demand for livestock products, and particularly meat. Prices are kept far below their costs, and far below the level at which supply and demand can balance, by a subsidy which has now reached gigantic proportions. Relative prices of meat are, from any economic standpoint, far too low. So far, at least, the Soviet government's policy has been to maintain them at this level, and this policy has been reaffirmed in the five-year plan through to 1985. High priority is being given to the expansion of output of meat and other livestock products. Yet four mediocre harvests in a row (1979, 1980, 1981, 1982) have made it impossible to expand production despite the high level of grain imports. Let us suppose that weather improves in the course of the next few years, and production in 1981–5 averages 215 million tons of grain, this having been the target in the previous quinquennium. This would imply a very substantial deficit of fodder grain. In practical terms the magnitude of the deficit must in some part depend on political decisions. How much priority will the Soviet state give to the building up of livestock herds? How much hard currency will it be prepared to devote to the purchase of grain? What will be the level of Soviet exports, bearing in mind the high dependence of the Soviet Union on oil for its hard currency earnings? Might the government take courage in both hands and double the retail price of meat? Might it decide to ration meat, or to go on tolerating chronic shortage for five more years? How successful will its efforts be to increase the supply of fodder other than grain?

If one adds to the picture the uncertainties of the international situation and the possibility of an accelerated arms race, to make any forecast is very hazardous, but it seems not unreasonable to expect the Soviet purchases to continue at a level of between 25 and 30 million tons annually, unless the weather turns exceptionally favourable or remains exceptionally unfavourable. The Soviet Union could also enter the world market on a large scale as a purchaser of meat, though here again there is a political choice to be made. Another relevant factor is the crisis in Poland. Relative to its size and population the Poles have been importing more grain than the Soviet Union in recent years, and the balance-of-payments situation in Poland is so catastrophic that such imports cannot continue without large-scale aid, some of it from the USSR. However, the most likely outcome would be Soviet loans in hard currency to purchase grain in the West rather than Soviet deliveries of grain to Poland.

Addendum

Since the above was written several important decisions have been taken, which must partially modify the foregoing analysis.

1   There has been a decision to increase substantially the state purchase prices for agricultural produce, reflecting the high and rising costs of production. In the absence of any increase in retail prices of staple food-stuffs, this will cause an escalation of the already enormous subsidy bill.

2   A new co-ordinating hierarchy of 'agro-industrial' administration, from the all-union level (where a committee of the relevant ministries is placed under a deputy-premier) all the way down to the rural districts (*raiony*), has been created. Its task is to ensure that all the various government agencies and enterprises (agricultural machinery, procurements, food industry, trade, rural construction, Sel'khoztekh-nika, Sel'khozkhimiya, etc.) pull together and aim at the highest final output. *Kolkhozy* and *sovkhozy* fall within this governing and co-ordinating complex, and one cannot help wondering whether this bureaucratic solution of a bureaucratic problem can possibly assure the necessary co-ordination, and whether the insufficient autonomy of the farm management will not be still further reduced.

3   Major investments will be directed to coping with the needs of infra-structure (roads, storage space, etc.) and packaging materials, and also rural housing and amenities.

4   An important change: in the decree of May 1982 and even more clearly in the speech of the Politbureau member in charge of agriculture, M. Gorbachev (*Pravda*, 20 March 1983), there is explicit recognition of the need to introduce the *beznaryadny* or *podryadnyi* (contract) system, based on the small brigade or the *zveno*. This is now (1983) being introduced all over the country. The problem one can anticipate is the ability (perhaps also the desire) of the *kolkhozy* or *sovkhozy* to carry out their side of the contract, due partly to habits of command over, rather than contractual

Table 9.3 Yields Compared, 3–Year Averages, 1976–9   (centners per hectare)

	USSR	Hungary	GDR	Poland	Romania	Czechoslovakia
All grains	16·3	40·2	34·8	24·8	29·9	36·1
Wheat	16·5	38·9	41·1	30·1	26·4	39·1
Barley	16·9	31·1	37·1	28·1	29·8	36·3
Maize (for grain)	32·4	47·6	48·0	40·4	33·5	44·6
Flax (fibre equivalent)	3·6	6·1	—	6·4	5·0	6·6
Sugar-beet	242·0	328·0	264·0	294·0	252·0	331·0
Potatoes	123·0	140·0	174·0	198·0	149·0	172·0
Fodder root crops	239·0	334·0	439·0	361·0	431·0	392·0
Hay (perennial sown grasses)	27·5	44·6	90·8	53·3	47·0	69·5

Source: Comecon Statistical Annual, 1980, pp. 217–22.

responsibility towards, their own members/employees; but most of all because they in their turn will be unable to obtain the necessary supplies, spare parts, and so on, from industry.

An example of admnistrative confusion, still occurring a year after the May 1982 reforms, may be quoted from *Pravda*, 25 and 26 May 1983. A new ministry of vegetables and fruit (*plodo-ovoshchi*) is supposed to ensure, within the agro-industrial complex, production and distribution of these products. Results: other food shops stop selling vegetables and fruit, to the inconvenience of customers, *and* the *sovkhozy* and *kolkhozy* specializing on these items are now under dual subordination, in that their other activities (growing other crops, or keeping livestock), and indeed their global output and financial plans, are still within the competence of the Ministry of Agriculture. Orders to grow more vegetables conflict with established crop rotation schemes. Allocation of the needed industrial inputs is also subject to division of responsibility, with disputes between two republican ministries as to whose *fondy* (items subject to allocation) are supposed to provide for these farms. All this is a classic illustration of bureaucratic crossed lines, a consequence (yet again) of not granting decision-making powers to *farms*, and – as the Russian saying goes – of 'having too many nannies'.

Notes: Chapter 9

1 Deduced from V. F. Garbuzov, *Planvoye khozyaistvo*, 1977, no. 7, p. 17, and V. Voronin, *Voprosy ekonomiki*, 1980, no. 6, p. 118.
2 *Voprosy ekonomiki*, 1981, p. 60.

10 The Soviet industrial enterprise

This essay was originally published in I. Jeffries (ed.), *The Industrial Enterprise in Eastern Europe* (New York and Eastbourne: Praeger, 1981), pp. 29–38. It ended with a reference to an 'imminent' shake-up of the ministerial form of control. Since it was written the signs of imminent change have multiplied, with loud criticism of the ministries and all-union *obyedineniya*, and the airing of projects designed to strengthen simultaneously central control over 'basics' and managerial powers over current output and the diffusion (and production) of new technology. How far any of this can be made effective so long as material allocation quotas, delivery contracts and current output targets are administratively imposed remains an unanswered question. 'Freedom of choice' in acquiring inputs clearly requires freedom both to sign contracts and to produce in accordance with user requirements embodied in these contracts, and this in turn requires freedom to acquire by purchase the inputs needed to produce what the customer wants. At the time this book goes to press (1986) there is still no sign that changes so drastic are about to occur. But we may be due for some surprises.

Let us begin with a glance at the 1965 reform. It will be recalled that this eliminated the regional economic councils (*sovnarkhozy*), restored the industrial ministries and sought at the same time to increase the powers and functions of directors at enterprise level. Many compulsory plan indicators were declared abolished, and the role of profits (profitability) in the computation of bonuses was enhanced. A price reform introduced in 1967 sought to eliminate loss-making sectors and did indeed substantially increase average profit margins, out of which a capital charge had to be paid into the budget. Supposedly, ministerial plan instructions were to be confined to the following indicators: value of output sold; profits and/or profit rate (*rentabel'nost'*); payments to state budget; wages fund; centralized investments.

There was a declaration about the desirability of more direct commercial links between customer and supplier, and a shift towards trade in (as distinct from administrative allocation of) the means of production. Material and technical supply functions at the centre and in the localities were to be concentrated in Gossnab (State Committee on Material-Technical Supplies) and its republican and local offices.

Subsequent history was one of virtually continuous retreat from the principles of 1965. The best and most detailed survey of the stages through which the reform was itself reformed is that by Gertrude Schroeder.[1] The number of compulsory indicators increased, formally and informally. Thus Aganbegyan reported that '80 per cent of directors [in a sample survey covering 1,064 directors] reported that their superiors imposed compulsory indicators (such as costs of specific products, the numbers employed by category, and so on) which in accordance with the economic reform measure were not to be laid down from above'.[2] Ninety per cent of directors considered that their powers were too small. Alongside this apparently unauthorized exercise of ministerial authority was a steady increase in the list of indicators which ministers were allowed, indeed instructed, to impose: labour productivity, material utilization norms, delivery obligations for the more important items, introduction of new techniques, quality improvements and others specific to particular sectors. Above all, output plans in physical terms (tons, square metres, etc.), with some breakdown in nomenclature, continued to be imposed as obligatory plan targets and the fulfilment of these targets was a precondition for payments into the incentive funds. The magnitude of the payments into these funds was based on a complex and supposedly stable set of rules, related in various ways to sales (*realizatsiya*), profits and/or profitability (*rentabel'nost'*). In fact the rules governing payments of these funds were repeatedly and arbitrarily altered.

Why did the 1965 reform develop (or rather fail to develop) in this way? The following reasons suggest themselves.

1   First and foremost, prices remained based upon what Soviet reformer critics call the *zatratnyi printsip*, that is, on costs, without reflecting demand, utility, or the relative scarcity of either inputs or outputs. The 1967 price reform did indeed eliminate loss-making sectors, but profitability varied greatly, especially with the passage of time, and the variation had no connection at all with use-value or shortage. Under these circumstances profits could not be used as rational indicator of effectiveness in any enterprise which could change its product mix.

2   There was in fact no serious move towards trade in means of production. Administrative allocation remained the rule, and so output and delivery plans were imposed in the usual way.

3   The economy continued (and continues) to operate in conditions of shortage, with all the resultant consequences. There is a 'seller's market', and this, plus the practice of tying customers to particular suppliers through the supply plan, provides good reasons for administrative rationing of resources.

4   It is unusual for plans to be either internally consistent or to be

drafted in time. Hence, frequent changes: 'in the course of one year, among only a part of the enterprises examined, there were 1,554 amendments to the production plan, and this without any changes in financial indicators'.[3] Under such circumstances there could be no stable plans. Indeed, numerous published statements attest to the fact that plans were altered not only because of unforeseen needs or shortages, but also to ensure that ministries could report that plans have been fulfilled; the successful were given extra tasks, sometimes a few weeks before the end of the year, and the less successful had their plans reduced. It was impossible for directors to have any confidence about what would be 'earned' for their incentive funds; the 'rules of the game' could be changed at any time, and the funds themselves were subject to arbitrary maxima.

It was hoped that the 1965 reform would discourage the concealing of productive potential, by increasing rewards if a plan were ambitious. This notion underlay the campaign to persuade enterprises to propose 'counter-plans' (vstrechnye plany); they were to be encouraged to propose a plan higher than the obligatory one, and would be rewarded even if the outcome were below the 'counter-plan', so long as they fulfilled the (lower) obligatory target. This, predictably, failed to make any impact. Plans were not only based 'on the achieved level'[4] but were the subject of argument and bargaining at the stage of their formulation and liable to alteration during the period of that currency, for reasons already explained. Obviously only a foolish manager would propose a 'counter-plan', since this would (and did) lead to an upward revision of the obligatory plan.

The same fate has befallen another well-meant effort to stimulate managerial initiative and to economize on labour. It is a notorious fact that labour is hoarded, for the same reason as materials (to keep a reserve against unexpected changes of plan or future need, and so on). To encourage the shedding of surplus labour the so-called Shchekino method was devised – an enterprise that reduced its labour-force, or operated additional productive capacity with the same labour-force, was to be entitled to keep the major part of the resultant economy in wages, for distribution to the remaining employees. However, the ministries have behaved as usual, arbitrarily changing the rules and in practice preventing enterprises from reaping the benefit from the economies they have achieved.

A source of repeated criticism is the practice, which was embodied in the price reform of 1967, of removing to the state budget the whole 'free remainder of profit' (svobodnyi ostatok prybili), which removed the incentive to increase profits, given the arbitrary changes in the rules governing the incentive funds, while at the same time also removing the impact of penalties (e.g. for non-fulfilment of contracts), since these are generally covered by that part of profits which would in any case be transferred to the state budget.

A considerable literature exists covering the petty restrictions on the decision-making process of directors. Yashkin[5] complains that he has to seek permission from the ministry about how to spend money allocated to the enterprise's incentive funds, though nominally they are within his decision-making competence; he describes the procedure as 'a marathon obstacle-race'. Then he is given annually a target for reducing administrative costs, which is often impossible. A limit is set even on travel expenses, a limit so severe that lengthy correspondence must frequently be undertaken to get the necessary permission to travel on business. He also complains bitterly that enterprises are punished for failing to produce goods which could not be produced because of the absence of the necessary materials, or because of an impossible plan.

We must now turn to the important and complex theme of the creation of *obyedineniya* (associations). The process had already begun in the 1960s, but a formal decision was taken in 1973 to base industry on *obyedineniya*. The process has been slow, but most of industry is now run on this basis, and the process of 'obyedeninizatiya' (to coin a phrase) should be complete by the start of the next five-year plan, but this is not by any means certain. As of 1 January 1980 there were 3,947 'production' *obyedineniya* in industry, containing 17,516 formerly separate enterprises, but only 147 were formed during the whole of 1979. In the Ministry of Light Industry, the 546 *obyedineniya* in existence produce 44 per cent of the total value of output of the ministry.[6] *Pravda* complained publicly of resistance and obstruction by those who regard the whole idea 'with scepticism'.[7]

What difference have *obyedineniya* made to directorial power? This should be the subject of a whole research project. I can indicate only some of the complications, and the inconclusive nature of the evidence.

Obyedineniya are of many different kinds, a fact which is in itself evidence of a flexible approach, but which makes generalization difficult. Some are all-union or republican, and these may sometimes replace the former ministerial *glavki*, and differ from them only by being on *khozraschyot*, that is, to possess a profit-and-loss account. The personnel may be the same, and the relationship with the ministry and with their subordinate directors may be unaltered, though no doubt it is possible that the more direct interest in financial results may affect the kind of instructions which are issued. Thus in the Ministry of Machinery for the oil and chemical industries the *glavki* have been replaced by ten all-union *khozraschyot obyedineniya*, one of which has its headquarters in Baku. Under them are thirty-five 'production' and five 'science-and-production' *obyedineniya*, except that some of the larger are directly under the ministry itself.[8] Other ministries make different arrangements.

The production associations (*proizvodstvennye obyedineniya*) and, in those cases in which they are linked with a research centre, the science-and-production (i.e. research-linked) associations, also vary immensely.

Some are a merger of small factories within a relatively small area, some have their production units spread over hundreds of miles and more, within or outside a given republic. Some relate to the final product (e.g. footwear, in an area), some to a process (e.g. spinning and weaving). Some very large enterprises have in effect achieved the status of *obyedineniya*, with some smaller units subordinated to them as *filialy*; this is the case, for instance, with the ZIL works and some large machinery factories.

Another very important distinction exists: namely, between those production *obyedineniya* within which 'enterprises' retain their separate existence under that name, with their own *khozraschyot*, legal personality and bank account, and those in which formerly separate enterprises become mere branch workshops. In January 1980, of the 17,516 enterprises which were merged into *obyedineniya*, 7,300 retained their separate identity.[9] There are instances of both types within the same *obyedineniya*: thus the Skorokhod Footwear Association, based in Leningrad and covering all north-west Russia, has treated its factories in Leningrad itself as workshops, but those outside the Leningrad area remain 'enterprises'. The press from time to time criticizes delays in creating *obyedineniya*, the small size of many of them, and the large number in certain areas and under certain ministries in which the enterprises retain their identity. In general, the very long and still incomplete nature of the re-organization is evidence of resistance, certainly within ministries and probably also in some localities; mergers which subordinate a factory in a town to an association with a headquarters in a different area cannot be in the interest of the local party's secretariat.

What has been the effect of all this on management and its role? What, furthermore, is likely to be the effect of the implementation of the 'reform' measures decreed in July 1979? It is very difficult indeed for any outsider to generalize about the internal relationships within any large organization, anywhere. Much necessarily depends on informal links and the human factor. One recalls the evidence deployed in the book by Andrle[10] based on his Birmingham doctoral dissertation. A Hungarian economist once remarked that, in even the most apparently centralized command system, 'most commands are written by their recipients'. It is one of the main contradictions of the Soviet economic system that, while on the one hand the task of subordinates is to obey plan instructions which supposedly embody the needs of society and the best means of providing for them, everyone in fact knows that much depends on the initiative, proposals and information (or the withholding of it) by or from management. Quality, punctual deliveries, technical progress, the details of the product mix (and the satisfaction of user needs) depend in practice on management. Paradoxically, the growth in the number of obligatory instructions and compulsory indicators may not reduce managerial freedom, since these instructions are bound, in the nature of things, to be contradictory, thus giving management a wider range of choice as to which instruction to obey. Breakdown in supply arrangements, rendered inevitable by the colossal scale of the task of the supply and production plan agencies, causes management to set up its own small workshops for self-supply, and to establish with other managers informal extra-legal links which become a parallel supply system, the scale of which is the subject of a great deal of guesswork. The large number of *tolkachi* has been the subject of repeated critical comment in the Soviet press, and the cause of the phenomenon is widely discussed. Some instructions are evaded. Thus the low pay of office staff and frequent orders to reduce their number can lead to the sort of phenomenon illustrated by a *Krokodil* cartoon: an elegant lady is typing and her boss says, 'She is a fine secretary, so I have classified her as an instrument mechanic of the fifth grade'.

The conversion of a *glavk* into an all-union *obyedineniye* should make little difference to the way in which central powers can be exercised, and it is intended not as an act of decentralization but as a streamlining of the control apparatus, giving it greater concern with financial results. But quite obviously the mergers affecting thousands of enterprises must reduce the powers of their directors, whether or not they formally retain that status. Instead of having a remote ministerial 'boss', they now find themselves under a super-manager who is much closer to them in function and geographically. It is one of the purposes of the change to empower the production *obyedineniye* to sub-allocate plan tasks, to promote specialization and indeed to issue instructions on a wide range of topics in its capacity as the hierarchical superior of the production units under its authority.

The all-union *obyedineniya* appear to lack powers *vis-à-vis* the ministry in some important respects. Thus the Soyuzreaktiv, with the Ministry of Chemical Industry, reports that it is 'not allowed to redistribute resources between production, disposals and research, it is not allowed to make agreements with outside research, experimental-construction and project-making organizations, machinery enterprises, etc.'. Similar problems arise in the science-production *obyedineniya* under Soyuzreaktiv such as Biokhimreaktiv, where the production and research sides are separately financed. Even the bonus rules and pay-rates of branches of management staff are different, and it is clear that it is not within the competence of the all-union body to alter them, since the paragraph ends with the words: 'to strengthen *khozraschyot* in the all-union-industrial and in the science-production *obyedineniya*, it is essential to increase the rights of their leaders'.[11]

What, therefore, are the powers of management of the production *obyedineniye* itself *vis-à-vis* its superiors? A number of complaints have been registered to the effect that the 'general directors' of *obyedineniya* have neither higher salaries nor greater powers than the common-or-garden directors.[12] Indeed, one motive and effect of their creation is to reduce the number of units which the central organs administer, and this could give them more time to issue orders. Other things being equal, it seems reasonable to surmise that the net effect of the creation of *obyedineniya* is to strengthen the powers of the central organs, of Gosplan, the ministries and the all-union *obyedineniya*, the latter seen as ministerial sub-units. This can be only a preliminary judgement, however; there is much research to be done.

A great deal depends on the organization of supply, and on certain potential effects of the July 1979 reform. I shall discuss the latter later, and deal now with the supply question. Its vital importance is obvious, from the standpoint both of the smooth functioning of the process of production and of the effective powers of management. Nothing can be produced without inputs and, if these are 'rationed' by the supply organs, nothing can be produced unless and until they authorize the necessary supplies. As already mentioned, 'trade' in the means of production remains insignificant, but much has been said and written about 'long-term direct links'. As far as can be determined, these links are under the authority of the supply agencies. In other words, they do not, as a rule, arise from the free decisions of those concerned. A is attached to B as a supplier, with negotiations only concerning detailed specifications and timing. The links are long term if the planning agencies decide that they be so: that is, A is to supply B with material X for several years. In practice these links can be disrupted as and when the planning or ministerial authorities consider it necessary to do so. There seems no fundamental change here. Far more stress is laid on the fulfilment of delivery obligations, but that raises another very important question – how to enforce such obligations – which I will not go into in this essay.

Now let us turn to the reform of July 1979, and to its possible consequences (in the aspects relevant to the present study). It is laid down that the role of the actual production units in the formulation of plans be enhanced; plans be balanced (i.e. the necessary inputs should be available); plans be stable for five years ahead (the five-year plan be split into five annual plans); and various 'norms' be stable too. These 'norms' are to include those governing the rules for incentive funds, a fixed relationship between net output and the wages fund, and for retention of profits (with the residual profits no longer being automatically transferred to the state budget). These measures seem, on the face of it, to be steps in the direction of increasing managerial functions. However, apart from the large number of compulsory plan-indicators, of which more later, this part of the reform document suffers from vagueness; certainly plans should be drafted in consultation with those who carry them out, undoubtedly output is impossible without the needed inputs, and plans and norms should be stable and should not be frequently altered, but have we not heard all this before? Why should we expect any change now? Thus plans are not stable because unforeseen circumstances and emergent shortages compel a change. Indeed it would be absurd to have stable (inflexible) plans for five years ahead, unless one were to assume perfect foresight and no uncertainty. (The better mathematical planning models describe themselves explicitly as of a 'stochastic' character, and rightly so.) Of course, if inputs (and outputs too) became less scarce, if shortages became less pervasive, there would be less need for 'rationing', a better chance for stable norms actually to be stable. But here again there have been declarations of good intention before. Did not Brezhnev declare at the Twenty-Fourth Party Congress that consumers' goods output should rise faster than incomes, so as to diminish shortages, and did not the opposite occur? He might well repeat this declaration at the Twenty-Sixth Congress in February 1981.

The revised and consolidated list of plan indicators, contained in the July 1979 decree, must be seen as a move towards greater *centralization*. The emphasis is *less* on profits and monetary aggregates relative to the financial performance of the production unit. There appears to be an increase in the number of centrally planned and allocated products and in the number of imposed targets of various kinds. Thus, for instance, there will be an increase in detailed planned nomenclature of machinery, and 'there will be an expansion in the number of compulsory indicators for technical improvements'.[13] While plan indicators will vary in different branches, and only a limited number will be used in determining payments into incentive funds, the following are mentioned in explanatory articles in the specialized press, and/or in the decree itself as subjects of obligatory targets and plans (though doubtless not all at once in every sector): physical output for principal items of output (sometimes corrected by coefficients to take quality into account); the carrying out of principal delivery obligations; labour productivity; increase in the volume of sales; numbers of workers and employees; percentage reduction in un-mechanized hand labour; percentage reduction in utilization of materials and fuel; profitability; cost reduction; relationship between net output and the wages bill; proportion of goods of first quality; introduction of new techniques; payments into the state budget; various targets connected with investments.

A decision published in *Ekonomicheskaya gazeta*[14] recommends that no more than two or three indicators should be used in determining payments into the incentive funds, but ministries are clearly given the right to issue obligatory orders on other matters, not necessarily included in the above list. Thus, for instance, factories in the chemical industry are given a plan for increasing the range of their products (which they sometimes fulfil by literally producing a few grammes of something new even if the customer wants much more than this!).[15] All the evidence suggests that control over enterprises will be tightened. This is true both of the *vstrechnye plany* and of decentralized investments, both of which are now to be included in the central plan. The motive is apparently to ensure the necessary material supplies and to reduce unpredictable demands on resources. Every production unit has to have a so-called 'passport', giving full details of its capacity, to facilitate the task of the central organs controlling it.

Labour productivity and the wages bill are to be calculated by reference to normed value-added, or net output. But note the word 'normed'. The calculation is vastly complex, and many articles have been devoted to explaining it. The essential point is that it is a *notional* sum made up of notional labour costs and profits, based upon sectoral averages, and not the actual costs and profits of the actual production unit. This introduces a contradiction to the basis of *khozraschyot*, which, surely, implies an emphasis on *actual* costs and profits, and some very odd relationships between the notional and the actual are bound to emerge, as for instance when producing more of product X increases 'normed' net output but in fact adds to costs and reduces profits. The price reform now being undertaken is being used to calculate net product norms for millions of products, along with their new prices.

In his comment on the reform Baibakov claimed that, as a result, differences in profitability lose their influence on the product mix.[16] This is supposedly to be based on contractual obligations, imposed or confirmed by the supply organs, but, for familiar reasons, no plan can possibly be fully disaggregated, and, under the prevailing conditions of a seller's market, with the role of profitability diminished, it is hard to see how the new system can be made to respond adequately to user requirements. Surely, in the words of the economist Kheinman, 'there must be created the conditions which guarantee the user *freedom of choice*, thereby compelling the producer to improve and modernize his product'.[17] He refers to the words of the decree of July 1979 that speak of the need for adequate reserves, and hopes that there will be no more 'planned deficits' in inputs in relation to output plans. But what meaning has 'freedom of choice' if one is attached to one supplier by the plan, and there is no provision for making it worth the producer's while to satisfy demand?[18]

Finally, I return to the vital question of prices. Effective decentralization, which in the view of many far-sighted Soviet reformers is an indispensable precondition for efficiency, can be based only upon a price system which reflects economic reality, namely, scarcity, need, use-value, and so on. There is a sizeable literature on this, a good deal of which is related to mathematical programming and optimization. It is quite clear that the new prices which will be fully operative in 1982 will be based upon traditional cost-plus. The evidence is contained, *inter alia*, in two articles, one by Glushkov, the chairman of the Prices Committee,[19] and the other by Yakovets.[20] There are, it is true, certain improvements. Thus prices have been raised to eliminate losses in the coal and timber industries, and certain charges have been more fully included in costs and prices, among them social insurance contributions, timber-cutting levy, charges for the use of water, geological prospecting, and so on. The idea is for costs to express social cost more fully, with some reduction in profit margins. In addition, some measures have been taken to provide for higher prices for better quality. However, it is clear that prices are intended to be fixed for at least the quinquennium. Then, the article by Yakovets appears to imply that while 'sector norms of profitability' will continue to be based on the value of basic funds, the percentage varying by sector, 'profits of specific products will be included in normed net output proportionately to cost of processing'.[21] It is not too clear to me just what this will mean, but it certainly does not mean that prices are intended to have any significant influence on choice at managerial level, choice of either output or inputs; and, of course, by being fixed for many years on end, prices will not be flexible.

This reform will hardly touch the basic ills from which the system is suffering and which are linked directly and indirectly to overcentralization. There is much discussion at present on 'planning by complexes', and experiments have been undertaken in the setting up of territorial production administrations. This may overcome one of the least satisfactory features of the *obyedineniya*; these are still, in the main, within ministries and so they cannot overcome the disease of 'departmentalism'. One must bear in mind that a very large number of items, especially machinery, components and consumer durables, are made in factories under the control of numerous ministries. Thus, materials-handling equipment is made in factories under the control of more than thirty ministries, and manufacture of components, forgings and castings is almost universal. Ministerial self-sufficiency, and the resultant loss of economies of scale, is the subject of sharply critical comment in the already-cited article by Kheinman. The reform of July 1979 envisages the designation of particular ministries as principals for the production of items made by many ministries, but how can this – and the territorial complexes – be fitted into a structure in which ministries are the sources or channels of plans, finance, materials allocation and investment funds? Furthermore, many enterprises and *obyedineniya* make a large number of different products which are also made elsewhere under other ministries. A considerable shake-up of the ministerial form of control over industry may be imminent.

Notes: Chapter 10

1 G. Schroeder, 'The Soviet economy on a treadmill of reform', in *The Soviet Economy in a Time of Change*, Vol. 1 (Washington, DC: Joint Economic Committee of the US Congress, 1979).

2 *Pravda*, 12 November 1973.

3 A. Aganbegyan, in ibid.

4 See I. Birman, 'From the achieved level', *Soviet Studies*, vol. 30, no. 2 (April 1978), pp. 153–72.

5 I. Yashkin, in *Pravda*, 1 November 1979.

6 *Ekonomicheskaya gazeta*, 1980, no. 28, pp. 12–13.

7 *Pravda*, 14 September 1979.

8 *Ekonomicheskaya gazeta*, 1980, no. 28, p. 12.

9 loc. cit.

10 V. Andrle, *Managerial Power in the Soviet Union* (Farnborough: Saxon House, 1976).

11 *Planovoye khozyaistvo*, 1980, no. 6, p. 30.

12 Evidence cited in A. Nove, *The Soviet Economic System* (London: Allen & Unwin, 1977), pp. 82–3.

13 *Ekonomicheskaya gazeta*, 1979, no. 33, p. 3.

14 ibid., 1980, no. 28, p. 11.

15 *Planvoye khozyaistvo*, 1980, no. 6, p. 30.

16 *Pravda*, 22 August 1979.

17 S. A. Kheinman, *Ekonomika i organizatsiya promyshlennogo proizvodstva*, 1980, no. 5, p. 39.

18 The articles in ibid., 1980, nos 5 and 6, by Kheinman are interesting and should be required reading.

19 N. Glushkov, *Planovoye khozyaistvo*, 1980, no. 6.

20 Y. Yakovets, *Voprosy ekonomiki*, 1980, no. 6.

21 ibid., p. 16 and p. 18.

11   *The economic problems of Brezhnev's successors*

This was originally published in *Washington Papers* (Center for Strategic and International Studies, Georgetown University), vol. 6 (1978), pp. 59–72, and was written in 1977. It is interesting and instructive to compare it with the 'leaked' memorandum written by Academician T. Zaslavskaya, whom I evidently ought to have included in my imaginary committee. Not very surprisingly, there are similarities, because the many criticisms published in the Soviet Union formed the basis of the 'committee's' report. There is no doubt that Gorbachev has had placed before him a similar diagnosis and at least some of the proposed reforms. He has shown himself well aware of the need for *systemic* change: 'the historical fate of our country, and the position of socialism in the contemporary world, depend in large measure on how we will now act' (*Pravda*, 24 April 1985). However, at the time of writing the signs are that the measures being taken will be partial, and quite possibly self-defeating. Thus no amount of exhortation and bonus schemes to improve technology and quality and to encourage managerial initiative can be effective so long as material allocation is bureaucratically administered and prices are uninfluenced by supply and demand. It would be surprising of Gorbachev or his more intelligent advisers were unaware of this, and it is possible that major restructuring of the planning system will be put before the party congress due to meet in February 1986. Yet the obstacles to systemic change still look formidable.

Let us imagine a report to Brezhnev's successor, written by a committee consisting of such influential but critical economists as A. Aganbegyan, S. Shatalin, D. Valovoy and V. Krasovsky, whom we will assume have been appointed for just such a purpose.

(Imaginary) report by (imaginary) committee

DIAGNOSIS
Growth rates have been falling, according to the official statistics, and it must be admitted that our official figures tend to overstate the real rate of growth, because the price index used to 'deflate' the rouble totals under-

states the real increase in prices. This is due to the introduction of new products at higher prices: for example, 'new equipment delivered to enterprises is usually 3–5 times dearer, or more, than the analogous old equipment, while its technological productivity is only 1·5–2·5 times higher, which causes a fall in the rate of return [*fondo-otdacha*] . . . which is one of the basic reasons why enterprises delay technological reconstruction and put off entering the new equipment in their accounts'.[1] The current five-year plan envisaged some decline in growth, but even the official figures show that we will not fulfil it, in terms of national income or industrial or agricultural production. Quite clearly the plan will not be fulfilled for such key commodities as electric power, steel, timber, paper, chemicals and most kinds of machinery, as well as for textiles and consumer durables. Of course we still *do* grow, unlike some capitalist countries in the grip of crisis, but the quantitative results have been disappointing.

Efficiency has not been rising. As the late Comrade Brezhnev and Comrade Baibakov had said, this *must* be a quinquennium of quality and effectiveness to make up for the inevitable slowdown in the rate of increase of the labour-force, and also the small increase in total investments which the plan provided for through 1980. We have not found the means of encouraging quality or the production of *use*-values (as against global statistics in tons or roubles). The diffusion of technical progress remains too slow, the machinery is too often obsolete and high-cost. Far too often the product mix and deliveries do not conform to the needs of industry or of the citizen. Nor have we been able to discourage the various forms of waste which a member of this committee (D. Valovoy) has vividly described in *Pravda*. Too much metal, fuel and other materials are used up, in manufacture and in construction, and those who do this are rewarded by the perverse working of our incentive and success indicator system. Repeated attempts to remedy these faults, and to stop the chronic over-commitment of investment resources to too many projects, have not been successful. Costs are rising, as may be seen from the steady fall in industrial profitability (from 20·5 per cent in 1970 to 14·4 per cent in 1976, expressed as a percentage of capital assets).

Agriculture has failed to free us of dependence on imports from the West, and this has contributed to the large size of the hard-currency payments deficit. Progress there has been, but the cost has been grossly excessive. Agriculture has absorbed 26 per cent of total investment, and the subsidy for livestock products is huge and rising (yet we do not dare increase the excessively low retail prices of meat). Mechanization has been incomplete and of poor quality, and labour has not been efficiently used. Every year we have to mobilize millions of townspeople to help with the harvest, thereby disrupting urban industries and education, and even our armed forces have to contribute millions of man-hours. We thus demonstrate to the world our inefficiency. This is highly embarrassing; it is a poor advertisement for our system. There is also a chronic shortage of skilled labour in rural areas, adversely affecting maintenance and repair. Fertilizer is much more abundant than ten years ago, but is frequently misapplied. Vegetables, fruit and other perishables cannot reach the consumers in sufficient quantity because of bad organization and lack of transport, storage and packaging.

Distribution is often to blame for *frequent shortages*, but equally to blame is the planning system itself, which fails to link producers with requirements. Complaints from citizens have been increasing. The existence of black markets, bribery, a growing gap between official and free market prices of food, the very large increase in cash savings, all show that hidden inflationary pressures are strong. As Comrade Smirnov pointed out,[2] even if we fulfil the 1978 plan, output of industrial consumer goods will have risen by 11·9 per cent in the three years from 1976 to 1978, against the original plan of 14·1 per cent. There is also much amiss in respect to quality.

Defence requirements are an important contributory cause of shortages and inefficiencies, as they absorb the best managers, labour and materials, and almost half the output of the machinery and engineering industries.

Planning and administration still cause grave problems. Reforms have been half-hearted and have not resulted in any radical change. The central organs are still overloaded with the impossible task of issuing orders on current output and allocation of materials to thousands of productive units. Prices remain in a state of confusion, and inevitably so when there are 12 million products to be priced. How can we expect Comrade Glushkov and his Prices Committee to cope? The *obyedineniya* ('corporations') have insufficient powers, and neither the ministries nor the regional party officials seem prepared to relinquish their powers. There must be fundamental rethinking about planning methods, for many of our inefficiencies stem from the persistence of old ways of controlling from the centre of those things the centre is unable to control effectively.

Finally, our *foreign economic relations* are not satisfactory. Fine resolutions about Comecon integration are put into effect at a slow pace, bilateralism persists, and our Comecon allies drag their feet and (like the Poles) ask us for help instead of putting their house in order. As for our deficit with the West, and the debt burden, we cannot rely so heavily on exports of fuel and raw materials, which are badly needed in our own country, and yet we seem unable to expand exports of manufacturers, and our trade pattern is still that of any underdeveloped country. Some Western commentators exaggerate the extent of our dependence on Western technology and the 'leverage' that it supposedly gives them. But the fact remains that we would be stronger *vis-à-vis* our Western rivals if we could improve the quality of our own machinery output and cover our needs for grain. It is also a source of concern that we, the world's second industrial power, cannot exercise *economic* power even in such backward areas as Africa, and must depend so much on *arms* exports to maintain influence there. Greater economic efficiency is vital for its impact on our foreign relations and on the worldwide power and impact of the USSR. True, we appear to have a large trading surplus with the less developed countries (over 2·3 billion roubles in 1977), but this mainly consists of arms sales for which we are seldom paid in convertible currency.

POLICY OBJECTIVES

There are several objectives which we *must* pursue. Disagreements concern the efficacy of various remedies to the ills outlined above, the priority of the various objectives, and the trade-offs between them (the pursuit of certain objectives, e.g. the concentration of the best resources in the defence industries or effective controls over incomes and prices, must be at the expense of others, e.g. the improvement in the quality of civilian machinery or greater reliance on a flexible market mechanism).

The agreed objectives are as follows:

(1)   Much greater efficiency, more rapid technical progress, much less waste and much better links between producer and user are required, with rewards to producers related to the *result* of their activities. Imbalances and inconsistencies in plans must be eliminated.

(2)   Shortages are a dangerous source of discontent. It is essential for security and order to improve supplies to the population. In this matter, we are impermissibly far behind the Czechs and Hungarians, and even the Poles.

(3)   All this is to be achieved while maintaining the priority of the defence industries, avoiding inflation and wage explosions.

(4)   It is essential to develop speedily the mineral resources of Siberia, which have such tremendous potential. This also has a most important political aspect: China. Oil and gas are particularly vital for our economy and for export.

(5)   It is essential to redeploy the labour force, which is at present both regionally and sectorally unbalanced. Thus, Siberia is short of labour, while the Central Asian republics are overpopulated and have a high birth-rate – in contrast to the low birth-rate in European Russia.

(6)   Comecon integration must develop further and faster.

(7)   Relations with the capitalist countries must be carefully reconsidered, in the light of policy choices to be discussed below.

POLICY ALTERNATIVES AND RECOMMENDATIONS

Let us look at these matters in greater detail.

The most difficult is *efficiency*. Essentially, there are two schools of thought on this issue. One aims at *streamlining the existing centralized system,* eliminating its rigidities and distortions. The planning mechanism could still operate on the existing principles, but improvement in organization of decision-making and in incentives to management would make it work better, with computers and programming used to 'save' central planning. The other is to change the system in fundamental ways. Your committee is of the opinion that the first of these two approaches leads nowhere, briefly for the following reasons. The errors and distortions of centralized planning arise essentially not from human stupidity or organizational inadequacies, but because micro-economic control from the centre cannot of its nature be efficiently carried out, despite computerization. Bureaucratic fragmentation, conflicts, inconsistencies and waste are inescapable, unless the path of radical reform is chosen. One can see this vividly in the (unsuccessful) attempts to devise a 'net output' or 'value-added' indicator.

Some non-economist comrades may not understand this last point, so let us spell it out. Strong criticism has been directed at the 'gross output' indicator, because it includes in plan fulfilment statistics the value of inputs. The 'sales' indicator suffers from the same defect. Therefore, enterprise management is in effect rewarded for producing goods using expensive materials. This takes the form both of trying to persuade the planners to include high-cost materials in the supply plan and in the selling price, and also of choosing a product mix containing the more expensive materials relative to the value added at the factory. Matters are even worse where the plan itself is expressed in quantity of work done, as in the building industry or in transport. Economy is penalized, as the plan is then not fulfilled. As has been repeatedly pointed out, we need to achieve results with a *minimum* expenditure of intermediate goods and services, yet we discourage economy in them.

Evidently, a possible solution is to base enterprise plans on *net* output, or value added, calculated by subtracting material inputs. The effect can be illustrated as follows:

	Cost of materials, etc.	Cost of labour	Profit margin	Price
Good X	100	20	10	130
Good Y	60	25	8	93

Under our existing system, it would clearly pay the enterprise to produce good X, although the value added (labour cost plus profit) is higher in the case of good Y. If we switch to a *net* output indicator it will 'pay' to produce good Y. But do we necessarily need to move from a material-intensive to a labour-intensive product mix? Labour is also short. In any case, what we need is to produce goods X *and* Y *in the proportions needed by our economy and society*. One method would produce too much of

X, the other too much of Y; neither ensures the needed proportions. There are also grave problems in the way of calculating net output of any particular product; thus, what share of the overhead and of the profits is attributable to this product when a factory may make many others? This has driven our economists and statisticians to concoct complex methods of calculation of 'normed' net output, i.e. in effect requiring the calculation of what the net output in each instance should be. For clearly the indicator must not be such as to reward the amount of work actually done at the factory, since some of it could be wasteful or unnecessary.

These problems illustrate the impossibility of devising output and plan-fulfilment indicators that would be free of serious defects. What we need is to produce and supply what the users actually require, in the most efficient and economical way. If anyone can devise ways of achieving this objective without the sort of changes that we are about to recommend, we can only urge that these alternative ideas be put forward to the Central Committee as quickly as possible.

The essential features of any effective reform would be as follows:

(1)   Abandon the central 'directive' planning of current output. No more output targets in roubles, tons, square metres, and so on. Management should determine this in negotiation with its customers (other enterprises, the trade network, etc.).

(2)   As a necessary corollary, abolish the system of administrative material allocation, with much more *trade* in means of production, as was indeed intended in the 1965 reform.

(3)   Reorganize the price system to eliminate (except when deliberately subsidized) loss-making and excessively profitable activities, so that what is needed is profitable to produce. As the necessary flexibility cannot be achieved with universal price control, move as soon as possible to decontrol of a large proportion of prices. A precondition of this is the elimination of the hidden inflationary pressures that exist at present. Some comrades say: but if we free prices, they will rise, and then we have inflation, and also the diversion of effort to produce those items whose prices are not controlled. This danger would be real indeed if there is excess demand; however, our Hungarian comrades have shown that a sound incomes, credit and price policy can prevent these consequences. Many Hungarian prices have been decontrolled (and this applies to producer goods and consumer goods) without any major price rises, and indeed in Hungary (unlike the USSR) there is no appreciable difference in prices between state shops and the free peasant market.

(4)   Rely more on the profit motive, while simultaneously ensuring, by progressive taxation, that excessive income inequalities do not result.

(5)   Encourage enterprise and competition, realizing that without competition the profit motive and market forces can produce perverse results. Allow producers' co-operatives to be formed to fill the many gaps

that exist in supplies, both of specialized equipment and components and of a variety of consumer goods, of types to which small-scale production is often particularly well suited. Cease treating would-be enterpreneurs as speculator-criminals, by providing an avenue for their legitimate (controlled and taxed) activities, which are now frustrated.

(6) To encourage technical progress, we must:

(a) devise means of encouraging risk-taking by management;

(b) relate designs of new machines more closely to the needs of users, and enable the latter to pay more for improved designs;

(c) encourage competition between design bureaux, such as has for long benefited the aircraft industry;

(d) stop obstructing innovation, by freeing management from the need for allocation certificates, permits, price authorizations, etc.;

(e) allow much greater scope for obtaining bank credits for small and medium-scale investments.

(7) Encourage labour to move, while eliminating the many instances of overmanning. Unemployment must be avoided, but not at the cost of inefficient under-employment. Workers must be convinced that redeployment of labour plus higher productivity has a quick effect on living standards, and that higher real wages are inconsistent with total security of employment in their existing jobs and locations. Otherwise, how can we cope with the labour problems of Siberia?

Some comrades may say: this is an attack on planning. Surely (they might argue), you do not believe the recent experience of Western countries gives ground for having much faith in market forces? And what of the doctrines of Marx and Lenin, who looked forward to the day when commodity production would disappear? We would answer as follows. First, we do not attack planning, which is necessary indeed, but which should relate primarily to the creation of new productive capacity, i.e. to large investments, which affect the structure of our industry and our society. Thus, for example, we rightly plan at the centre the fuel policy of our country, rightly decide at the centre to expand oil production in Siberia, to make major efforts in the field of nuclear power generation, to build long-distance electricity transmission lines, and so on. Compare this with the flounderings of President Carter in relation to energy policy. But we must recognize that we cannot plan centrally the product mix of footwear, or the production and supply of carburettors and pins, by existing production units. Our attempts to do so are simply self-defeating. To recognize reality cannot be contrary to the ideas of our revered teachers, Marx and Lenin. Under full communism, no doubt, there will be no commodity production, no money, no profits, no wages, no state (even no party), but until that day comes we must use the economic mechanisms and incentives relevant to our existing stage of development, which we all now call 'mature socialism.'

Better living standards are evidently linked with the elimination of *shortages* of goods and services for the citizens. Monetary incentives are ineffective unless people can buy what they want (unless it is vodka, pornography and American pop records, of course). Supply-and-demand balance is impossible unless some prices are increased. This is particularly clear in the case of meat, where the huge subsidy maintains a price at which demand cannot possibly be met. Negative phenomena associated with a sellers' market also must be overcome by a rise in output of a wide range of goods and with improvements in quality, achieved (we hope) as a result of greater reliance on market and incentives on the lines of our 'efficiency' proposals. We appreciate the initial unpopularity of price increases, and would recommend that they be linked with some rise in minimum wages *and* an increase in supplies, so that people can see that higher prices mean better goods more freely available.

Given a policy that will exclude excess demand, there is no reason to fear that supplies to the military sector will be affected. Comrade Ustinov should not worry, but we fear he will. It is necessary to persuade the military that a healthier, more productive, more innovative economy is *also* an important aspect of Soviet power in the world. Of course, much could be gained from economies in military expenditure, but this raises issues wider than we can discuss.

Siberian development and labour deployment are linked issues. So are labour redeployment and the more rational use of labour in agriculture. It is astonishing, with so high a proportion of the people engaged in agriculture, that, as we have said, we still have to 'import' labour from the towns, and mobilize the army, to get the harvest in. Cautious experiments with small autonomous work-teams have shown what can be done if courage is shown in introducing these new methods, which increase productivity and save labour (problems and tensions are also caused, but progress without problems and tensions is not possible). Another source of Siberian workers is the Central Asian republics. The natives are attached to their way of life and language, and a bold solution would be to set up townships in Siberian industrial areas as Central Asian enclaves. (This was done in France with Polish miners, who lived in Polish settlements; Comrade Gierek was one of them.)

Long-term credits and technical aid from Japan would be of great help in eastern Siberia. Surely, Comrade Gromyko should look again at the intransigent attitude shown to Japan over the Kurile Islands, which, apart from discouraging Japanese participation in Siberian investments, is encouraging Japan to collaborate with China. The worsening of relations with the United States has its negative economic aspects, and we trust that those who advise a tough policy in Africa and elsewhere are aware of them. On economic grounds, we would urge increasing and deepening the worldwide division of labour, and with it the interdependence of East and West. However, since East–West trade plays a bigger role for the East than it does for the West, interdependence could be dangerous if, with a worsening international climate, the West chooses to use selective economic pressure, which could cause the economy serious damage. So, if the international barometer shows unsettled or stormy weather, caution may be the appropriate attitude. The contradictions and confusions of the Western capitalist economies can affect policy in several potentially conflicting ways. On the one hand, capitalists seeking orders at a time of recession will be generous with offers of credits. On the other, protectionist tendencies will grow, and this, plus business stagnation, will inhibit Soviet exports. Political instability in the West could yield dividends, but could also result in a dangerous lurch to the extreme right.

Finally, Comecon. We would like to express support for those (like our Hungarian comrades) who wish to liberalize intra-Comecon trade, to get away from bilateral quotas, to achieve meaningful currency convertibility, to align prices and exchange rates to relative scarcities and costs, and to encourage integration on the basis of an 'Eastern' common market. The same principles of competition and greater freedom to decide what to produce by negotiation with customers, which are part of our recommendation for the USSR's own economy, will do much to improve Comecon's performance. We must cease the practice of bartering second-rate goods with one another. Integration through supranational centralized planning will not work effectively – though no doubt there is scope for joint investments and international specialization agreements for particular industries.

Here the imaginary report and recommendations end. As matters now stand, they would be rejected, the committee members who drafted them would be thanked and sent back to their respective institutions, and a more amenable committee appointed instead (imaginary membership: E. Kapustin, A. Boyarsky, N. Drogichinsky and N. Bunich). This committee would stress the risks of radical change (which do exist), the advantages of having centrally imposed priorities, the ideological heresy of relying too much on markets and (worse!) competition, the dangers of relaxing price control, and the existence of still unrealized opportunities of improving the traditional system.

They would have some powerful arguments to deploy. The logic of the 'radical' committee's recommendations would be to challenge many received ideas, to tread not only on ideological corns but also on a whole complex of vested interests. The party-state machine, at the centre and in the localities, is engaged in running the economy and in correcting as best it can the many distortions and shortages generated by the centralized system. A Moscow satirical theatre once put on a sketch (which I saw) in which a petty official said: 'Comrades, shortages have made me who I am, shortages make me a person of substance and influence; so, comrades, what we want is shortages.' No one, of course, could openly advocate inefficiency for self-seeking purposes, but the instinctive feelings of the entire control apparatus must be hostile to changes that would affect adversely their status and career prospects. These instinctive feelings would surely be reinforced by the fact that the sort of solution envisaged by the 'radicals' does raise many very real problems. The conservative committee would list them, and do so quite sincerely. It is no easy matter to combine the advantages of centralization (which exist for some sectors and some categories of decision) with those of decentralized flexibility. It is easy to say, 'control the big, the macro, and let the micro take care of itself,' when, adapting a Scots saying, many a micro makes a macro. The techniques of indirect control, of regulating a market, are difficult and (in the USSR) untried. If controls are relaxed, might there not be chaos? Would prices not rise, would not some managers make large and un-deserved bonuses by 'playing the market', would there not be dangers of inflation and a threat to supplies and production in key strategic sectors, including the military? Would the workers tolerate a lessening of their security of employment?

As for ideology, the present atmosphere of dreary conformism would have to change before a man such as Aganbegyan would be appointed to head my imaginary committee. Let me stress at this point that not only is the committee imaginary, but so (to a considerable extent) are the opinions which I have arbitrarily ascribed to its members. No doubt several of them would indignantly deny the view I have ascribed to them, and so perhaps it would have been better if I had called them Bushkin, Kukush-kin, Lozhkin and Vilkin – in other words, imaginary comrades as well as an imaginary committee. All I wished to convey is that there certainly exist some Soviet economists (not necessarily the ones I have named) who think along the lines indicated. Their chances of having much influence are not large, unless the change of leadership produces a new situation, which at present seems unlikely.

So, unless one of Brezhnev's successors deliberately nails the flag of radical reform to his mast, the strong combination of state planners, ministerial officials, Central Committee and regional party officials, the military-industrial complex and the hard-line ideologists will be much too powerful, and conservatism will win. Of course, measures *will* be taken to develop Siberia, to improve investment decisions and planning tech-niques, to discourage waste, to encourage innovation. Quality, effectiveness, rewarding management for satisfying social need (as distinct from producing for plan-fulfilment statistics), these are all declared party objectives. The problem is, can they be reached without the sort of radical changes that challenge the traditional forms of party domination and central control, and that introduce new, risky expedients which could have unpredictable results?

The most likely outcome is that the post-Brezhnev leadership will adopt cautious recommendations and ignore the more radical ones – so much so that the more radical reformers would not be members of the advisory committee in the first place, or, if they were, they would consider it pointless to make recommendations for radical reform. The leadership will probably listen to those of the 'mathematicians' (like N. Fedorenko) who claim that streamlined centralization can work if computers are more systematically utilized. It may take several more years for them to appreciate (as the more reform-minded mathematicians have appreciated long ago) that microeconomic decentralization (to a 'controlled market mechanism' *à l'hongroise*) is a precondition for the application of computerized programming on a manageable scale. *Note*: Gorbachev has put forward some radical proposals to the 27th party congress in February 1986, and Aganbegyan is said to be one of his principal advisors!

Notes: Chapter 11

1 *Planovoye khozyaistvo*, 1978, no. 1, p. 59.
2 *Planovoye khozyaistvo*, 1978, no. 5, p. 19.

PART FOUR

Politics and Law

12 Some aspects of Soviet constitutional theory

I must admit that the inclusion of this essay is in part a sort of sentimental indulgence. I had just left the army and this, in 1947, was my first attempt at serious academic writing. It was published by the *Modern Law Review*, vol. 12, no. 1 (January 1949), pp. 12–36. It began as a review of Vyshinsky's book, and expanded when other sources came to light. It may none the less still be of interest for several reasons. First, it analyses details of the so-called 'Stalin' Constitution, which was replaced only a few years ago. Secondly, it shows what sort of impact the reading of Soviet constitutional materials and texts made in the late 1940s on a rather sceptical but also somewhat imperfectly informed reader. It now seems to me that I devoted unnecessarily close attention to the formal structure, but the text does show that I was properly sceptical as to its real significance. At the same time, recent work has emphasized the paradox that the same Vyshinsky who prosecuted in the notorious Moscow trials of the 1930s also played an important role in trying to strengthen legal norms and procedures. It is as if, as an old professional lawyer, he wished Stalinist arbitrariness to observe codified rules. In fact there were (and are) many examples not only of blatant illegality but also of precise observance of protocol. As will be seen, I did not fail to mention the centralized and dominant role of the party, and that it 'controlled all important appointments', but would have said more about the *nomenklatura* system had I known more about it.

The new Constitution differs in some (not many) respects from the old, and the tone and style of Soviet commentaries on constitutional law are now more moderate and scholary (see, for instance, the excellent survey of Soviet political science by Archie Brown in Neil Harding, ed., *The State in Socialist Society*, London: St Antony's/Macmillan, 1984). It must be stressed that the powers of the secret police (the KGB) have been much diminished; they are no longer entitled to arrest and deport without trial, and there are no 'Special Councils' with powers to isolate anyone thought to be socially dangerous. It seems also, from many subsequently published memoirs, that those arrested under Article 58 of the Criminal Code were in practice often sentenced without any trial at all, and here too the change is one of substance. Article 58 no longer exists in its old form, but there are other provisions to deal with dissidents through the courts. The compulsory move of Sakharov to Gorki seems to be an example of a recurrence of the practice of administrative exile, but it does seem that there is usually a trial, even if the outcome is politically determined. Penalties are much less severe. Since 1954 no one has been executed for a political offence, and party leaders who fall from grace are allowed to retire peacefully, in contrast with such blood-letting as the so-called Leningrad affair (1949–50) which saw the execution of Voznesensky and the entire Leningrad party leadership. There are now far fewer political prisoners, but conditions in detention camps are harsh.

Other reforms introduced since 1947 and worth noting are the elimination of tuition fees in secondary and higher education, and of the decrees adopted in 1940 making lateness and absenteeism subject to criminal penalties. It would be interesting to discover whether the rules on duplicators cited below are still operative and have been extended to cover Xerox and other 'reproducing' equipment. I have been unable to discover any source referring to the subject more recently than 1946. One of the notes (82) refers to the fact that the Yevtikhiev and Vlasov book, from which the quotation on duplicators is taken, was criticized and was to be rewritten. So it was, with such details as these omitted!

1   The purposes of the Soviet State machine

It is a common failing of both friends and enemies of the USSR to apply to Soviet institutions criteria of judgement which are quite irrelevant, both to the avowed purpose of these institutions and to their actual functioning. The aim of this essay is to examine the structure of, and the theories behind, the Soviet system of government, as these are viewed by Soviet constitutional theorists.[1]

It is impossible to appreciate Soviet ideas on the state, law, or justice without some knowledge of the Marxist-Leninist terminology which all Soviet lawyers employ. This is no place for a general discussion of Marxist theory, so it will suffice to state simply that the following concepts are accepted as axiomatic by Soviet theorists in this field:

(a) 'The state always has been, and is, a coercive apparatus, with the help of which the ruling classes impose obedience on their "subjects".'[2] So long as capitalism survives, 'the exploiting classes need political rule in order to maintain exploitation, i.e. the selfish interests of an insignificant minority against the vast majority of the people'[3] and, indeed, 'the more democratic [the capitalist state is], the cruder, the more cynical is this capitalist rule'.[4] While the limited rights of the people under capitalist democracy make it worth defending against fascism, 'this, however, in no way weakens the description of *any* bourgeois stage . . . as an apparatus for the suppression and oppression of the toiling masses'.[5]

(b) The Soviet state, too, is an instrument of suppression, of 'dictatorship', wielded by the working class in alliance with the peasantry, i.e. by and in the interests of the mass of the people, towards the building of communism. Although this state does, and must, restrict the freedom of those who oppose it, it is, by definition, 'a million times more democratic than the most democratic bourgeois republic'.[6] There is no contradiction, in Soviet eyes, between the dictatorship of the proletariant and democracy, because the dictatorship is wielded by and for the vast majority, in their own interest, through the Communist Party, which always represents their interests.

(c) As the state is an organ of class suppression, it follows that it must eventually 'wither away' after classes are abolished.

(d) Laws are 'forms by which the ruling class in the given society sets norms of behaviour for all other classes, according to what profits and suits that ruling class'.[7]

(e) Abstract justice, in any ethical sense, cannot be invoked as a basis of law. Justice is itself purely relative; under capitalism there can only be 'capitalist justice', and Soviet justice, as well as Soviet law, must express the needs of a socialist transformation of society.[8]

Both Marx and Lenin concentrated, in their theoretical formulations, on emphasizing the evil character of the bourgeois class state and class law, and this, allied to the theory of the withering away of the state, led to the rise in the 1920s of a Soviet school of law which regarded the state and law almost apologetically, as a transient phenomenon. They interpreted the increasing preoccupation of the Soviet state with economic regulation as the beginning of the withering-away process. Professor Reissner went so far as to question whether there is any need to 'dress up the proletarian dictatorship in some mysterious legal formulae'.[9] Another leading Soviet lawyer of the period, Pashukanis, emphasized in his teachings that legal forms were a survival of the pre-socialist class epoch, about to wither away with the state. Much of Lenin's *State and Revolution* can be, and was, quoted to support this view.

These theories were decisively rejected by 1936, and their advocates removed from any influence on affairs. Pashukanis, indeed, was liquidated as a 'spy and wrecker', and his theories were officially deemed to have been the means by which he deliberately sought to weaken the Soviet state for treasonable ends – a typically Soviet approach to the subject of political error.[10] In their place, new theoreticians produced the ideas which found their institutional expression in the 'Stalin Constitution'.

In the early years of the Soviet regime Lenin and his colleagues were not unmindful of the need for 'revolutionary socialist legality', in the sense that Soviet officials had to act in accordance with Soviet rules. However, in a period in which the small trader and the individual peasant farmer had to be painfully liquidated, the situation required administrative flexibility of a kind which did not take kindly to legal restraints. By 1935, however, these processes were complete. The state really did fully control the economic life of the USSR, and Stalin declared that the socialist society had been built. No 'exploiting classes' remained.

Clearly, the new and widespread tasks of the Soviet state, especially in the field of economic planning, required effective organization and effective obedience to the state authorities. Furthermore, a new degree of *social* stability (reflected by increased income differentiation, inheritance laws, life insurance policies, the greater stress on family life, and so on) had to find its reflection in the legal structure of the Union. 'Stalin teaches us to strengthen socialist legality, underlining the full importance of the stability of Soviet laws for our further progress. This idea of stability is reflected in the great Stalin Constitution . . .'[11]

This concept of the Soviet state is clearly quite at variance with the idea that it is about to wither away. Stalin himself was responsible for a reformulation of the official theory. 'The withering away of the state will come not through the weakening of the power of the state, but through its uttermost strengthening, which is necessary for the purpose of completing the destruction of the remnants of the dying classes and to organize defence against the capitalist environment.'[12] Only when people are willing to work without compulsion, drawing from the common pool in accordance with their needs, only when the capitalist states no longer threaten the security of the Union, will it be possible to think of the withering away of the state. These vast changes in the human character and the international situation cannot occur for a great many years, and meanwhile the USSR 'must proceed not by lessening the class struggle but by strengthening it'.[13]

At the Eighteenth Congress of the Communist Party in 1939, Stalin formulated the tasks of the Soviet state as follows: 'defence of the country against external aggression, protection of socialist property, economic-organizational and cultural development work', contrasting these functions with the task of liquidating hostile classes which played so large a role in Soviet affairs before 1936.[14] On this interpretation, the coercive measures taken within the USSR in the period following the promulgation of the Stalin Constitution were part of the 'defence of the country against external aggression'; this accords with the official representation of all political opponents of the regime as agents of various foreign powers.

This is what Vyshinski's textbook has to say about the nature of the Constitution:

> The dictatorship of the proletariat solves the problem of the proletarian revolution also with the help of law and in accordance with measures strictly defined by law, through administrative and judicial organs. The dictatorship of the proletariat, creating its own laws, uses laws, demands the observances of law and punishes breach of law. It does not entail anarchy or disorder; on the contrary, it entails

strict order and firm government, acting on strict basic rules, set out in the fundamental law of the proletarian state, the Constitution. The problem of strengthening the power of the proletarian dictatorship faces the Soviet state in all its acuteness and strength . . . The greatest expression of proletarian democracy, and at the same time the organic synthesis of the principles of proletarian dictatorship, is the Stalin Constitution.[15]

Denisov echoes him, quoting Stalin's dictum: 'The present Constitution leaves in being the dictatorship of the working class.'[16]

While the Soviet state axiomatically represents 'the highest form of democracy that is possible',[17] all bourgeois states, whatever the party in power, inevitably act according to 'the juridical principles of the dictatorship of the bourgeoisie'.[18] (The English lawyer would be amused to see in Vyshinski's volume how easily English constitutional theories can be exploded. For instance, a quotation from Engels about the class prejudice of English country JPs in 1875 is held to prove the utter hypocrisy of the whole contention that there is an independent judiciary in Great Britain!)

Soviet theorists make much of the democratic forms of the Stalin Constitution. This form, as we shall see, does not correspond in its content to Western democratic ideas. However, it does not in the least follow that the Constitution is therefore a mere sham. It has a significant part to play in Soviet life, and so have the institutions it has called into being.

The reader who is unfamiliar with the Soviet Constitution may find some value in the following very condensed summary: A part (Articles 1–10) of the Constitution contains a series of sociological propositions which do not directly enter a lawyer's purview (e.g. 'the USSR is a Socialist state of workers and peasants', or 'from each according to his ability, to each according to his work'). There is a section on basic rights and freedoms, to which allusion will be made later. Finally, there is a detailed account of the system of governmental organization. This is based on an elected assembly, the Supreme Soviet, which is divided into two houses, the Soviet of the Union (elected in proportion to the population by electoral districts throughout the Union) and the Soviet of Nationalities, in which the sixteen republics comprising the Union are represented equally, regardless of population, by twenty-five members each.[19] The two Houses meet normally for two sittings a year, each lasting less than one week. In between sessions, power is exercised by a joint standing committee of the two Houses, the Praesidium, subject to the ratification of important decisions by the Supreme Soviet. The Council of Ministers (formerly People's Commissars) is elected by the Supreme Soviet and is responsible to it and to the Praesidium. The general supervision over the administration of law (and the legality of administration) falls to the

Attorney-General of the Union ('Generalni Prokuror'), who is appointed by the Supreme Soviet. The USSR itself is, in law, a voluntary union of national republics, each with a constitution of its own. Finally, the interpretation of the Constitution and of the laws is the responsibility of the Praesidium.

While there cannot be attempted in these few pages a detailed description of the Soviet system of government, it is of considerable interest to examine some individual features of the system outlined above, and to examine critically how Soviet theory and Soviet practice deal with the traditional problems which face the constitutional lawyer: constitutional amendments, sovereignty, federalism, separation of powers, legislation and its enforcement, and so on.

2 Constitutional amendment

A relative inflexibility of the Constitution is formally recognized by the requirement, in Article 146, of a two-thirds majority vote of both Houses for any amendment or new article.

This provision has not been of real importance for two reasons. The first is the fact, to be referred to later, that all voting in both Houses is always unanimous. The second lies in the fact that the Praesidium has, by decree, several times amended the Constitution, and the amendment took effect before its subsequent ratification. Thus numerous new ministries were set up by decree ('ukaz') of the Praesidium (e.g. the Ministry of Rubber Industry on 5 June 1941, Ministry of Machine Tool Construction 14 October 1945). As the setting up of ministries affects the powers of the republics of the Union, all ministries are listed in Articles 77 and 78 of the Constitution; yet it was not until March 1946, that the requisite amendments were put before the Supreme Soviet, and were carried unanimously and without discussion.[20] Meanwhile the relevant ministries had been functioning in their new form on the authority of the Praesidium. Another example among many may be cited: on the submission of the Supreme Soviet's Committe on New Legislation, the Praesidium promulgated on 10 October 1945 an 'ukaz' changing the minimum age at which a deputy could be elected to the Supreme Soviet from 18 to 23, thus amending Article 135 of the Constitution. The wisdom of the measure is not in question, but it is interesting to note that the elections of 1946 were carried out with this 'ukaz' in effective operation, and it was the newly elected Supreme Soviet which ratified the change, *ex post factum*, unanimously and without discussion.[21] It is not unfair to conclude that formal constitutional rigidities have little chance of interfering with administrative expediency. Formally, only the Supreme Soviet can make laws; the Praesidium can only issue 'ukazes', which must be based on powers conferred by the

Constitution or on existing legislation. It is clear from the above that in actual fact its ukazes can not only have the force of law but can also effectively amend the Constitution; formally, however, it is not till a vote of the Supreme Soviet is taken that the ukaz becomes a law ('zakon').

Even the Council of Ministers has been known to ignore the Constitution. For instance, Article 121 of the 1936 Constitution guaranteed free secondary and higher education. In 1940 a ministerial order introduced fees. Article 121 was amended by the Supreme Soviet . . . in 1947.

3   Sovereignty and the Union republics

The official teaching on sovereignty is closely linked with the federal nature of the Soviet state, and it is convenient to treat both together. (For reasons of space the important subject of the 'autonomous republics', that is, federal subdivisions of the Union republics into which the USSR is divided, is being left on one side.)

Sovereignty is defined as follows in Vyshinski's textbook: 'the supremacy of state power, which makes it unlimited and independent within its own borders and independent in its relationship with other states'.[22] Granted this definition, it must be said that Soviet theory advances a series of propositions which no lawyer outside its own borders would regard as mutually compatible. Thus: 'In the USSR sovereignty belongs to the multinational Soviet people, who exercise it through its socialist state and through the supreme organs of state power';[23] and again: 'the supreme organs of state power in the USSR . . . incarnating the will of the whole multinational Soviet people, fully and indivisibly exercise its sovereignty'.[24] But at the same time 'every Union republic is a sovereign state',[25] 'the Stalin Constitution confirmed . . . the sovereignty of the Union republics',[26] 'the sovereignty of the USSR does not contradict the sovereignty of the Union republics'.[27]

What reasons are given for this apparently untenable proposition? First, that the USSR was formed on the basis of voluntary union, in which the union republics voluntarily surrendered certain powers to the central USSR government. Second, that each republic has the formal right of secession from the Union (Article 17). Third, that the boundaries of each republic cannot be altered save with its consent. Fourth, that each Union republic possesses all residuary powers, i.e. those not specifically granted to the centre in Article 14 of the Constitution. Fifth, that the republics participate in central decisions by sending their representatives to the Supreme Soviet, and in particular to the Soviet of Nationalities within it, and these decisions are (by definition!) in the general interest of all. Sixth, each republic has the right to enter into relations with foreign states and to maintain its own military formations. Finally, that without the protection of the Union, the republics would not be able to defend their own sovereignty. 'Bourgeois' teaching on the subject is false, because sovereignty never belongs to the people in reality, but only to the ruling class; and none but the largest states are independent except in an unreal, formal sense.

The views of Vyshinski and his fellow lawyers, summarized above, are not in accord with Soviet reality. Vyshinski is fond of judging 'bourgeois' institutions by their real nature-in-action, as distinct from their formal-juridical nature, and it is only right to return the compliment by subjecting the 'sovereignty' of the Union republics, two of which have separate representation within UNO, to a brief factual scrutiny.

It is necessary to begin with a reference to two concepts, 'democratic centralism' and 'dual subordination', an understanding of which is essential in this context.

The term 'democratic centralism' was originally coined to describe the form of organization which Lenin prescribed for the Bolshevik party: iron discipline and full obedience to the elected leadership. This system was also applied to the Soviet state: 'Democratic centralism assumes, in the structure and in the activity of the state machine, unity in essentials and variety in detail . . . The necessity of unity is founded on common basic interests of all nationalities and administrative units of the Soviet state and of the state as a whole.'[28] Or, put another way, the system implies 'the strictest obedience to the directives of the party and the government', while ensuring 'fullest consideration of local conditions and peculiarities'.[29]

The above principles find their organizational expression in the so-called system of 'dual subordination'. At each level below that of the central government, one often finds state organs nominally responsible to two masters: one on the state's own level, and one above it. For example, the council of ministers of the Ukrainian republic is responsible both to the Council of Ministers of the USSR and to the supreme soviet of the Ukraine; the Ukrainian minister of textile industry is at one and the same time the Ukrainian subordinate of the Minister of Textile Industry of the USSR and a member of the Ukrainian 'cabinet'; the Kiev city health department is also the Kiev branch of the Ukrainian ministry of health, and so forth. Within this system, the orders of the centre have all the legal force of a valid instruction from a hierarchical superior. From top to bottom, 'the soviet on a higher (hierarchical) level controls the inferior one, and the instructions of the higher soviet are obligatory on the lower one; the former checks on the legality of the latter's actions, and is responsible for these actions'.[30] The same degree of subordination applies to any administrative unit of the Union republics vis-à-vis its equivalent in Moscow. The fact that a republican minister, for instance, is responsible to the cabinet of which he is a part, as well as to his superior on USSR level, must be viewed in the light of the fact that the Ukrainian cabinet collectively is fully subordinated to the USSR cabinet.

It is with the above points in mind that one can appreciate the significance of the 'residuary' nature of the powers of the republics, that is, their right to do anything not specifically assigned to the centre by virtue of Article 14 of the Constitution. It must be added that Article 14 defines the competence of the Union so vaguely that anything could be included within its orbit, and that in case of dispute the Praesidium is the sole arbiter of the Union's competence (there has, needless to say, been no dispute to date).

A brief mention of points relevant to the powers of the Union republics will now be given.

(1)   We have already seen how far the councils of ministers which each republic possesses are under the authority of the centre. With a few exceptions of purely local significance, the individual ministries on republican level are branches of ministries in Moscow (these ministries are known as 'Union-republican'), operating under the principle of dual subordination. In these cases, the ministry at Union level 'exercises its authority through identically named ministries at Union-republican level'.[31] The degree of autonomy actually delegated by the centre must vary considerably but, for example, an economic ministry on republican level receives instructions from Moscow on 'the organization of work, piecework norms, wages, financial organization and so on, the construction of new undertakings, the organization of raw material supplies, preparation of cadres, and so forth', and the ministry's budget and production plans require central approval.[32] It should be added that large industrial units of all-Union significance are controlled directly from Moscow.

(2)   Even this limited degree of local autonomy applies to a small section of the Soviet state's activity, particularly in the economic field. Of the fifty economic ministries which existed in Moscow at the end of 1947, only fifteen were Union-republican. The remaining thirty-five are known as 'Union ministries', that is, ministries which conduct their affairs within the republics through subordinates who are responsible *only* to the centre.

(3)   Since 1944 some of the republics possess their own ministries of foreign affairs. Under the amended Constitution 'foreign affairs' is on the list of Union-republican ministries, and the normal principle of hierarchical subordination to the centre, which is a normal feature of a Union-republican ministry, must apply to this field. The textbook lays down that the centre remains responsible for 'the general rules concerning the relations of the individual Union republics with foreign countries' and 'for representing the Union as a whole in international relations'.[33] It is difficult indeed to think of any subject which, say, the Ukraine could discuss with a foreign country without in some way affecting the Union as a whole – and therefore necessarily requiring the guidance of Moscow. 'It is natural that the decisive rights in this field belong to the Union.'[34]

(4)   There is a ministry of the interior in each of the republics, but these are fully subordinate to the minister in Moscow, having no responsibility whatever to the republican council of ministers. 'In this respect the ministry of the interior is in the same position as a Union ministry'.[35] The individual republics therefore have no control over the secret police formations, labour camps, convoy troops, frontier guards and even fire brigades functioning on their territories.

(5)   The 'sovereign' republics are forbidden to alter their own administrative-territorial divisions, which are listed in Articles 22–9 of the Union Constitution.

(6)   The budgets of the republics require approval by the centre. (In 1946 all the sixteen republics' budgets combined totalled 63,000 million roubles, while the Union's budget was 320,000 million roubles.)

(7)   The Union republics have, since 1944, the right to maintain their own armed forces. This is, on paper, an impressive manifestation of sovereignty. However, this is how the right is interpreted by a Soviet commentator:

> The unity of the Army is now being still further strengthened, as the military formations of the Union republics will be component parts of the Army of the USSR. The Army of the Soviet Union must continue to be unquestionably one, unquestionably centralized. The whole Red Army will have a single set of regulations, a single mobilization plan, a single command. The basic rules of organization of the armed forces will be laid down by the Union organs.[36]

(8)   The supervision over the legality of administration within each republic's territory is carried out by the Prokuror's department. However, the officials of this department are appointed by, and are responsible to, the Prokuror-General of the USSR, and they are *not* in any way responsible to the republican authorities. The Prokuror is barred from challenging any acts of the central government.

(9)   'The councils of ministers of the Union republics are forbidden to undertake any reorganization of their administrative apparatus, to create new organizations or offices, or to alter the nomenclature or salaries of their officials, without the permission of the Central Establishments Commission' (in Moscow).[37]

(10)   Most important of all, the Communist party is highly centralized on an all-Union basis, and in a one-party state it is the degree of autonomy granted to local party functionaries which really determines the extent of local rights. The party statutes lay down that 'on all questions, party groups are obliged strictly and undeviatingly to obey the decisions of the leading organs of the party' (paragraph 71) and this applies to the party leadership of a Union republic *vis-à-vis* the centre.

There remains the formal right of secession from the Union. When the new Constitution was being discussed in 1936, Stalin said: 'The USSR is a voluntary Union of republics with equal rights. To omit from the Constitution the articles relating to freedom to secede from the USSR would be a breach of the voluntary character of the Union.'[38] It is certainly a tenable proposition to say that the republics have equal rights (whatever views one may hold as to the extent of these rights), but the right to secede is purely fictional, and must remain so for as long as public advocacy of secession remains a *de facto* criminal offence. No one with the slightest knowledge of USSR politics would deny that if any Ukrainian (for instance) stood up in a meeting in Kiev to advocate independence for the Ukraine, he would court instant arrest. Indeed, Stalin himself has written the following revealing paragraph:

> There are occasions when the right of self-determination contradicts another and higher right, the right of the working class to strengthen its power. In these cases – it should be frankly stated – the right of self-determination cannot and must not obstruct the rights of the dictatorship of the working class. The former must give way before the latter.[39]

Soviet federalism rests on the need to adjust the policies decided at the centre to the varied national cultural and linguistic requirements of a vast country. 'The toiling masses of each nation within the USSR are free in deciding the national form of their participation in the common work of building socialism.'[40] Considerable local initiative in carrying out centrally devised policies is encouraged, but strictly within the framework of these policies.

Soviet delegates at international conferences defend the principle of national sovereignty. It should be clear from the above that in Soviet parlance the Ukraine and Azerbaidjan, for example, are sovereign states. So long as Western lawyers judge Soviet lawyers' pronouncements at their *Western* linguistic value, they will be unable to follow their case.

4 The Communist party and the Constitution

The position of the Communist party in the Soviet state is the subject of much misunderstanding. The Webbs defined it as follows: 'The party members who are office-bearers, and who are all pledged to complete obedience to the dictates of the party authorities, have assumed as their main vocation the supreme direction of policy and the most important part of its execution, in every branch of public administration of the USSR . . . The Communist Party Central Committee, and especially the inner

Politbureau which it appoints, not only prescribes the line to be pursued by all party cells throughout the USSR, but also co-ordinates and directs the policy and executive action of the Council of People's Commissars and of all party members who constitute the most important part of the staffs in these commissariats. It is in this way, in fact, that is exercised the dictatorship of the proletariat.'[41]

The Webbs wrote before the Stalin Constitution came into force. There is no doubt, however, that the above passage in no way underrates the role of the party. Denisov's textbook, after comparing the party with the heroes of Greek mythology, state the following:

Party leadership is the basis of the fruitful activity of each state and social organization, and of all these organizations taken together. They all take instructions from the party, which has its members in the state and social organizations of the masses, forming the directing nucleus and ensuring that the given state or social organization carries out the decisions of the party. That is why the opportunist 'theory' that non-party organizations should be independent of the party organization has been shown up by Lenin and Stalin as incorrect and harmful . . . In general, the whole Soviet system and Constitution rests on the directing role of the party . . . The party controls the selection, distribution and training of the personnel of the whole Soviet state apparatus, and checks on the work of the organs of state and government. Not a single important decision is taken by the state organs of our country without previous instructions and advice from the party.[42]

The Communist party is specifically mentioned in Article 126 of the Constitution, in which the following clear statement of its functions occurs:

The most active and conscious citizens from the ranks of the working class and other toilers join together in the All-Union Communist Party (Bolsheviks), which is the advance guard of the toilers in their struggle for the strengthening and development of the socialist order and *constitutes the directing nucleus of all toilers' organizations, both social and governmental.*

Particular attention must be drawn to the last sentence (emphasis mine), because in it is to be found the key to all Soviet constitutional practice and the explanation of much of the theory. The leading role of the party permeates all Soviet life.

The unity of the administration is ensured by the political leadership of the party, whose directives and slogans have the force of a practical decision which must immediately be carried out; the executive organs carry out their functions in full accordance with the directives given by the party.[43]

A large proportion of the more important executive orders are published as coming jointly from the Council of Ministers and the Central Committee of the party.

The Soviet theorists are, of course, right when they point out that their Constitution at least honestly emphasizes the supremacy of the party, while Western constitutions usually ignore the existence of parties, although these are by no means without significance to the real working of any 'bourgeois' constitution. But the existence of a highly disciplined party with a long-term political monopoly creates a quite special situation and, as we have seen, there is a profound sense in which a pronouncement of the Central Committee of the party has practically the force of law, despite the oft-repeated desire of the party leaders to carry out the task of government exclusively through the Soviet state machinery.

The party itself, like the Soviet state itself, is run on the basis of 'democratic centralism', that is, unquestioning obedience to orders from superior authority which, however, is itself elected. There are some who hold that such a system gives to the party chiefs powers over the process of election itself, and certainly the higher organs of the party seem to be endowed with powers which one cannot see effectively challenged from below. It should be stated in this connection that while the party statutes lay down that a Congress should be held every three years, no Congress has been held since 1939.★

5 The constitutional guarantees

The freedoms guaranteed by the Constitution must be interpreted, and are interpreted by Soviet jurists, in the light of the nature and purpose of the Soviet state. Personal freedom, in the sense of freedom from want, is 'guaranteed' by the provisions relating to old age pensions, sick pay, freedom from unemployment, and so on.[44] When it comes to such matters as freedom of the press, of meetings, demonstrations, or of speech, Article 126 of the Constitution makes these freedoms conditional upon their being used 'in accordance with the interests of the toilers and with the aim of strengthening the socialist order'. Explaining these provisions, the textbook lays down: 'In our state there is not, and of course cannot be, any freedom of speech, of the press, etc. for the enemies of socialism.' As for

★Congresses were held in 1952 and thereafter.

demonstrations, 'in the USSR the fullest initiative is granted to social and toilers' organizations, and in the first place to the directing nucleus of all these social and governmental organizations, the Communist party.'[45]

The Soviet jurist does not consider that these limitations in any way contradict his concept of democracy; he considers that the capitalist basis of the Western states makes nonsense of their formal constitutional guarantees, and that only in the USSR (and the countries of the 'new democracy' in Eastern Europe) is there to be found the material basis of real freedom, directed in the interests of the mass of the people.

However, it is difficult to see how Vyshinski would justify the immense precautions taken to make sure that unorthodox views do not find their way into print. The following quotation tells its own story: 'Permits for obtaining and using duplicators and accessories thereto are granted by the local police department to the head of the secret department within the undertaking, office, or organization acquiring the duplicator,'[46] 'or, where there is no secret department, to the head of the undertaking, office or organization . . .' Once the permit is received, 'the duplicator must be registered in the local office of "Glavlit",'[47] and 'the sale of duplicators is permitted only with prior permission of the police department, while accessories may only be obtained on production of the duplicator's registration certificate, bearing a wax seal of the police department'.[48]

6   The separation of powers

Soviet theorists strongly attack the theory of separation.

> The basic content of the principle of the separation of powers in a bourgeois state consists of ensuring the independence of the executive, as the firmest prop of the power of the bourgeoisie, as against the elected representatives of the people, who at a time of wider franchise are less reliable from the point of view of bourgeois interests.[49]

In Vyshinski's textbook, both Ramsay Muir's and Lord Hewart's criticisms of the growth of delegated legislation are quoted with approval.

Soviet theory insists on 'the supremacy of the elected representative assembly in the Soviet state'.[50] The Supreme Soviet, or its standing committee (the Praesidium), has supreme powers. 'All other activities of the state are subordinate in character. Forms of subordinate powers are: the executive . . . the judiciary.'[51] In accordance with these principles, ministers are appointed by , and are responsible to, the Supreme Soviet, while the Praesidium interprets the Constitution and the laws; the judges of the High Court and the Prokuror-General of the USSR are also appointed by Supreme Soviet.

The declared opposition of Soviet theorists to the principle of separating the powers arises, too, from the theoretical consideration that there is no need to protect different sections of the community against the state, or one part of the state against another. Such an idea would run counter to the present-day Soviet notion that Soviet society contains no internal contradictions. Indeed, the Soviet state is held literally to embody the general will in Rousseau's sense;[52] it must therefore be illimitable.

7 The Supreme Soviet and its Praesidium

The Supreme Soviet requires a long essay of its own. All that will be attempted here is a brief discussion of three aspects of its existence: its unanimity, the theory behind its second chamber, and its Praesidium.

It has already been stated that the Supreme Soviet is, in law, the sole body entitled to legislate for the whole Union.[53] This was not true of its predecessor under the 1924 Constitution, the Congress of Soviets. That body, indirectly elected, met every two years, and was more like a mass meeting than a legislature (about 3,000 delegates attended). It elected a Central Executive Committee (Vtsik) of some 600 members, which met at more frequent intervals and exercised all the Congress's powers. When Vtsik was not in session, all its powers (including that of legislation) were exercised by its Praesidium. Finally, the Council of People's Commissars was also empowered to pass valid laws.[54]

Although the Supreme Soviet is now of manageable size and not just a mass meeting, the Western observer cannot but be struck by its unanimity on *all* issues, including the election of its own officers and committees. This unanimity does not mean that there is no criticism. Reports of sessions are full of speeches calling for more and better construction projects in a given area, or demanding greater efficiency in various branches of the administration. These criticisms, however, are never taken to the point of registering a hostile vote (unless, of course, that vote is itself unanimous). Criticism concentrates on details of execution, but not on the policy itself.

Soviet theorists maintain that the Supreme Soviet is 'a working institution, which does not spend time and energy on political quarrels and arguments . . . in its activity is expressed moral-political unity, a bolshevik business-like approach'.[55]

In fact, the practice of unanimity arises naturally from the one-party system. The large majority of deputies are party members, and the others may be fairly described as fellow-travellers. In consequence, any disagreements are ironed out behind closed doors in meetings of the party group, and no doubt nominations to committees, and so on, are similarly arranged, for only one name is generally put forward for any one vacancy.

Needless to say, party control over the legislature is by no means peculiar to the Soviet Union! What *is* unique is the pursuit of the fetish of unanimity, even where (in the election of a minor committee, for example) it has no clear purpose. It might well have been argued that only under a socialist state could deputies cast their vote quite freely, unencumbered by vested interest or narrow party considerations. This is not, however, the line taken in the USSR, where the 'sure compass' of dialectical materialism is held to provide one 'correct' answer to any problem, and where the party controls all important appointments.

The 'second chamber' of the Supreme Soviet, the Soviet of Nationalities, is composed of twenty-five representatives directly elected by the people of each of the Union republics, plus eleven from each autonomous republic, and lesser numbers from smaller national groupings. This represents in the highest organ of Soviet power the multinational principle of the Soviet state, and is intended to safeguard the specifically national interests of the various national groupings. Originating in a committee within the People's Commissariat of Nationalities, the Soviet of Nationalities was set up under the 1924 Constitution as a special section of the Central Executive Committee (Vtsik). The Soviet of Nationalities under the Stalin Constitution is fully equal in all formal respects with the Soviet of the Union. At joint sessions the Speakers of the two Houses take the chair at alternate meetings. Deputies are elected to both Houses for four years, at the same general election. In case of disagreement between the two Houses, a joint committee (on which they are equally represented) is provided for in the Constitution; if after all efforts by this committee the Houses still disagree, the Praesidium dissolves them and there is a new election. For no reason other than the above can the Supreme Soviet be dissolved before the end of its term. In practice this provision is without significance, as both Houses have always been unanimously of the same opinion on any issue.

The Praesidium is, perhaps, the most original contribution by the USSR to the practice of government.[56] It is composed of a chairman, sixteen vice-chairmen (one for every Union republic), fifteen other members and a secretary, all elected at a joint session of the two Houses of the Supreme Soviet (Article 48). Its powers are:

(a) *Legislative.* Although it has the formal right only to issue decrees (ukazes), we have seen that in effect the Praesidium may legislate effectively by Ukaz on any issue, and may expect its acts to be subsequently ratified by the Supreme Soviet. (In any case, being itself the interpreter of the Constitution, it is hardly likely to find itself guilty of illegal acts.)

(b) *Executive.* The Praesidium's functions under this head cover a field which, in most other countries, belongs either to the cabinet or to the head of the state. Thus it calls meetings of the Supreme Soviet, appoints and accepts resignations of ministers (between sessions of the Supreme Soviet), declares war, appoints ambassadors, receives letters of credence from foreign envoys, exercises the prerogative of mercy, awards decorations, appoints and dismisses commanders-in-chief of the armed forces. Vyshinski stresses that the Chairman of the Praesidium has no powers, except those arising simply from his being the chairman; he takes the chair, he signs laws and ukazes, but he can issue no instructions save in the name of the Praesidium. 'The Praesidium of the Supreme Soviet is the "President-in-Commission" [*kollegialny president*] of the USSR.'[57]

(c) *Judicial.* The Praesidium interprets the Constitution and the laws and has the power of declaring any act of a Union ministry, or republican ministries, or any other administrative act, void if it deems them to be not in accordance with the law.

The Praesidium is 'accountable to the Supreme Soviet for all its activities'.[58] It has no right of veto over legislation, and cannot dissolve the Supreme Soviet save if the two Houses fail to agree. In practice, with the Supreme Soviet meeting at frequent intervals, the Praesidium naturally has very wide powers, which it exercises without any instance of challenge or even question from its 'master,' the Supreme Soviet.

A member of the Praesidium who became a minister resigns from the Praesidium, but ministers can be deputies to the Supreme Soviet, though this is not always the case.[59]

8   The executive

The Council of Ministers is responsible to, and is appointed by, the Supreme Soviet and its Praesidium, and its instructions must be based on either laws or ukazes issued by these bodies (Articles 66–7).[60] These instructions (*postanovlenia* – laying down norms, and *rasporyazhennia* – deciding a specific case) have the force of a statutory rule. There has been no case of a rule being challenged, but presumably such a challenge would have to go up for decision to the Praesidium. In practice the Council of Ministers must work closely with the Praesidium, as is inevitable in view of the wide powers of the latter.

In the composition of individual ministries one peculiarity is worth bringing out: in every ministry there is, under the minister, a council (*kollegia*) to whom all important questions must be referred; this council is appointed not by the minister but by the Council of Ministers. Its members consist of the minister's deputies and of some high civil servants, and, if they disagree with the minister, these have the right to appeal to the Council of Ministers. Indeed, before 1934 the *kollegii* issued instructions on their own responsibility; this caused confusion, and they were abolished, only to be revived in 1938 without the power of independent executive action. Only the minister can issue a valid instruction for the ministry as a whole.

One ministry is peculiar to the Soviet Union and deserves a brief special mention. This is the Ministry of State Control, born of a marriage between the Workers' and Peasants' Inspection and the party's Central Control Committee. This ministry has the double task of preventing abuses in the administrative machine, and of ensuring that orders given by the higher authorities are in fact carried out. Its officials have powers of access to all relevant documents, and 'it is compulsory for all ministries, commissions, departments and other organs' to provide 'explanations, reports and all other information'.[61] The ministry has its men working throughout the administrative machine at all levels (it even has its inspectors in military stores and army divisions). The ministry's officials are empowered to take disciplinary action against offenders or, in serious cases, to hand the case over to the Prokuror for criminal prosecution before the courts. The Ministry of State Control plays an important role in that system of inspection and cross-checking, which is a feature of Soviet administration (other 'checkers' include the secret police, the Ministry of Finance, the planning authorities and the Establishments Commission).

9   Electoral procedure

The procedure for elections to the Supreme Soviet is, on paper, fully consonant with the democratic principle. The legality of election procedure is watched over by a system of electoral commissions, who represent social and workers' organizations (the names of members are confirmed by the local soviet in the area in which they function). A widely representative Central Electoral Commission, whose members are confirmed by the Supreme Soviet or its Praesidium, supervises the elections on a nationwide scale, and hears appeals against any decision by the local commissions. It renders a report on the conduct of the elections to the mandates commissions of the two Houses of the Supreme Soviet.

Candidates may be nominated by 'social organizations or societies of toilers – that is, Communist party organizations and other societies registered in accordance with the law'.[62] Religious organizations are excluded.[63]

Now it has already been remarked that the Constitution itself lays down that the Communist party is 'the directing nucleus of all social organizations and societies of toilers'. It follows, then, that the candidate is effectively selected by the Communist party (whether that candidate is himself a party member or not). In the two elections that have been held to the Supreme Soviet since the promulgation of the Stalin Constitution

(1938 and 1946), there has not been a single case of a contested election. A Soviet lawyer would view the matter thus:

> The moral and political unity of the whole Soviet people results in the fact that, in practice, only one candidate is nominated in each constituency, and he receives unanimous support from all social organizations and meetings of the working masses of the given area . . . Soviet elections are a brilliant demonstration of socialist democracy in action.[64]

Indeed, at the last election 99·7 per cent of the electors voted, and less than 1 per cent failed to vote for the official candidates. As a charmingly naïve article put it, 'not a single deputy in a bourgeois parliament . . . can ever have received or can ever receive such a majority . . .'[65] At any rate, we must admit that the organization which gets people to the poll must be very efficient.

The Constitution provides for the recall of individual deputies by the electors if the latter are dissatisfied with them, but the machinery for doing so has never been brought into operation, and the right is purely theoretical to date.

10 A note on the judiciary and the political police

The Soviet judicial system requires an essay of its own, and only the briefest reference will be made to its position in the constitutional structure of the Union. At the top of the hierarchy of people's and regional courts stands the Supreme Court (strictly the High Court) of the USSR. It is divided into five 'collegia': civil, military, criminal, rail transport and water transport. It has a president, sixty-eight judges and twenty-eight 'assessors'. The collegia are responsible for hearing appeals from the lower courts, which may be initiated by an aggrieved party or by the prosecutor (Prokuror); in addition, there are cases of national importance, for which the relevant collegium of the High Court acts as a tribunal of first instance. On these occasions, two assessors sit with the judge (as is the practice in the lower courts). The military collegium heard the cases of Zinoviev and Bukharin during the purges, because it covers 'cases of treason, espionage, sabotage, and so on, by whomsoever committed',[66] as well as appeals from courts martial. The transport collegia hear appeals from the special transport courts, whose main task is to enforce labour discipline, and who appear to have powers similar to courts martial. The two transport and the military collegia are staffed by judges who have risen in the hierarchy of these special courts. From the decisions of the collegia there is no appeal (save to the Praesidium, which exercises the prerogative of mercy).

However, cases may be reviewed by the plenum of the Supreme Court, which is a meeting of all the judges, attended also by the Prokuror-General and the Minister of Justice, held at least every two months. The plenum reviews those judgments of the collegia which are brought to its notice by the President of the Court or the Prokuror-General, and issues directives to the lower courts. These directives lay down the principles which the lower courts must follow in applying the laws, and frequently embody valuable safeguards for the public.[67]

The Supreme Court's powers to interpret law arise primarily from its own casework. In carrying out this function, however, it is subordinate to the Praesidium of the Supreme Soviet, which has the overriding right to interpret the Constitution and the laws.

The Supreme Court judges are appointed for five years by the Supreme Soviet, and Article 112 of the Constitution lays down that they are 'independent and subject only to the law'.

As in most other Continental countries, the preparation of a case against the accused (including interrogation of witnesses, and so on) is undertaken by a judicial investigator (*sledovatel*) who operates under the guidance of the 'prokuror'. For political cases, however, the organs of the Ministry of State Security (i.e. the political police) act as judicial investigators, with the usual powers of interrogation and detention which such officials possess.

The Minister of Justice exercises a general supervision over the functioning of the courts. He may not intervene in the hearing of a case (save to overcome delays and red tape), but he 'watches over the correctness of the application of the laws to civil and criminal cases'.[68] If the minister feels that a new instruction to the courts is called for, he puts a proposal to that effect before a meeting of the Plenum of the Supreme Court.

Space compels total omission of fascinating problems connected with procedure and application of the laws. But no review of Soviet constitutional practice can omit some reference to the Ministry of Home Affairs and the Ministry of State Security, usually known by their initials – MVD (NKVD) and MGB. These two ministries were at one time one, and the exact boundary between their functions is a well-guarded secret. They jointly exercise the powers of the former OGPU, and many more besides. There is nothing in the Constitution about the wide powers of arbitrary imprisonment practised by these ministries and their local organs. However, a series of laws and orders regulate their functions, and many pages of the textbook on administrative law are devoted to listing them. We have already seen that the MVD and MGB organs act as preliminary investigators of any political case. If they should come to the conclusion that a citizen is 'socially dangerous', the 'Special Council' (Osoboe Soveschanie) may exile him or confine him to a concentration camp for up to five years – and 'control over the release of the detainee is exercised by the local organs of the MVD in the area of exile or detention'.[69] The Special Council at Union level consists of the Minister of the Interior, his highest subordinates and the Prokuror-General; the latter may appeal to the

Council of Ministers against an unjust detention order. But if the security organs have built up a case against the accused (for instance, under the many sub-paragraphs of Article 58 of the Criminal Code, which define counter-revolutionary activities), he is tried and sentenced by the regular courts of the land. The choice seems to rest with the secret police, who undertake the preliminary examination.

The MVD also exercises the functions of the Registrar-General, controls fire brigades, the uniformed police, a large and well-equipped Security Army, frontier guards, road-building, prisons and concentration-labour camps. With the MGB, it is a power in the land; during the great purge of 1936–8 it was able to cause the total disappearance of deputies, ministers and even members of the Politbureau.*

11 The prokuror

The institution of 'prokuror' in the Soviet state has no clear parallel in Western countries. He is at one time the public prosecutor and the guardian over legality in the field of both administration and justice in the area in which he functions. The hierarchy of local prokurors are appointed by, and are entirely subordinated to, the Prokuror-General of the USSR; they are totally independent of the local or Union-republican authority. The Prokuror-General is appointed by the Supreme Soviet for seven years, and we have seen that he plays his part in the plenums of the Supreme Court in determining the general 'policy' of the Soviet Courts. He also personally prosecutes in important cases before the Supreme Court; thus Vyshinski, who was then the Prokuror of the USSR, prosecuted Zinoviev, Bukharin, etc. before the military collegium of the Supreme Court.

The prokuror in the localities exercises the following functions:

(a) While 'he does not settle administrative problems himself', the prokuror 'must see that the settlement of such problems by local state authorities corresponds to the provisions of the law. In case of any illegal instruction being issued by anyone, or of any illegal act or omission, the prokuror's office must challenge the illegality, that is, bring the matter to the notice of the next highest organ of state power. If the decision of this organ is also inconsistent with the law, it can be challenged in its turn. In this way 'the problem can go up to the highest organs of the state, which then give a binding decision'.[70] In acting thus, the prokuror is expected both to use his personal initiative and to follow up complaints from citizens.

* The MGB is now the KGB, with modified powers.

(b)   In his capacity as public prosecutor, the prokuror represents the state in all judicial proceedings. If in his view any decision of the court is wrong, he can challenge it and take the case to the next highest court, right up to the Supreme Court.[71]

(c)   The sanction of the Prokuror or of a court is required for any arrest.

(d)   The judicial investigators operate under the prokuror's authority.

There is a close tie-up in practice between the prokuror system and the party and state security organs.

In order that it should be a strong and flexible weapon in the hands of the working-class dictatorship in its struggle for communism, the prokuror must work under the closest supervision of, and in the closest contact with, the party organizations which offer the most effective guarantees against local or personal influences.[72]

In his task, he must co-operate 'with the organs of the NKVD and with the courts in a decisive struggle against all remnants of the Trotsky-Bukharinite bandits, the hirelings of fascist intelligence services, spies, wreckers, thieves, hooligans' and so on.[73]

First and foremost, the prokuror is 'the guardian of socialist legality, the executor of the policy of the Communist party and Soviet power, a fighter in the cause of socialism'.[74] His position is deliberately intended to be outside the system of elective organs of state power in the various republics and the local government areas. He must watch over the local administration and the local machinery of justice, and keep them to the laws, ukazes and directives of the supreme authorities of the Union. It is doubtful, in view of the above quotations, whether he is likely to protect the citizen in cases where 'political unreliability' is involved, but a conscientious prokuror can do much to defend citizens against abuse of power by local authorities or officials.

12   The citizen and the administration

The reader who has some knowledge of Continental law will be looking for a Russian equivalent of the special administrative courts, a Russian 'Conseil d'État' for hearing citizens' cases against the state. There is, however, no hierarchy of this type of administrative courts in the USSR. State prosecution of citizens or officials for any serious offence not committed on the transport system is heard by the ordinary courts. The following means exist for an aggrieved Soviet citizen to obtain satisfaction against the state.

(1)   The right of complaint is 'the most important means of ensuring

legality in Soviet administration'. 'The right of complaint in the Soviet State has the essential characteristic that . . . it is the means of defending the legal rights of citizens . . .'[75] An elaborate procedure exists by which the complaint must be investigated within a given period of time, and the complainant is shielded from repressive acts save in cases of malicious and libellous complaints. The complaint may be addressed to the head of the office committing the alleged illegal act, or to the prokuror, or to a state control office (as well, of course, as through party channels). If no satisfaction is obtained, the complainant may make representations to the next highest administrative level. The party is enjoined to assist in this system of complaints, as its proper functioning helps to keep the administration on its toes.

(2) The right of appeal to the courts is limited in scope principally to 'the prevention of breaches of socialist legality in the levying of administrative fines and non-payment of taxes'.[76] A variety of state and other institutions have the right of imposing fines (for example, city officials of Moscow may fine citizens for non-compliance with by-laws). The accused has no right of appeal on the substance of the case; he may, however, refuse to pay the fine, and then the case is heard by the courts – who confine themselves to deciding whether the authority in question was *intra vires* in levying the fine and do not consider the rights and wrongs of the decision of the administrative organ. Where the fine is levied by an institution (for instance, by an office or factory for spoiled work), no appeal to the courts is possible, and the money owed is simply deducted from pay.

(3) The prokuror, as already stated, watches over the legality of administrative acts. Citizens' complaints may be taken up, and the prokuror's office may challenge the illegal act all the way up the administrative hierarchy, up to the government and ministries of the USSR, whose acts are not challengeable by the Prokuror-General.

(4) A hierarchy of state arbitration tribunals hear disputes between the various economic organizations of the state. Where an organization can persuade the prokuror that it has been unfairly treated, the latter can appeal to the Chief Arbitrator, who is attached to the Council of Ministers. The decision of state arbitration tribunals is binding on both parties. Disputes within the same sphere of ministerial responsibility (for example, beween two trusts of the Ministry of Heavy Industry) are heard by the ministerial arbitration tribunal, whose decision is final. Arbitration is not relevant to cases 'where one of the parties is below the other in the same hierarchy, as the orders of the superior organization are binding for its inferiors'.[77] With all industry owned by the state, the significance of these arbitration tribunals is clearly much greater than it would be in this country.

It will be seen that outside the small sector reserved to the courts, the citizen's rights against the state are confined to appeals to higher administrative instances, who are expected to reverse the decision complained of.[78] With the party in control at each level, it may be said that this system, while affording protection against illegal acts by individuals, is helpless in the face of any party-backed decisions, provided the party organ is high enough in the hierarchy to wield the necessary influence.

13   Some conclusions

The Soviet theory of state and law follows logically enough from the premisses on which it rests. If 'the party embodies the desires and yearnings [sic] of the people',[79] then the constitutional forms which give the most efficient expression to the party's policy represent a perfect form of democracy. If 'there can be no conflict in Soviet society between law and morality because both represent the ideology and outlook of the whole monolithic Soviet society',[80] then Soviet law axiomatically represents the general will of the people. If the interests of the state, in the Soviet classless society, must always be identical with the interests of the individual, then the omnipotence of the state (and of the party) is in itself a 'guarantee of the maintenance of the interests of the individual'.[81]

Of course, the above seems to the Western constitutional lawyer to be altogether too rosy a picture. The party may become corrupted, as others have been before it, by the unchallenged exercise of absolute power. Its leaders may come to identify the furtherance of their own power or privileges, or considerations of administrative expediency, with the interests of the people. Many instances might be quoted of legislation which seems to have little connection with the desires of the masses of the people (for example, the imposition of a fine of up to a quarter of the worker's monthly wage for being more than twenty minutes late for work). Absolute power, in the nature of things, is liable to be abused, and Soviet constitutional theory and practice seem to be well fitted for such abuse.[82]

Notes: Chapter 12

1 Detailed expositions of Soviet constitutional theory and practice may be found in the following (Russian) works:
A. Vyshinski (ed.), Soviet State Law (Sovetskoye gosudarstvennoye pravo) (Moscow: Academy of Sciences, Legal Section, 1938); despite the date of publication, still an invaluable guide to official theory.
A. I. Denisov, Soviet State Law (Russian title as above) (Moscow: Ministry of Justice, 1947).
Yevtikhiev and Vlasov, Administrative Law (Administrativnoye pravo) (Moscow: Ministry of Justice, 1946).
The above are textbooks for law students.

The Foundations of the Soviet State and Law (Osnovy sovetskovo gosudarstva i pravo), a symposium edited by Professors I. D. Levin and A. V. Karass on behalf of the Law Institute of the Academy of Sciences of the USSR (Moscow: Ministry of Justice, 1947); a textbook for students *not* specializing in law, and largely a condensed version of others books.

Articles in the periodical Soviet State and Law (Sovetskoye gosudarstvo i pravo) published by the Academy of Sciences, Legel Section.

Various pamphlets and books on the Soviet state, mainly transcripts of lectures, issued in Moscow in 1946 and 1947.

Stenographic reports of the sessions of the Supreme Soviet. Communist Party reports and resolutions; works of Lenin and Stalin; press articles.

2 Vyshinski, op. cit., p. 13.
3 V. I Lenin, State and Revolution (London: Lawrence & Wishart, 1933), p. 21.
4 Lenin, quoted by Vyshinski, op. cit., p. 13.
5 ibid., p. 14; original emphasis.
6 V. I. Lenin, The Proletarian Revolution and the Renegade Kautsky (London: Lawrence & Wishart, 1935), p. 30.
7 Vyshinski, op. cit., p. 21.
8 A useful historical survey of Soviet law and justice is contained in R. A. J. Schlesinger, Soviet Legal Theory: Its Social Background and Development (London: Kegan Paul, 1945).
9 M. A. Reisner, Law (Moscow: 1925).
10 This view of Pashukanis and his school is fully developed in Vyshinski, op. cit., pp. 58–61.
11 ibid., p. 54.
12 J. V. Stalin, Voprosy leninism (Leninism), (Moscow: 10th edn, 1934), p. 509.
13 loc. cit.
14 Summary quoted from Yevtikhiev and Vlasov, op. cit., p. 1; full version in stenographic account of 18th Congress of the Communist Party, p. 717.
15 Vyshinski, op. cit., p. 51.
16 Stalin, op. cit., 11th edn, p. 519.
17 Vyshinski, op. cit., p. 51.
18 Levin and Karass, op. cit., p. 89.
19 There is also special representation for 'autonomous republics' and for minor national subdivisions; these are themselves federal units of individual republics.
20 See stenographic account of 1st Session of the Supreme Soviet, Moscow, 1946.
21 ibid.
22 Vyshinski, op. cit., p. 262.
23 loc. cit.
24 ibid., p. 292.
25 ibid., p. 263.
26 Levin and Karass, op. cit., p. 130.
27 N. P. Farberov, The Sovereignty of the Union Republics, transcript of lecture (Moscow: Pravda, 1946), p. 12.
28 Denisov, op. cit., p. 260.
29 Yevtikhiev and Vlasov, op. cit., p. 17.

30   Denisov, op. cit., p. 261.
31   Yevtikhiev and Vlasov, op. cit., p. 27.
32   ibid., p. 294.
33   ibid., p. 171.
34   Levin and Karass, op. cit., p. 137.
35   Yevtikhiev and Vlasov, op. cit., p. 92. Presumably this applies equally to the Ministry of State Security, formerly part of the Ministry of the Interior.
36   Farberov, op. cit.
37   Yevtikhiev and Vlasov, op. cit., p. 40; even a rural district council in England has greater powers in this field.
38   *Report on the Draft Constitution of the USSR* (Moscow, 1936).
39   J. V. Stalin, *Marxism and the National and Colonial Question*, quoted in Denisov, op. cit., p. 232.
40   Vyshinski, op. cit., p. 218.
41   S. and B. Webb, *Soviet Communism* (London: Longman's, 1937), p. 354.
42   Denisov, op. cit., pp. 191–2.
43   Yevtikhiev and Vlasov, op. cit., p. 6.
44   But we have seen how one 'guarantee', dealing with free higher education, was disregarded in 1940.
45   Vyshinski, op. cit., p. 555.
46   My emphasis. No *individual* is entitled to acquire a duplicator. The 'secret department'is the network of secret police agents which functions within most Soviet institutions. It is rare to find a reference to it in print.
47   'Glavlit' is the body responsible for censorship of all published material, which must be submitted to it *before and after* its appearance.
48   Yevtikhiev and Vlasov, op. cit., p. 231. This is *not* a wartime security measure as it already existed in 1935.
49   Levin and Karass, op. cit., p. 94.
50   I. D. Levin, *The State System of a Socialist Democracy*, transcript of lecture (Moscow, 1946).
51   Levin and Karass, op. cit., p. 34.
52   This analogy is developed at some length in an unsigned leading article in *Soviet State and Law*, 1946, no. 2.
53   Article 32; but the Praesidium and the ministers have invaded this field (see above).
54   Webb and Webb, op. cit., and W. R. Batsell, *Soviet Rule in Russia* (Cambridge, Mass.: Harvard University Press, 1929), contain full descriptions of the pre-1936 system seen from very different angles.
55   *Soviet State and Law*, 1946, no. 2, p. 28.
56   The 'new democracies' in the Balkans have adopted some features of this institution.
57   Vyshinski, op. cit., p. 311; the words are Stalin's.
58   ibid., p. 310.
59   In 1938 Stalin himself was a member of the Praesidium, but he ceased to be a member when he became officially head of the government. He remains a deputy, however. Ministers, whether or not they are deputies, have the right to speak in either house.
60   In practice the Council of Ministers, usually bracketed with the Central Com-

mittee of the Party, has issued Orders making new laws and even, as we have seen, amending the Constitution.

61 Yevtikhiev and Vlasov, op. cit., p. 128.

62 Article 56 of the Regulations on Elections to the Supreme Soviet of the USSR.

63 Vyshinski, op. cit., p. 637.

64 Levin and Karass, op. cit., p. 215.

65 *Soviet State and Law*, 1946, no. 2.

66 Vyshinski, op. cit., p. 471.

67 Schlesinger, op. cit., contains much information on the general work of the Soviet courts.

68 Denisov, op. cit., p. 314.

69 Yevtikhiev and Vlasov, op. cit., pp. 191 and 245.

70 Vyshinski, op. cit., p. 473.

71 His right applies also to civil cases, and in criminal cases he has the right of appeal against a prisoner's acquittal. He may also undertake a civil case on behalf of a citizen if this is in the public interest. Recently the right to appeal against a sentence 'once it is legally in force' has been restricted to senior members of the hierarchy of prokurors.

72 Vyshinski, op. cit., p. 473; he is quoting Lenin.

73 ibid., p. 481. The political jargon is definitely '1938'; in 1948 there would be a reference to the Hirelings of Imperialist Warmongers.

74 ibid., p. 484.

75 Yevtikhiev and Vlasov, p. 137.

76 ibid., p. 117.

77 ibid., p. 134.

78 This applies to the administration at all levels, but not to economic undertakings; the latter are endowed with a legal personality and may be participants in a civil action. Thus a citizen whose suit was ruined at a state-run dry-cleaning establishment could sue that establishment for damages before the ordinary courts.

79 Levin and Karass, op. cit., p. 32.

80 ibid., p. 36.

81 Denisov, op. cit., p. 119.

82 It has come to my notice that one of the books quoted in this essay, *Administrative Law* by Yevtikhiev and Vlasov, has been the subject of official criticism and is to be rewritten by its authors. It is felt, none the less, that the quotations made are not without value.

13 The class nature of the Soviet Union revisited

This was originally published in *Soviet Studies*, vol. 13, no. 3 (July 1983), pp. 298–312. The debate continues.

I have had two bites at this particular cherry: 'History, hierarchy and nationalities' (*Soviet Studies*, July 1969), and 'Is the Soviet Union a class society?' (*Soviet Studies*, October 1975), both articles being reprinted in my *Political Economy and Soviet Socialism*.[1] I have discussed these ideas, formally and informally, in Glasgow, London, Paris, Budapest, even Moscow and Shanghai. With one exception (of course, in Glasgow), all accepted that the ideas were fruitful and interesting, but naturally there was also disagreement and criticism. Meanwhile the already sizeable literature on the subject has expanded considerably. So it seems worth making an attempt to revise, rephrase, rethink.

First, let us examine the question of *who* the rulers are, before tackling the issues of whether they should be designated 'class', 'caste', 'stratum', or something else, whether Soviet society represents a 'mode of production' unforeseen by Marx, and whether such a society is subject to any 'laws' (*zakonomernosti*, 'law-like regularities') peculiar to itself. I tried in my earlier articles to discuss the historical aspect, that is, how and why the system had evolved, together with such relevant matters as the Russian political tradition, the circumstances of revolution in a backward country, the functional logic of a centrally planned economy, and so on. These are important and interesting questions, but I will leave them aside for the present. The extent to which Marx's ideas contributed to Soviet reality have been fruitfully discussed by Kolakowski, Markovic, Gouldner and others,[2] and this too will be omitted from the pages that follow.

In both my earlier articles I expressed the view that the *nomenklatura* of the Central Committee is the best available approximation to defining the 'class of rulers', the 'establishment'. This is a view argued at length, and with much supporting material, in M. Voslensky's book of that name,[3] which has been a bestseller in France but is none the worse for that. Where nearly everyone who is anyone holds official rank, membership of the *nomenklatura* of the Central Committee defines those whom the system

itself recognizes as occupying posts of social, economic, or political significance. There may, of course, be individuals who are rich and/or influential
who are not on any *nomenklatura*; actors, dancers, inventors, astronauts, for
instance. This, however, does not constitute a challenge to a definition that
seeks to identify those who rule, and not those that happen to acquire money
or fame. In our own society, a film actor, jockey, or disc jockey may be rich,
but we would not for this reason include him in a definition of a ruling class –
unless he used his riches to become a capitalist or a landlord, in which case he
would acquire the power that ownership of property brings. His Soviet
equivalent cannot do this. To acquire political, social and economic
authority and *not* to be on the *nomenklatura* is something irregular, contrary
to the system's own nature, so to speak. It can happen, but – as in Poland in
1980–1 – it is a challenge to the entire system.

Is this a perfect definition of the ruling stratum? No, but critics must
devise a better one. It can be, and has been, criticized in several ways.
Thus, when I presented these arguments in Paris, objections were raised
on the following lines. Such a definition makes too hard-and-fast a line
between those above and those below it; it implies total dominance,
and/or that those below the line have no influence on decision-making.
Another criticism was that the line was drawn, so to speak, too high on the
hierarchical pyramid; we should include more junior officials who are not
on the *nomenklatura* of the Central Committee. For example, *kolkhoz*
chairmen, directors of medium-sized industrial enterprises, or of a
republican research institute, are probably on the republican party *nomenklatura*, and it is doubtful if the Central Committee's apparatus takes
cognizance of army officers of the rank of colonel or major. It has also been
argued that we should base ourselves on the statistical categories to be
found in the census, covering those in charge (*rukovoditeli*) of state, social
and co-operative enterprises, offices, departments and their sub-divisions,
as everyone in these categories is in some position of authority or
command. Their numbers exceed 2 million.

In a hierarchically structured society any line that is drawn to indicate
'senior' civil and military officers is of its nature arbitrary. There is no
good reason to draw it at the equivalents of general, colonel, or even
lieutenant, and some lieutenants will become generals when they are
older. So if some prefer to enlarge the definition, to include the republican
nomenklatura, for instance, this cannot be ruled out or rejected. I am less
happy with the statistical categories taken from the census, because they
include far too many quite minor (and poorly paid) uninfluential petty
officials, such as 'directors' of rural co-operative stores or head librarians
in small provincial towns. The effect is to swell the total by over a million
individuals who are somewhat less influential, and much less well paid,
than a deputy manager of a Woolworth store in Grimsby. Yet the chief of
staff of an army corps might be omitted, because he is not the commander.

So would be the 'instructors' of the Central Committee itself, though many directors or even deputy ministers might tremble at their approach. Surely, the *nomenklatura* is a better guide.

Do people who are not of high rank also exercise some influence over decision-making? Of course they do, but who ever supposed otherwise? In every country, the decisions of senior officials and businessmen are affected by the actions (and proposals) of their subordinates. The 'ruling class' in any capitalist country, howsoever defined, is influenced and constrained in its actions by workers, company staffs and other members of the 'lower orders'. No more have the Soviet *nomenklatura* officials power to do just as they please. In any large hierarchical organization, subordinates have a range of choice, can amend or deflect instructions they receive; 'in a command economy', as a Hungarian economist once said, 'many commands are written by their recipients'. All this is by no means inconsistent with the view that there are commanders, and that senior officialdom, in a country in which ownership of the means of production is vested in the state, constitutes the nearest equivalent to a ruling or dominant class or stratum.

A different view is held by Konrad and Szelenyi,[4] who speak of a ruling class of *intellectuals*. I discussed this in a long review in *Telos*.[5] They are, in my opinion, mistaken. The 'intellectuals' they speak of are all those with higher education. It is true that, to reach the top positions, higher education has become a *sine qua non*, but officials do not achieve promotion through their intellectual gifts. Bienkowski wrote: 'promotion in the ruling group . . . excludes all meritocratic criteria such as qualifications or talent. The ruling apparatus takes particular care that nobody who even once betrayed a critical attitude towards any problem, who has not shown willingness to subordinate himself entirely, should be promoted.'[6] The large majority of graduates are poorly paid, receive no compensatory privileges and have lost ground as compared with skilled workers. Of course, one could argue that the radical *intelligentsia* (in the original Russian sense of that word) dominated the revolutionary parties, including the Bolsheviks. Indeed, at the turn of the century Makhaisky was claiming that the Marxist social democratic doctrine was the class ideology of the intelligentsia, by which it mobilized the masses to achieve its rule over them, using them to eliminate the capitalists and landlords. Even if Makhaisky were right about the original Bolsheviks, surely the events of the 1930s included the massacre of Marxist intellectuals, the emergence of a leadership of a quite different kind. Again, Bienkowski can be quoted in support:

It is striking that while the ruling cadres during the revolutionary period were made up of outstanding intellectuals, people with a strong theoretical training, several years after the revolution such people had completely disappeared. Obviously the main credit for this must go to Stalin, who almost totally exterminated the intellectual elite.[7]

The typical holders of *nomenklatura* posts have nothing in common with the *intelligentsia* in its pre-revolutionary meaning, and nothing in common either with the mass of the 'intellectuals' (in the Konrad–Szelenyi sense, that is, graduates) though they *are* graduates. A man can only play rugby for Oxford or football for Southern California by being a college student; generals have passed examinations at a staff college, but their nature and qualities surely cannot be labelled 'intellectual' for such reasons. Konrad and Szelenyi have expressed some very interesting thoughts concerning the relationship between claims to *knowledge* (including knowledge of Marxism-Leninism) and the achievement of high office. However, academic qualifications as such relate only to the first rung of a long ladder which leads to power.

Surely only the tiny minority who climb high up the ladder matter to us in the present context. Otherwise the millions of underpaid teachers and medical staffs (mostly women) must be included. Konrad and Szelenyi also confuse the issue by drawing a line between productive and unproductive labour; many if not most 'intellectuals' in their sense can be regarded as unproductive, but then so can a large number of others who are not intellectuals at all (cleaners, prison guards, policemen, nurses, filing clerks . . .). This is an inappropriate distinction in the context of identifying a ruling class or stratum.

No definition of a ruling class can ever be statistically and conceptually tidy, as attempts to apply this category to the reality of any country bear witness. Indeed, I would argue that the Soviet 'unihierarchy' makes the task easier. One could apply the *nomenklatura* principles to the tsarist rank system, say, of Nicholas I, defining the top four or six civil and military ranks as 'rulers'. This would be incomplete, as it would omit great landowners and textile millionaires, who held no official rank at all, but who had much influence and power in their capacity as property-owners. There are now no landowners or capitalists, there is the universal service state. This is one of the reasons why certain analysts – for instance, Bahro, Bienkowski, Gouldner – are attracted by the parallel with the Asiatic mode of production, where property rights were absent or minimal and the despotic state was all-powerful. Bienkowski, indeed, cites ancient Chinese doctrine to the effect that fully fledged despotism is only possible in a classless society (since any ruling or property-owning class must, by definition, have rights). Of course, the parallel must not be pressed too far. The Asiatic mode of production was economically static, and the state was headed by a hereditary despotic monarch. Even if Stalin was a despot too, he was not a monarch, and the fact that his personal rule conflicted with the formal ideology ('*ni dieu, ni césar, ni tribun*') contributed to the fact that he was not followed by another despot.

In my view, one is driven back to the *nomenklatura* definition, while conscious of its limitations. One is strengthened in this by evidence from many quarters to the effect that those actually occupying *nomenklatura* posts are very much aware of their own special status, that is, exhibit something close to class-consciousness. They also show themselves strongly opposed to the creation of any organizational structure which is not part of the official hierarchy. Conversely, as experience in Poland has recently shown, any steps towards real democratization necessarily involve a challenge to the principles of unihierarchy of which the *nomenklatura* system is an expression. Also significant is the refusal of officials and the censorship to allow any discussion of *nomenklatura* and of the rights and privileges it confers.

So far we have been discussing the problem of defining what segment of society we should be designating as rulers. Now let us pass to the different question of what they should be called.

An interesting and important debate centres on the applicability of the term 'class'. Some who would probably agree with the above definition of *who* rules would demur at the use of a label which could have misleading connotations. Ken Jowitt gives some cogent reasons for preferring the term 'regime cadres' or 'generalized elite stratum', in an article with the suggestive title of 'Soviet neotraditionalism'.[8] Another who rejects the term 'class' is Maria Hirszowicz. She points out that, except at the very top, even high officialdom

> must observe the rules imposed from above and follow the instruc-
> tions of their superiors. A hierarchy – or rather a network of hier-
> archies – within the party state implies for this very reason the con-
> cept of 'more' or 'less' power, rather than a simple division between
> rulers and ruled.[9]

She prefers to base her analysis on stratification. These are defensible positions, and it almost becomes a matter of personal preference whether 'class' is seen as misleading or clarifying in the present context. Others take a different view, basing themselves on the notion of some sort of collective control by the 'class' over the means of production and/or the surplus. For example, Gouldner:

> If control over the surplus, based on control over the instruments of
> production, helps to establish the hegemony of the proprietary class,
> consistency suggests that when state officialdom has a similar con-
> trol over the instruments of production – whether hydraulic systems
> or industrial technology – they too become a ruling class.[10]

Such quotations can be multiplied. A valuable survey of these and other interpretations is to be found in David Lane's recent book, *The End of Social Inequality?*[11] Lane himself prefers the term 'state-socialist society', in which there is 'a hierarchy in which some groups of men (and few women) have power, prestige and privilege, while others lack them'; he speaks of 'competing elites operating in a bureaucratic structure' (p. 159), and would reject 'ruling class'.

There is widespread agreement that 'class' in its conventional Marxist sense, that is, based on ownership of property, does not and cannot apply. So either we are to use the word 'class' in a new sense, designating those who exercise control over resources and over people, or we need a new term. Some critics would regard inheritance as a factor of great relevance, and deny the applicability of the term 'class' because privileges depend on the rank held and are lost when that individual loses his or her post. In my original article I probably over-emphasized the extent to which *nomenklatura* posts are *not* hereditary. True, it is quite exceptional for the topmost posts to be held by sons of holders of topmost posts. Only one member of the present Central Committee (as far as I know) is a son of a member, past or present, of the Central Committee. However, privileges in education plus influence ensure that they have 'the status and income that their father's rank required', to paraphrase a line from Hilaire Belloc's *Lord Lundy*. Thus young Brezhnev is a deputy minister of foreign trade, young Gromyko the head of an important research institute, and some senior officers are sons of generals. None the less, there is also promotion from below into the hierarchy, and indeed it is important to keep open a door through which ambitious and intelligent children of workers can rise into the *nomenklatura* ranks.

All this seems to me predictable and to present no great conceptual puzzle. A purely hereditary system would be a *caste*. The tsarist *dvoryanstvo* estate (*soslovie*) was mainly hereditary, but anyone could be promoted into this estate by achieving senior rank in the civil and military service; the formal hereditary element was surely greater than is the case with the official class today, but the word *soslovie* may appeal to some as a better one than *klass* to designate the group we are discussing. At the other extreme one could conceive of a pure meritocracy, with all top ranks filled by promotion from below by a series of competitive examinations. This would presumably give rise to so high a degree of social mobility that neither 'class' nor *soslovie* would be an appropriate term. Of course, the Soviet ruling group is *not* a 'meritocracy'! Nor is it hereditary. A mixture of inherited privilege plus some upward social mobility appears to be not at all inconsistent with such terms as 'class'. Some capitalists were 'self-made men'.

Let us look at other possible terminologies. I mentioned in an earlier article Rakovsky's attempts to grapple with the problem. He and other left oppositionists spoke of *klass pravyashchikh*, 'class of rulers', or 'class of officials'. It may be worth quoting their exact words, as they sound so 'up-to-date', so similar to those of some neo-Marxists today:

> Before our very eyes there has been and is being formed a large *class of rulers* with their own subdivisions, growing through controlled co-option . . . What unites this peculiar [*svoeobraznyi*] sort of class is the peculiar sort of private property, namely, state power.

After some discussion as to whether Marx regarded state bureaucracy as a class, another group of exiled oppositionists argued that, on the contrary,

> the bureaucracy is not a class and will never become one . . . It will degenerate, it is a nucleus of a class, which will not be the bureaucracy but another hitherto unknown one; its appearance will mean that the working class will become another oppressed class. The bureaucracy is the nucleus of some kind of capitalist class, controlling the state and collectively owning the means of production.[12]

Debates on this topic were already raging among oppositionists in the later 1920s. Ciliga's remarkable book refers to such debates.

> Some of us thought that there still existed a dictatorship of the proletariat, though it had a bureaucratic slant; others that there was no proletarian dictatorship left, but there were relics of it . . . still others that there was no dictatorship of the proletariat at all and that we were faced by a new social regime that was neither bourgeois nor proletarian. Opinions on the Soviet economy were equally divergent: socialist economy, transitional economy, typically bureaucratic economy, capitalist state economy.

Ciliga himself wrote of 'a new type of exploitation', and criticized Rakovsky for not quite reaching the conclusion that 'the bureaucracy was nothing but a new ruling class', while paying tribute to the depth and quality of his analysis.[13]

Bienkowski prefers 'caste' and speaks of a 'process of feudalization' associated with older forms of despotism. Quite independently, Voslensky speaks of 'feudal fiefs' in discussing *nomenklatura*. Bienkowski (correctly, in my view) rejects the term 'bureaucracy' to define a structure from which some bureaucratic charateristics ('rationality, professionalism, a division of competence . . . established rules, legal norms') are conspicuously absent. The term 'elite' evades definitional precision, and can be stretched all the way from the top leadership down to underpaid production engineeers and foremen, all the way to uneducated managers of rural retail stores. My own preference oscillates between 'official class' (or *klass pravyaschchikh*) and some new terms combining elements of 'caste' and 'estate'.

Whatever one calls them, are they 'ruling'? Ticktin claims that they only very partially control the means of production (evidently they do not *own* them).[14] However, this turns on the meaning attaching to the word 'control'. One is reminded of the controversy over the applicability to the Soviet Union of the 'totalitarian' model. If one were to define totalitarianism sufficiently narrowly, it is easy enough to prove that the term is not applicable; pressure groups and coalitions exist, orders are sometimes not obeyed or their execution is distorted, and so on. Similarly, if 'control' is understood to mean *total* control, then it does not exist in Russia, or indeed anywhere. Markus, in a most percipient paper, speaks of 'a complicated process of semi-institutionalized *competition* and *bargaining* between the various horizontally and vertically articulated bureaucracies, i.e. functional constituents of the unified apparatus of power'.[15] In my own book I headed a chapter 'Centralized pluralism',[16] to express the same thought. Maria Hirszowicz refers to 'bureaucratic pluralism'. Markus also pointed out, in analysing this 'system of social domination', that

> this does *not* mean that in these societies the politically constituted top of the apparatus . . . has the arbitrary power to determine – at least within the limits of material possibilities – the direction of economic developments. The once constituted *institutional structure* again imposes its own principle of selectivity.

In an unpublished paper, Valerie Bunce also emphasized the element of bargaining, of the combination of a strong hierarchical state with what she calls 'state corporatism', which involves co-option and compromise.[17] *Nomenklatura* officials at all levels must take into account not only each other (for instance, in competing for scarce investment resources) but also their subordinates, not least the workers. While autonomous workers' organizations are not tolerated, a widespread go-slow and general slackness are. This, and much else, imposes constraints on the rulers. But where, outside of inferior textbooks, are rulers unconstrained?

A different and more difficult question is, can the system survive, has it the needed degree of stability? This is relevant to the issue of whether the Soviet Union is an example of a new mode of production. If it is *inherently* unstable, this would provide some support for the view that there *is* no resting-place between capitalism and socialism, that what we have is either 'transitional' or a non-viable hybrid. Indeed Bettelheim, as we shall see, claims not only that the USSR *is* capitalist (run by the 'state bourgeoisie') but that the October revolution itself was bourgeois, that capitalism (in *his* definition) merely changed its spots.[18]

The question of stability has been discussed by many writers. My own views too have evolved, as the USSR faces increased economic difficulties and we are witnessing the spread of what can only be characterized as general demoralization. Bienkowski points to 'the enormous hiatus between content and form, between what is done and what is said', between 'the real political system and the fictitious one', which 'constitutes a permanent *source of demoralization of the regime and of society*' (his emphasis). He develops a theory of 'petrification'; all institutions, bureaucratic ones especially, show a tendency towards petrification, unless challenged. While the Soviet system certainly *had* a dynamic, it has now

> fallen into complete inertia . . . deprived of any stimulus from a paralysed society, it is in no condition to change direction, even though it is in the clear interest of those in power whose immediate interests obscure all prospects for change. One might ask what plays the greatest role in this hopeless inertia: fear of disturbing the *status quo*; the lack of any kind of conception of the direction in which adaptive processes should go (for half a century political problems have been completely banished from intellectual thought); or, a third possibility, the blockade of the system based on a kind of balance of power within the ruling groups, each of which is prepared to oppose any initiative on the part of any of the others in order to maintain the existing balance.[19]

He then refers to 'what might be called the "feudalization" of social relations'. All this represents a fetter on productive forces, especially in an age of rapid technological change.

Jowitt notes a process that he calls 'political corruption', at all levels. The great tasks of transforming society are not now on the agenda, centrifugal forces assert themselves, indiscipline spreads. The desire, indeed the necessity, for greater efficiency is in constant conflict with the ethos and *modus operandi* of the party apparatus. Markus, in the paper referred to earlier, notes how the 'institutional requirements dictated by the existing system of social domination' repeatedly obstruct urgently necessary changes in industry and in agriculture. Gouldner, in a chapter entitled 'State and class in Marxism', writes that of course the ruling class is 'not a military conqueror', does satisfy its society's needs, is 'committed to the maintenance and reproduction of those under them and is involved in reciprocities with them'.[20] But then he goes on, by a different route, to conclusions similar to those already cited.

> Investing control over production in the state – as Marxism saw in the A[siatic] M[ode of] P[roduction] – threatens the economy with

stagnation . . . If the socialist economy is managed by the state with a powerful bureaucracy, will they not themselves become a powerful new ruling class which plunges the rest of society into a new and more debilitating dependence, crippling the liberative intent of socialism?[21]

Gouldner notes, in my view correctly, that 'the hyper-development of the state in Marxist collectivism' arises in part 'from a kind of default: that is, some agency is needed to manage the property expropriated from the proprietary class'. But suppose, argues Gouldner in his chapter, 'Nightmare Marxism', suppose 'private property really turns out to be the basis of civilization', that the 'new collectivist state brings a new stagnation to the economy rather than a new productivity'?[22] In the Soviet context, where the state and party claim both omniscience and total responsibility, stagnation and economic troubles have directly political consequences – in the West it is by no means so clear to see 'who is to blame'. So it follows from Bienkowski, Bunce, Gouldner, Jowitt, Markus and indeed a number of others that crisis and instability may well be of threatening proportions. In fact 'the chronic crisis of the centralized system may be reaching an acute stage, with consequences as yet unforeseeable', this time to quote myself.[23]

However, I do not wish to imply that there is danger of imminent collapse, and other analyses stress not only the system's deficiencies and contradictions but also its durability. Thus Szelenyi:

despite all the ups and downs of their history, [the Soviet-type societies] represent a spectacular continuity, coherence, vitality and stability. They are obviously in a permanent 'transition', like any other society or social formation in human history, but they still seem to represent their own logic, including their own and in many ways unique system of political oppression and economic exploitation, they deserve to be acknowledged as at least relatively autonomous new formations.[24]

Mark Rakovski, writing in Hungary in the early 1970s, also saw Soviet-type societies as new and solidly established formations, and as 'class societies', neither capitalist, nor socialist, nor transitional, with specific characteristics. He makes a distinction between the 'class in power' (or political leadership) and specialists or technocrats, who also have influence but must be distinguished from the party-apparatus officialdom. Indeed, in discussions with 'new leftists' in Hungary I heard the argument advanced that actual or potential splits between 'those who know how to do things' (technocrats) and 'those who claim to know the laws of society' (political leaders cum ideologists) provide opportunities for critical intellectuals to exploit.

A very different approach indeed is Bettelheim's. In his latest work, cited above, he inclines to the view that what took place in 1917 was 'essentially a *capitalist revolution*, leading finally to a radical expropriation of the direct producers . . . The October insurrection *presented itself in the illusory form of a socialist revolution*, whereas it opened the way to a *capitalist revolution* of a specific type' (p. 13; emphasis in original). His concluding pages are headed: 'Un capitalisme d'un type nouveau'. So evidently he would regard the USSR as a class society, but a *capitalist* class society.

In a valuable and as yet unpublished paper, the *émigré* Czech sociologist Zdenek Strmiska provides a highly stimulating critical analysis of various theories of the nature of Soviet-type societies. This includes a critique of the Bettelheim position. He (correctly) notes that Bettelheim's definition of socialism is utopian. As Strmiska puts it:

> socialism is conceived as a social order not much different from communism . . . An integrated society, liberated from deeper structural contradictions, a society in which there is no separation of one type of producer from another, or separation of the producers from the means of production . . . In this society all social relations are based on community relations, the identification of the subject with society as a whole . . . a reciprocity of exchange is not considered a necessary form of social relations, but as part of bourgeois reality and bourgeois ideology. In a society as integrated as this no class differences are thinkable . . . We arrive at a conception of socialism without any essential internal differentiation, without exchange, without classes, without a state, without relations of power. It is impossible not to consider such an idea as utopian *par excellence*; a socialist society conceptualized in this way, as if all its social problems were *a priori* solved as a direct result of its own nature . . . In its conspicuous negativity and its fictitious perfection such a definition of socialism cannot but resemble the conception of God in negative theologies.

Those who characterize the Soviet system as 'state capitalism' have, Strmiska argues, this quite unreal picture of socialism, so that 'not only societies of the Soviet type but also other possible types of future society will be capitalist . . . merely because they necessarily diverge from the ideal-type model of socialism'.[25] It is necessary to add that Bettelheim's ideas on socialism are changing, and that Strmiska himself has now circulated a second part of his analysis, in which he speaks of what he calls a 'politocracy' as a 'group that is formed on the basis of the administrative political functions in society',[26] and which in this sense is in no way different from other 'ruling' classes; but he makes no attempt at any precise definition as to who they may be. Various references to other strata (for example, the 'intelligentsia') suggest that he might opt for a narrower definition than one based on *nomenklatura*.

Among other individuals of a semi-Trotskyist persuasion, one should also remember Bruno Rizzi, who as early as 1939 advanced the theory of a new and specific class structure in his book *La Bureaucratisation du monde*.[27] Among our own contemporaries it is also necessary to mention the interesting ideas of Bernard Chavance who, in seeing the USSR as a class society, distinguishes between 'state capitalism' (*capitalisme d'état*) and 'etatist capitalism' (*capitalisme étatique*). The point of the distinction is that in the former version the state plays the role of capitalist, but in the latter (which he supports), the role is played by specific individuals (officials, managers) within a system in which ownership is formally vested in the state and in which these specific 'concrete persons' act as 'capitalists'.[28]

Voslensky is so sure that this is a new class society that he heads his chapters with a series of qualifying epithets: 'the hidden class'; 'a new dominant class'; 'the directing class'; 'the exploiting class'; 'the class of the privileged'. Jean Ellenstein, in his introduction to the French edition of Voslensky's book, sees it as a class society unforeseen by Marx, that is, as a mode of production, a view that would be supported by Szelenyi and Gouldner. It seems to me a fruitful hypothesis, which leads to a search for defining characteristics and its specific *modus operandi*, a question to which I shall turn in a moment. First let me dispose of the question of stability and durability. On this, obviously, opinions differ. I doubt if any of the contributors to the debate would for a moment deny that there *are* elements of instability, even of crisis, in Soviet-type societies at this time. But this implies neither that the leadership is necessarily incapable of making the changes necessary for survival, nor that the changes, if made, would radically alter the 'mode of production' or the class nature of the system. Agreed, the efforts of the 'official class' to hold on to their monopoly position, to maintain what Harry Rigby calls the 'mono-organizational society', run counter to the needs of efficiency, and contribute to potentially dangerous immobilism. The inherent conservatism of the leading cadres is doubtless reinforced by the worsening international situation; the system is at its most effective when 'the disjunction between production and consumption is completely eliminated', that is, in the military sector, as Markus correctly points out. The Reagan–Weinberger theory (if it can be dignified with such a word) by which US pressure can force reforms upon the system is surely quite wrong-headed. Reforms, if they happen, would do so *despite* American policy.

However, whether change will be in the direction taken by Hungary, or on the contrary towards a more despotic form of centralization, the dominant group will still be 'the class of rulers', the official estate. The possible emergence, as in Hungary, of a few private enterpreneurs would not change the nature of the system, which would and should be defined in terms of its dominant characteristics, not by the tolerated exceptions to the general rule.

What, then, *are* its dominant characteristics? One, too obvious to need more than a mention, is this dominance of officialdom, of the 'class of rulers', the *nomenklatura*, its rejection of any competitor, a firm grip on all communications media, the censorship, the rejection also of any but small-scale private enterprise. In its social as well as in its economic aspect, this view finds its clear expression in Markus's exceptionally well argued article: the 'goal-function of the "planned" economic activities of the state is the maximization of the material means (as use-values) under the global disposition of the apparatus of power as a unified whole'. Of course they *also* desire efficiency, but 'what is effectively accumulated outside the domain over which [the apparatus] can directly dispose does not count as an element of "national" wealth, but constitutes a threat . . . because it can confer a degree of economic independence upon those who own it formally or practically'.[29] This makes good sense. Applied to agriculture, it enables one to see *both* the genuine anxiety to increase production at least cost, *and* a built-in preference for state farms as against co-operatives, and for either as against private, though their cost-effectiveness is in reverse order. Other writers speak of maximization of power (Voslensky), of the exploitation of the direct producers, that is, of the surplus (Konrad and Szelenyi), of accumulation (Bettelheim), which can be seen as variations on the same theme. Indeed, Voslensky finds the source of Soviet aggressiveness internationally in the drive by the *nomenklatura* to maximize its area of power, and he draws a parallel with a capitalist's tendency to enlarge his profits. This seems to me rather farfetched. There are many and complex reasons to account for expansionism, which can be studied in many very different societies (tsars, oriental despots, Great Britain in the nineteenth century, and other numerous examples come to mind).

These 'maximands' are presumably intended to be the equivalent of profit maximization under capitalism. They do have analytical value, but I am unhappy with the use of the concept 'maximize', whether this is used in Chicago or by neo-Marxists. Suppose a firm makes a 15 per cent profit, is this the 'maximum'? Could its directors have increased it by working harder and not going on holiday? All that we know is that the profit *was* 15 per cent. The concept of 'satisficing' would fit the facts just as well. When Stalin defined socialism as a system in which 'maximum satisfaction' of the citizen's needs is achieved, we know this to be meaningless apologetics, which asserts that whatever is available to the citizens is the maximum possible, subject, of course, to constraints. Applied to individuals, it implies that, being 'maximizers', *whatever* they do must maximize their welfare, at least in intention. While there *is* some sense in the proposition that a competitor in a race is exerting himself to the maximum, because the constraints are physical (heart, lungs, muscles) and the objective clear and unambiguous, one is on a slippery conceptual path if one applies such terms to socio-economic behaviour. Yes, the Soviet *nomenklatura*, taken collectively, wants to invest more, but it is also concerned with heading off potentially dangerous discontent on the part of the workers (or else 'Poland' can threaten), and tolerates much slackness and indiscipline on the factory floor. It has a built-in preference for collective as against individual consumption, this being a form of consumption which is more controllable and plannable, but we hear no more now of *fabriki-kukhni* and much more of the virtues of separate family apartments with their own kitchens. Private plots are a *pis-aller*, but right now they are being encouraged, as food is in short supply. Accumulation used to grow at 10 per cent per annum and more, but the eleventh five-year plan provides for something much nearer 1 per cent. If one wishes to call this maximization under constraint, well and good, but does this help our understanding? Is it not better to speak of tendencies, propensities, preferences? One can then analyse their relative potencies, as well as those of counter-tendencies, and also the contradictions that arise if several inconsistent aims are simultaneously pursued. And indeed it is a most important fact that the present form of the Soviet system, the *way* in which the 'official class' exercises its domination, is in increasingly obvious conflict with the requirements of a modern industrial economy. This point is appreciated by an increasing number of the senior officials, and they say so.

Markus – whose article is well worth circulating to students – has much of interest to say about the ways in which the system generates excess demand, making also the point that this provides its own justification, since de-control or decentralization under conditions of chronic shortage threatens chaos. The separate administrative units of which the system is composed compete for resources, especially investment resources, with relative institutional weight or influence being the determining factor, rather than considerations of economic rationality or need. Indeed it is useful to see here a contrast with Western capitalism. Here, if toothbrushes or babies' nappies happen to yield above-average profits, more will tend to be produced. In the USSR, the rank of the officials in charge of toothbrushes and babies' nappies is bound to be quite modest, and it is this, and not just some ideological preference for steel, that gives steel the edge, so to speak. In fact the same factors operate *within* the producers' goods sector (department I): thus small-scale equipment, needed for *malaya mekhanizatsiya*, tends not to be produced because the bureaucratic heavyweights are not responsible for its production. 'Mini-technique, mini-attention', to quote *Pravda*.[30]

The existence of 'administrative competition' for resources within a nominally centralized system is, of course, a fact, and is used by Bettelheim to support his argument that the USSR is really capitalist, since what is taking place is 'a relationship of struggle between different fragments of social capital', analogous to competition under classical capitalism.[31] The difficulty with this argument is that it implies the possibility of the existence of some system in which social capital is totally unified, and in which those in charge of its different segments do *not* compete for resources, a situation only conceivable if there is 'abundance', that is, no opportunity cost, in the sense of mutually exclusive alternatives; once again, one is then driven to the (untenable) conclusion that any system likely to exist in the foreseeable future must be 'capitalist' on Bettelheim's definition, whether or not every capitalist and landlord is or is not liquidated.

Other commentators also have interesting things to say about the system's functioning. Thus Jowitt discusses what he calls 'status societies', and suggests that the 'political corruption' of the Soviet elite brings them closer to 'traditional type patrons and "big men" '. In his view, 'the convergence occurring is more with peasant-status societies of the Third World than the class societies of the West'.[32] Noting the amalgam of 'charismatic, traditional and modern features', Jowitt argues that they find expression in 'the central place of "heroic" and "booty" orientations in Soviet political economy', the importance of *blat*, what he calls 'arithmetical' planning (for instance, physical output targets), and also the pervasive secrecy. The charismatic, 'be he feudal noble or party cadre, "rejects as undignified all methodical methods of rational acquisition" '.[33] The quotation within the quotation is from Weber. Some activities are seen as appropriate to party-led heroic achievements; the big project is favoured, as against light industry or services. Interpersonal relationships between different units of the ruling stratum take the form of *blat*, 'and not impersonal, strictly accountable standards of value', and we must all be aware of the complex network of informal links at all levels and of its importance. But simultaneously there are also modern as well as traditional features within the system, and there are tensions between them. As Jowitt puts it,

> this framework recognizes methodical economic action but favours 'heroic' storming, values professionals but subordinates them to tribute-demanding *apparatchik* notables, attempts to upgrade contract as a mode of economic predictability but debilitates its institutional integrity with *blat*, strives for a scientific industrial economy but approaches it 'arithmetically' . . .[34]

He has other fruitful and thought-provoking insights. Thus

> the Soviet elite may be expected to disdain as well as fear a social order based upon the skills and ethos of businessmen and politicians and to avoid the benefits and terms of private/market ownership: they are too threatening.[35]

He refers to a tendency towards 'political not entrepreneurial capitalism', that is, 'the sponsorship by cadre-patrons of quasi-legal or illegal activities and the gratitude, deference, fear and "tribute" they receive', and explains this as 'a major adaptation of a Leninist organization lacking a combat task seeking to preserve its political exclusivity and perquisites'.[36] This approach helps us to understand the dislike of high officialdom for the market mechanism. Of course, in a hierarchical system the official desires privileges and (especially) promotion, not *ownership* of the particular segment of the economy he may be at that moment managing.

Also relevant to our understanding is Valerie Bunce's concept of 'state corporatism'. The ruling stratum cannot ride rough-shod over sectional interests, must try to satisfy as many as possible, and this becomes more difficult as growth slows down and the competition for the remaining resources intensifies. This can contribute to a growing instability. It is also inconsistent with an analysis conducted in terms of 'maximizing' in relation to one single aim or objective.

So, after this *tour d'horizon*, what conclusions is it proper to draw? One is that there is a great deal still open to legitimate debate. Another is that our terminology (including the word 'class') needs to be adapted to new phenomena, that Soviet-type societies do not fit our inherited labels. The definition of who falls within the ruling group (class, stratum, or estate, regime, cadres, or whatever) does and will necessarily present problems. The *nomenklatura* has the advantage of being based on the system's own self-definition – though of course the detailed contents of the Soviet *tabel' o rangakh* are a strictly-guarded state secret. Alternative ways of identifying the rulers seem less satisfactory. Of course, the 'unihierarchy' is also a set of competing hierarchies, though each tends to show a facade of unanimity to outsiders, and together they defend their common interest to prevent others from challenging their monopoly right to rule. There has surely been a qualitative change in the nature of the ruling stratum since the days when Stalin terrorized it; office tenure is far more secure, the privileges are institutionalized. The official class came to power in the process of revolutionizing society, expropriating peasants, purging the revolutionaries themselves, preparing for and waging a deadly war. Petrification, 'political corruption', a regression into neo-feudalism even, these are some of the ways in which the recent evolution of the system has been characterized by percipient observers. Whether this deserves the name of socialism, howsoever qualified (state-, etatist-, proto-, etc.) depends on the degree of utopianism with which 'socialism' is defined.

Hélène Carrère d'Encausse's *Le Pouvoir confisqué* makes many good points, but the title is, in my view, misleading. It is consistent with the notion of a workers' state that had somehow degenerated, as if the masses *did* rule and the party apparatus usurped power. It seems to me that Bienkowski and Gouldner (and many other critics) are right; the 'dictatorship of the proletariat' is an inherently meaningless concept. Dictatorship can only be exercised by a relatively small group of rulers. One cannot replace the functional necessity of command and co-ordination with slogans. It is not the *existence* of a ruling stratum that is new, but its nature, recruitment, background experience, age, its style of ruling, its job security, which have indeed altered.

A question arises which can only be lightly touched on here, but which is of great importance for socialist theory. What *would* we accept as a classless society? Does the existence of a distinction between rulers and ruled imply that the society possesses a ruling class (stratum, elite, estate) *and* is therefore not socialist? Are the rulers 'exploitive' because they rule, or because of the manner in which they allocate resources (for instance, to themselves)? Can one envisage a socialist society in the foreseeable future *without* rulers? Or is the key question one of the relationship between commanders and commanded, that is, elections, responsibility, freedom of criticism and of organizing opposition, trade unions, and so on? It seems to me that it is here, in its self-selection and lack of any effective institutional responsibility to those below them, and the secret nature of its privileges, that the Soviet ruling stratum conspicuously fails even the most non-utopian socialist test.

Bienkowski expresses well both some of the specificities of the system and its resistance to change:

> This specific configuration of tendencies – industrialization, feudal-ization and elements of social policy derived from socialist ideology – created an original hard alloy insusceptible to further working. It was not enough to be aware of the inadequacy and the archaic nature of these forms; fear of unbalancing the whole construction prevented any attempt to change one of the elements.[37]

'Feudalization' expresses a similar thought to Jowitt's 'neotraditionalism', a partial regression to older forms, in conflict with the requirements of modernization.

In the absence of 'heroic' goals and of a powerful despot-ruler, there is clear danger that the *nomenklatura* will degenerate (has already degener-ated) into conservative, bureaucratic immobilism. With no effective chal-lenge from below or from competing political and social forms, the 'class of rulers' can be made to change its ways only from above. This brings one back to the related issues of stability and adaptability. The forces of inertia are immensely strong, but a sense of self-preservation may none the less compel the leadership to impose change upon their unwilling subordi-nates. Thus there may be some combination of economic reform *à l'hongroise* with a campaign against indiscipline both on the factory floor and in party and government offices. There *may* be, waiting in the wings, some successors to the present gerontocracy who could try to put through drastic reforms (perhaps Andropov himself might try), and so it is not impossible that instability in the second half of the 1980s may be due to unforeseen effects of radical but contradictory change, rather than to the consequences of continued immobility. But of course we should never forget that modern industrial society is presenting challenges to established institutions, theories, habits of thought here in the West, as well. Gorbachev *is* trying!

Notes: Chapter 13

1   A. Nove, *Political Economy and Soviet Socialism* (London: Allen & Unwin, 1978).
2   Kolakowski's and Markovic's ideas are developed in their excellent contributions to R. C. Tucker (ed.), *Stalinism: Essays in Historical Interpretation* (New York: Norton, 1977); Alvin Gouldner's in his *The Two Marxisms* (London: Macmillan, 1980), esp. pt III.
3   M. Voslensky, *La nomenklatura* (Paris: Belfond, 1980).
4   G. Konrad and I. Szelenyi, *Intellectuals on the Road to Class Power* (New York: Harcourt, Brace, Jovanovich, 1979).
5   *Telos*, Summer 1980.
6   W. Bienkowski, *Theory and Reality* (London: Allison & Busby, 1981), p. 207.
7   loc. cit.
8   K. Jowitt, 'Soviet neotraditionalism: the political corruption of a Leninist regime', *Soviet Studies*, vol. 35, no. 3 (July 1983), pp. 275–97.
9   Maria Hirszowicz, *The Bureaucratic Leviathan* (London: Martin Robertson, 1980), p. 93.
10 Gouldner, op. cit., p. 334.
11 David Lane, *The End of Social Inequality?* (London: Allen & Unwin, 1982).
12 *Byuleten' oppozitsii*, 1929–30, nos 17–18 and 15–16.
13 Ante Ciliga, *The Russian Enigma* (London: Noonan Hurst, 1979), orig. pub. 1938; with thanks to Dr S. L. White for the reference.
14 For instance, see *Critique*, no. 9 (1978).
15 G. Markus, 'Planning the crisis: some remarks on the economic system of Soviet-type societies', *Praxis International*, no. 3 (1981), p. 247; original emphasis.
16 A. Nove, *The Soviet Economic System* (London: Allen & Unwin, 1977).
17 Valerie Bunce, 'The Soviet Union under Brezhnev', mimeo.
18 C. Bettelheim, *La Lutte des classes en URSS, 3ᵉᵐᵉ periode* (Paris: Maspéro, 1982).
19 Bienkowski, op. cit., pp. 186, 206.
20 Gouldner, op. cit., p. 334.
21 ibid., p. 340.
22 ibid., p. 382.
23 A. Nove, *The Economics of Feasible Socialism* (London: Allen & Unwin, 1983), p. 113.

24 I. Szelenyi, 'Whose alternative?', unpublished paper, Flinders University, 1980.
25 Z. Strmiska, 'The social and structural contradictions in societies of the Soviet type', part I, circulated for the conference on The Experiences of the Prague Spring, 1968, Paris, April 1980, pp. 103–4.
26 ibid., part II, p. 99.
27 Bruno Rizzi, *La Bureaucratisation du monde* (Paris: Hachette, 1939).
28 Bernard Chavance, 'La nature du système soviétique', *Les Temps modernes,* June 1981.
29 Markus, op. cit., p. 245.
30 Pravda, 4 May 1981.
31 Bettelheim, op. cit., pp. 299–300.
32 Jowitt, op. cit., p. 277.
33 ibid., p. 278.
34 ibid., p. 283.
35 ibid., p. 288.
36 ibid., p. 286, K. M. Simis also refers frequently to 'tribute' in his recent book *USSR: Secrets of a Corrupt Society* (London: Dent, 1982).
37 Bienkowski, op. cit., p. 185.

Index